HAVE I SAID TOO MUCH?

CAROLE WHITE

My Life In and Out of
The Model Agency

arrow books

1 3 5 7 9 10 8 6 4 2

Arrow Books
20 Vauxhall Bridge Road
London SW1V 2SA

Arrow Books is part of the Penguin Random House group of companies whose
addresses can be found at global.penguinrandomhouse.com.

Penguin
Random House
UK

First published by Century in 2013

www.randomhouse.co.uk

A CIP catalogue record for this book is available from the British Library.

ISBN 9780099576693

Printed and bound by CPI Group (UK) Ltd, Croydon CR0 4YY

Penguin Random House is committed to a sustainable future for our business,
our readers and our planet. This book is made from Forest Stewardship
Council® certified paper.

MIX
Paper from
responsible sources
FSC® C018179

HAVE I SAID TOO MUCH?

D1368340

Carole's agency, Premier, formed with her brother Chris, has been at the forefront of fashion since 1981 and most recently came to prominence when the agency let the TV cameras in for the fly-on-the-wall documentary *The Model Agency* for Channel 4.

Carole lives and works in London and has a daughter who also works at Premier.

To my wonderful family who always support me in
everything I do, and take care of me.

ACKNOWLEDGEMENTS

Of Hack and Sheila's unconditional love, unwavering support and belief in me.

Thanks to Stephanie Pierre for so much input and loyalty.

Alison Taylor for listening to my story and writing it with my sense of humour.

Paul Rowland for being my friend and for being a genius source of inspiration.

Steve Dellar and Gerald Marie for their advice and making me laugh.

To my staff, past and present, for their tireless hard work.

To Huggy for her great images.

To all my lovely Premier models, past and present.

Special thanks to Suzanne Wallis, Jeanna Ridout, Christophe Sanchez-Valhe, Paul Hunt for his great sense of humour, Jamie Ellis, Mariella 'The Schnitzel-Knows-Best', Annie Wilshaw for her great eye and for being my friend.

My brothers Chris Owen and Michael Owen for trying to sort my life out.

My husband who never complains that I am always on the phone and cooks me lovely food.

Aidan Jean Marie for his patience with me.

Sissy Best for me telling me like it is, Jack Best for telling me like it is too.

Subreena for her work ethics and for sticking by me.

Jack Singh for crunching numbers.

Elizabeth Rose and her Man's team for making things happen.

Sophie Wood.

Mick White.

Simone and Steve Barten for always bringing me down to earth.

INTRODUCTION

'People think we're all like Joan Collins, constantly
having our nails done and wafting around. We might
waft around a bit but we'll be doing it in jeans and
T-shirts and smoking fags'

Carole White, 2013

When I found out about my Twitter alter ego 'Carole
Shite', I decided the best thing to do was invite her to
lunch. Shite appeared when *The Model Agency*, a seven-
part fly-on-the-wall documentary about my company,
Premier, was first aired on Channel 4 in February 2011.
We didn't realise when we signed up for it that the show
would be so big but here I was suddenly signing auto-
graphs on the street and inspiring joke avatars. Surreal,
to say the least.

It was like we became famous overnight. I'd go with

my team for dinner near the office in Covent Garden and everyone would know our names and come over to talk to us. Taxi drivers and builders in vans would drive past and lean out of their windows shouting 'Hi, Carole!' while I had a fag outside the office. Even the dustmen were watching it and would chat to me about it in the morning while they emptied the bins. I'd walk down the street and strangers would come up to me and say, 'I know you.' It was incredible really how something on at ten o'clock at night and a bit leftfield could reach so many people. I was approached at an airport luggage carousel once by a quizzical-looking lady: 'My friend said you look like Carole from *The Model Agency* but I told her it couldn't be you because you wouldn't be on a Monarch flight to Turkey.' I said, 'Your friend's right, actually.' She rushed back to her friend, squealing, 'Lynn, Lynn, look, it is Carole!' Hilarious.

The recognition was definitely fun but it could also be a bit disconcerting, mainly because I'd get confused, thinking the person saying hello did actually know me. I'd think, *shit, it's a client!* And because I'm so bad at remembering people's names I'd automatically go, 'Hi, how are you, darling?' I've never met them, they've never met me, yet here I am pretending I know them! The whole thing really took on a life of its own. It was more powerful than anything we'd done before on television and I think that was partly down to social media and the fact that kids could watch it online too. Suddenly everyone was talking and tweeting about it, including Carole Shite.

At first I was horrified by Carole Shite's tweets. I took her as a personal affront. We even tried to get Twitter to take the account down because we didn't really get the joke, which is rather hysterical, thinking back. But then the penny dropped – which is when I decided to befriend Carole Shite instead of making her my enemy. She was evasive at first but then started to be quite nice to us in Carole Shite land. When the programme finished we had a 'phew it's over' wrap party and invited my alter ego (she couldn't make lunch). She was actually two guys – comedians – who were hilarious. I think they do a spoof Kerry Katona, too, so I guess I'm in good company.

Another thing that took us all by surprise in the wake of *The Model Agency* was the reaction of our peers. Fashion people and the cool magazine press loved us, from *Vogue* to *Dazed & Confused* and *i-D*. We knew from the start that we were taking a huge risk with our image in a business where image is everything. Had the show been naff – gosh, I dread to think . . . but we genuinely hadn't considered that possibility. Luckily we managed to gain a sort of cult following which was very cool for us. Had it not gone that way, we would have been really cringing.

We weren't that lucky with the papers – they hated us. They like to use the model industry to create 'compelling' copy, usually about size zero, role or underage models, as it is such easy prey. Journalist Jan Moir from the *Daily Mail* wrote a vitriolic piece spewing forth such niceties as: 'Carole smokes like a chimney, has skin like a kipper and doesn't know how to work a camera.' My response to that was to order a box of kippers and send them to her at Daily Mail Towers. She redeemed herself by accepting them with good humour and sending me a thank-you card with the note: 'I eat children, too.'

The nationals thought that we were superficial and horrible, which is not a new criticism to be levelled at our industry. It often returns to the size zero weight debate, a topic I will explore in more detail later. I've always been really outspoken on this particular issue because to my mind it is entirely media-invented, so 'faux' and politically correct and, frankly, bollocks. It's like anything in life: of course there are some anomalies where some people aren't as healthy as they should be but most models are naturally that thin. It's genetics. Unfortunately, thin is now inextricably linked to 'sick' but I can honestly say that in forty years in this business I've sent home three girls because they were genuinely sick from eating disorders.

More generally I think people – and the press – feel uncomfortable with a job that is focused on looks. Critics tore into the frank discussions we'd have on the show about a model's appearance. They'd find it distasteful, cruel even, but I say it's the same as any job. If you were a coach for an athlete you'd be analysing their running, in a constructive way one hopes so they can improve it, but there would be criticism – and it would be frank. Or if you're a ballerina your tutor will be critiquing your performance after the fact. Everyone strives for perfection and so do we: we expect our girls to be like athletes, to feed themselves like athletes and exercise like athletes because we want healthy girls. Yes, there are difficult things in our job but there are difficult things if you're a ballerina, too. You're not going to be a fat ballerina, are you? Nobody would be able to lift you up! Dancing, athletics, modelling . . . you do things to make sure you're fit and healthy so that you can do your job well and live life to the full.

I agreed to do *The Model Agency* (after a lot of persuasion) because I wanted to show the public the reality of what we do. It gave us the opportunity to demonstrate what a difficult job it can be, how hard the bookers work and how committed we are to our models. People think we're all like Joan Collins, constantly having our nails done and wafting around. We might waft around a bit but we'll be doing it in jeans and T-shirts and smoking fags.

Ultimately, modelling is a career, and we build careers. We can take girls from working- or upper-class environments and propel them into something that will open up a whole new lifestyle, education and security for the future. They'll be on planes to New York, Paris and Milan, they might spend time living in different cities and invariably they'll learn other languages – many models are bi-lingual or even tri-lingual. Even though some girls might not have had a good formal education, they've developed a talent and their world has opened up. Some girls might not know what an artichoke is and then they go to Italy and discover how tasty and healthy they are. It's all life education whilst you earn a living.

Yes, it can be a shallow business, a tough business, a rejection business, but it is a business nonetheless and it provides money for people. To slag it off and not be proud of it, which is so English, just gets me so mad because I'm proud of it. It can change people's lives and I think that's wonderful.

Back in 1981 when I first started Premier with my brother Chris in his living room, I'd been booking at another agency that had gone bust and, I'll be honest, my main motivation was that I needed a job and fast (more on that later). But very soon afterwards, I realised that I was good at it and became passionate about it and started to understand it. You never stop learning in this business – it's so quick.

I love the intricacies of booking and negotiation – it's like solving a crossword puzzle every day. I love coming to work. I love the fact that every day is different. I love firefighting and solving problems for my bookers. I love the drama and the characters that I meet.

Everyone in this business, including the bookers, is in charge of their own little island. They're responsible for making that job happen for that girl. It's down to their individual decisions, not some big corporate going, 'You're doing this.' It's all about your personal talent, from the hair and make-up people to the stylist and photographer, the creative director and the casting director. It's like one big pudding where all these different people with a talent come together in one big bowl to create something beautiful.

People are too quick to dismiss fashion as trivial.

Apart from the cold hard fact that it is now the second biggest industry in the UK, it is also extremely important for culture, individuality and self-expression. Fashion defines moments in history. I loved the era where it all started for me, the 1960s, because it was powerful and fun and a lot of it originated in London. The same is true of the Punks in the Seventies and New Romantics in the Eighties, when the King's Road became the epicentre of a countercultural revolution. We're so quirky and creative as a nation and I'm proud of that. It's also an individual thing. Every item of clothing that you choose to buy is yours individually – how you wear it and what you wear with it. You might get it wrong in my eyes, but it's your choice. It's creative. It's democratic. That's powerful.

If I had to commit, though, to the one thing that it's really all about for me, it has to be the girl. You're always chasing that special girl: the face that defines an era, the model that becomes a muse for an entire generation (yes, they do exist). That's very powerful to me, so sod the press. We're in the business of creating dreams and they *can* come true. Just look at me . . .

Hope you enjoy my story, love Carole x

1

GOLD COAST TO GUILDFORD

Pawpaw fruit, palm trees and 'houseboys' . . . I realise now that growing up in Africa in the 1950s was a fantastically different experience but, to me, having servants and an avocado tree in the garden was absolutely normal. As was being on constant mosquito, spider and snake watch and not being allowed out of the house barefoot for fear of 'jiggers' (a parasitic flea that burrows into your toes to lay its eggs). I developed a taste for tonic water (quinine), which I later learned to mix with gin – a wonderful elixir! The air was potent with the scent of the rusty-red African soil, laterite. It was extraordinary after the rains: healthy, earthy and so rich that you wanted to eat it.

I guess you could say that the first ten years of my life were like an adventure in another world. It was my wonderful world, and the only one that I knew, but it still had a sense of 'other' about it. I inherited that feeling from my parents: an awareness that we were living in a world that wasn't really ours and that could also be frightening and dangerous at times.

The first of many formative long-haul journeys took place six months after I was born (17 July 1950, Kent) when I was bundled with my mother Sheila aboard the *Accra*, one of the famous Elder Dempster fleet that ran between Liverpool and Ghana, or the Gold Coast as it was known then. I'm told Mum was sick throughout her entire pregnancy with me so I repaid her by being a sickly child, always crying and whining. I can only imagine what a nightmare that trip would've been for her, travelling alone for two weeks with a screaming, probably puking, baby.

I have strong memories of those huge vessels. We were put in the ships' nursery, probably so that my mum could go and be sick in peace. And get some sleep. On one crossing, when I was a bit older, I got really obsessed with this ginger-haired baby boy at the nursery. He was really heavy and I dropped him on his head! I can remember to this day all of these accusing eyes on me.

We'd be on the boat for a couple of weeks at a time, in a really pokey cabin with bunks. Even through a child's eyes it was grim. Add to this the constant stench of vomit and diesel and you'll get the picture. Without fail, we were all sick so it was pretty unpleasant. Ships then weren't that luxurious and those early experiences put me off them for life, although recently I've become quite fond of large yachts. There were *some* exciting aspects to being on those ships, like meeting the captain and playing on the decks, which were really slippery. There was also a pool where the sailors would play this game called the Greasy Pole, where the aim was to wallop their opponent off said greasy pole with a pillow. It was part of their crossing-the-equator ritual.

On arrival in Africa, the boat docked at Accra, the capital of the Gold Coast. However, we lived first in Kumasi, about 150 miles northwest, which was home to the headquarters of the Northern Territories of the United Africa Company, a Unilever company, where my dad worked. My parents met there a few years earlier when Mum went out to teach English and domestic science in a missionary school in Mampong. She was brought up by nuns so she was quite holy – though she originally trained as an opera singer and did a Cordon Bleu cookery course, both of which sound infinitely more glamorous to me. My dad, Harold 'Hack' Owen, came from Wallasey near Liverpool and he just wanted to get away from there. He'd inherited the moniker Hack after chivalrously coming to the aid of a woman being pestered by some guy at a party. There was a famous wrestling champion at the time called Georg Hackenschmidt and it just stuck. Better than Harold.

UAC traded in cocoa and gold and Hack was general manager for its gold department. Ashanti gold is the purest in the world and it was plentiful then. They would make everything and anything in gold. I remember these stunning chess sets crafted from solid gold – they were so shiny and really heavy. At the time, the Brits saw them as tacky and rather ostentatious, so nobody would buy them. They liked the more artistic mahogany and ivory carvings and not the gold, unless it was worked into something small like cufflinks, napkin holders or small trinkets. Of course if they had been smart instead of colonially snobby it would've been worth a fortune now.

Hack and Sheila were married in 1949. Our house in Kumasi was beautiful. It was a huge, Colonial-style building – all white with pillars out front, a second-level veranda and elegant windows. It was called the White House, aptly enough, and reflected Hack's status as the GM of the northern territories.

To add to the idyllic scenery, my mother had a pet duiker, a tiny deer that she looked after and kept in the garden. She loved it and treated it like a pet. My dad warned her that somebody would steal it for food but Mum didn't believe him. Sure enough, we woke up one day and the duiker was no more, to everyone's shock. It didn't help us kids that Disney's *Bambi* was doing the rounds of the club cinema. I was never told the almost-certain fate of our garden Bambi but I do remember feeling really traumatised one Christmas when they gave the turkey a spoonful of gin to get it drunk before lopping its head off. I found that really upsetting but that was life in Africa and Christmas dinner was an awesome feast.

After we'd been there a year, my brother was born. He was christened Christopher Rupert John and was called Rupert up to age seven, until his housemaster at school switched him to 'Christopher', or 'Chris', which he much preferred, so eventually we all switched to Chris. I'd been my dad's blue-eyed girl and then Chris arrived and I loathed him so much I hit him on the head with a crystal ashtray. Got in big trouble for that because I could've killed him. We used to have fights like brothers and sisters do but on the whole we got on well. We looked after each other and played together. We kind of had to: there was nothing else to do so we became very protective of each other at an early age and quite insep-arable.

Because it was so hot and humid, Mum made us have a siesta in the afternoons, which we never wanted to do. She would take a nap too, so Chris and I would take the opportunity to become ever more adventurous and decided it would be much more fun to explore. One day, we climbed on top of the wardrobe pretending to conquer Everest, which was crazy as it fell over with a massive crash. We weren't hurt but we screamed really loudly and Chris was stuck underneath it. Mum came rushing in wearing her green dressing gown. We got in deep shit for that but it didn't deter us from getting up to more mischief.

Eventually we moved to the capital, Accra, to a house on stilts. What a novelty! But we'd get bored there too and terrorise the ladies who'd be doing the ironing outside with those old-fashioned hot irons heated on charcoal burners. We'd fill empty coke bottles with water, lean out of the window and empty them onto those poor screeching women. Or we'd try to douse the fire completely, which would splash dirty water onto the washing. All hell would break loose, resulting in the farcical scene of two small children being chased around the garden by these huge, drenched women, shouting and shaking irons and threatening to beat us!

Brimah, our housekeeper, was constantly watching out for us; we absolutely loved him and he loved us. Chris was called the 'small master' and could get away with anything. I remember we used to pray alongside Brimah when he knelt and turned to Mecca. As well as Brimah and the ironing ladies, we had a cook, gardeners and houseboys. Brimah was in charge − he was the equivalent to head butler and a lovely man who also took it upon himself to look after Chris and me. All the white people had servants so we just thought it was normal.

The other 'normal' thing − that also happened to be really scary − was the nightmare-inducing scale and variety of bugs and creepy crawlies over there. Chris and I shared a bedroom and one night a huge fruit bat with a wingspan of about six feet flew in through the window! They're pretty big things anyway but to us it looked and sounded like a terrible monster, with very large scary eyes. Terrified, we screamed the house down. My parents lived at the other end of the house so Brimah came rushing in, with my father close behind him, wielding a cricket bat. To this day I don't like birds or bats or anything flappy like that. After that incident Chris was so scared that Brimah had to sleep on our bedroom floor next to him.

The main things we had to worry about were snakes and scorpions. It was the gardener's job to keep them at bay. There were black mambas, only one of the most aggressive and venomous snakes in the world! Not an ideal garden playmate for two young kids who just wanted to explore. Chris once caught a snake in the outside drain with a stick and Brimah and the gardener nearly had a fit trying to get him to leave it alone and back off as it wound its way up the stick. Chris dropped it and we ran for it and the poor snake was duly dispatched. Hack was furious and gave us a big lecture about snakes. There were driver ants, too, running around everywhere. We thought they were quite fun to play with until we were told that they made light work of eating a horse. An entire horse! Munch munch munch! Thinking about it, my mother was worried a lot of the time: all these dangers lying in wait for us – snakes, scorpions, bats, driver ants, jiggers. She made us wear frumpy Clarks sandals, gradually turning that orange sole black, and when we grew out of them Mum would cut off the toes to eke out a bit more wear.

Because she wasn't teaching any more, Mum's life centred around a dizzying social timetable of coffees, afternoon teas, cocktails and dinner parties. That was all the rage in the ex-pat community. For a kid it was quite comforting in a way, getting to know the routine of it and watching Mum and the servants prepare. Chris and I always loved watching Mum get ready for these occasions. She was really glamorous back then and fashionable too. She'd wear chic shift dresses and stilettos

– the new thing! – bought in Rome, en route from England.

She'd go back to see our grandparents and take us with her. It would take two days to get there on a plane because there were no jets then; it was still all propellers so the plane had to make frequent stops on the way. We flew on Lockheed Constellations, Boeing Stratocruisers and Bristol Britannias and were proud members of the BOAC (the forerunner of British Airways) Junior Jet Club. We had the log book and the T-shirt.

We always got airsick so they'd put us in first class, which was nice. It was like being in a five-star hotel. We'd eat delicious things like crêpes flambéed beside your seat. You don't see that nowadays – it'd be considered a fire hazard! On the way back we'd stop off in Rome so that Mum could buy the latest fashions from the Via Condotti. She would buy really quite cool stuff – the first stiletto-heeled sandals, sack dresses and amazing sunglasses. She'd go back to Accra with all this finery and people would think she was quite strange because she was so advanced in her style. That was my first exposure to the allure of fashion. I loved it.

As well as the boutiques, we were dragged around the Vatican and the Colosseum, which we didn't enjoy as much. I remember being given candles in the catacombs and Chris ate his and got into a lot of trouble. My mum was very keen for us to see the world. We'd stop off at the Rhine Falls in Schaffhausen to stay with Mum and Dad's great friends, the Stolls, in Bern with the Falkenbergs, then Zurich, Lake Como and finally

Rome. Sometimes, we'd take one of the big ocean liners and stop off in Las Palmas, which was an assault on the senses to say the least. You'd get off the boat and be greeted by a stampede of ladies in traditional Spanish dress with hibiscus behind their ears – the whole nine yards. They were flogging dolls, embroidered shawls, fans and castanets. We became experts in Spanish souvenir tat!

Mum would always make us go to museums, which of course we hated at the time but, looking back, she was cultivating us and introducing us to an amazing cultural education. She was very knowledgeable and well-read. If you asked her, 'Who painted this?' she'd tell you. She was incredible. For little kids it was pretty tiresome – we were bored rigid! – but she would stress that we were very privileged. We didn't understand how lucky we were, getting to visit all these exotic and fabulous places.

She would go all out dressing for dinner, even wearing a hairpiece to give her chignon more oomph. We'd watch her apply her Elizabeth Arden rouge lipstick and Femme perfume, and put on one of her new dresses and stilettos. Earlier in the day she'd paint her nails and then have a little nap while they dried. She was definitely one of the leaders of the social pack out there. The women would throw cocktail parties and try to outdo each other on the canapés. She'd serve honeydew melon and grapefruit with brown sugar and ginger on top, really avant-garde! And avocado with Worcester sauce, which is still a seriously awesome combination.

We weren't allowed to be at the dinner parties but we'd watch everything from behind the door. It was all silver service and the servants wore starched white jackets with gold buttons. It was very glamorous. The men would wear white dinner jackets and bow ties and the women would be fabulous in their Fifties dresses. All very colonial *White Mischief* style! Occasionally we'd be allowed to go to a cocktail party and we'd swig people's drinks when they weren't looking. Chris and I got absolutely plastered. They all drank Scotch (Johnny Walker Black Label) and soda, Gordon's gin and tonic or the ultimate in sophistication: pink gin (gin with Angostura bitters and a little soda). The tonic had quinine in it and was drunk to guard against malaria – at least that was the excuse, although everyone took a daily Paludrine pill. Everybody smoked Player's Navy Cut cigarettes (without filters) that they kept in elegant silver cases or ivory boxes. To me it all seemed terribly chic.

Getting a fridge and air conditioning was a huge deal out there and we were one of the first to get them. Before that, huge blocks of ice would be carried for miles on the head of some poor soaked soul and be half-melted by the time they arrived. These poor boys' teeth were chattering and they were in serious danger from frostbite. I remember the fridge had bowls of kerosene at the foot of each leg to prevent the ants climbing up. If you had a fridge with an ice compartment then you were the bees' bollocks. It was all about one-upmanship. The air conditioning was just in my parents' bedroom and when they got it they always kept the curtains drawn to keep it extra cool. We didn't have it – we just had a fan – and Mum wouldn't let us go into their lovely cold and dark room except on special occasions.

We'd get the most terrible sunburn because Accra was so close to the equator. In those days there wasn't any sun protection but they used to smear us in Nivea cream, thinking it was helping, but of course it was the equivalent of basting us like turkeys. Every kid was like this – smeared in white gunk.

Sometimes when it was really hot and we were suffering from third-degree sunburn they'd take us to the rainforest in Aburi. I can remember staring up at the trees and it being really cool. Then, we'd travel in a fleet of classic black and chrome Rovers to the Northern Territories, where there were crocodiles and other exciting creatures to see. We'd stay in these posh guesthouses – very English and military-style with waiters wearing red fez hats with tassels.

I can remember getting out of bed one morning and seeing this huge tarantula. Brimah came rushing in and killed it and then took it out between his toes. Brimah was from the Northern Territories and such a lovely man. He would have died for us, but he was obsessed with Chris, he just loved him. He was very kind and my parents really trusted him. He helped to protect us. After we left Ghana, Hack meticulously continued to send him a Christmas bonus every year and we stayed in touch with him via our Christmas letters – writing these was a traditional event that the whole family took part in.

One night in Accra the 'Juju men' came to the house. We kids were terrified of these black magic men who looked so menacing and I think my parents were equally scared. My dad and Brimah had a big confab on how to get rid of them, which ended up with my dad having to 'dash' (the African word for tip or bribe) them. It was scary stuff. We had to be quite wary of our surroundings and the people we were coming across. We were taught from an early age to question everyone and everything, which is quite a responsibility for a kid.

* * *

When I was five and Chris was just four we were sent to boarding school because there were no schools for white kids in Accra at the time. This meant we had to travel all the way back to England and be separated from our parents at a really young age. We just thought it was normal, of course. We were put into a school called King's in Essex. Because Chris was still such a baby the matrons loved him. He had curly hair and a cherubic face. They wouldn't cut his hair because of those curls so it grew really long – I was quite jealous because he was the cute angelic one getting all the attention. I did feel a responsibility to look after him, too, even though I was only five.

There was a period for maybe a couple of terms when Mum decided to try us at the international school that had just opened in Accra. We thought it was great because we didn't have to go to boarding school. We were taught outside, under the stilts of the school building. It didn't last long, though, because Mum didn't think it was up to scratch so it was back to boarding school for us.

This time, we went to High Trees in Sussex. After a while we started to travel with a chaperone, Mrs Ramsbottom. She came all the way to Africa to collect us and took us back home for the school holidays, which must have cost our parents a fortune. We couldn't actually say her name without having hysterics; it was a big family joke. In the end they decided she was too expensive so we started doing it on our own and were looked after by airport staff and the stewardesses. We had luggage labels with our names and address on, tied to our coats like Paddington Bear, in case we got lost. We'd have the big summer holiday and Christmas in Africa and then spend Easter and half-term breaks with our godparents George and Thelma Tipping in New Malden because the holidays weren't long enough to warrant the journey back. We'd be separated from our parents for long stretches of time and we really missed them, but we loved George and Thelma. They were really cool. They always followed the horseracing season at Ascot, Kempton Park and Sandown.

For a suburban couple they were very cosmopolitan. They'd go to the South of France every year, drink cocktails and put marmalade on their bacon and eggs – how exotic! They had an amazing house that was on a golf course – all these beautiful mansions that flanked the golf course. Everyone was very wealthy.

George was a very bright guy. He'd been in Army Intelligence (MI6) and spoke French and Italian fluently. He started work at the Midland Bank and ended up as a GM. George always answered the phone 'Tipping here'. He was very funny, with an extremely dry, very dirty sense of humour. The Tippings didn't have children and to us they were really glamorous because they had a bar in their living room with an El Cordobés bullfighting poster with George Tipping inscribed as one of the support bullfighters! The living room also featured paintings on velvet of sexy women (yuk). George and Thelma always seemed to be sipping on Noilly Prat martinis or nipping to the races in their Jag.

Thelma was really pretty and petite. She was from Gibraltar so she looked exotic, too; we adored her. She wore a lot of leopard print and pill-box hats. She was also mad about lilac. The whole house was done out in a wash of pale purple, including the bedroom wardrobes, which were adorned with flashes of gold. Her style was very feminine. She gave me a toy lilac poodle and it had a musical head for its top-knot.

I think George would've been a bit of a player back in his day. He used to have a rude calendar in the loo with pictures of women with their breasts on show. Thelma would always turn it around when we were there but we'd always sneak a peek. We loved it! The first thing we'd do when we got there was check out the calendar. It was so risqué! They didn't really know what to do with kids so she'd take us to Harrods and to some grand restaurants too. George gave us a tour of the bank

– very Mary Poppins. The Tippings moved to Esher after New Maldon and George Harrison was their neighbour, so the glamour just kept on rolling!

Much later on, George helped Chris to get his first job, as a trainee at the Midland Bank's PR and marketing department, which led to my first booking as a model, as the Midland Bank girl, so our godparents definitely had a big impact on our lives. They were very, very good to us because I'm sure we were quite forlorn little things.

I was known as 'Flibbertigibbet' at school. I was all over the place – bright but also attention-seeking. I was probably a pain in the arse, actually. If you did something wrong they whacked you with a ruler and if you were really bad you had to go and see the headmaster, stand on the mat and he'd hit you with a cricket bat on your bum. I experienced that a few times. Chris and I were not docile by any means; we explored everything and didn't take too kindly to discipline of any kind after the freedom and relaxed lifestyle of the tropics.

It was a strange school. We had to line up in our forms once a week and take our knickers off to show that we hadn't 'been bad' in them. Can you imagine that happening today? It would be a scandal. Of course, I, being a bright little girl, wised up to this quite quickly and started turning my knickers inside out so they were always pristine. If you had skid marks you were in deep shit, excuse the pun.

The food was disgusting. The meat was all gristle so I'd throw it on the floor to avoid having to eat it and get into massive trouble. The only good things to eat were the sweets. We had a tuck shop with lovely old-fashioned sweets – every mouth-watering classic you could think of: sherbet fountains, humbugs, liquorice allsorts, flying saucers, Milky Ways and Mars Bars. Our matron, Miss Smith, was vile – straight out of Roald Dahl with a mean mouth, lank grey hair, a frumpy, long, straight skirt and flat lace-up shoes. Spinster shoes. I like that preppy look now but when I see trendy girls wearing those shoes I always think of matron.

School at this age wasn't fashionable at all. We'd be kitted out every school year in a new uniform, the prime purpose of which seemed to be to dispense hellish discomfort. Coarse wool + heavy tweeds = itchy and vile. We had to wear liberty bodices – thick woollen vests – because it was so unbelievably cold. Literally, there'd be icicles on the *inside* of the windows. We'd come from the tropics to that! The vests were always too small and really itchy and when they went into the school wash they shrunk even smaller and dug into you. We were always trying to 'lose' them but if we did of course we were in serious trouble.

I've got a wool phobia now thanks to my early school days and so does Chris. I can't bear those harsher Guernsey knits; I'll only wear cashmere. They didn't have any idea of luxury in those days, which is why I loved Thelma because she was dripping with the stuff. We relished going to George and Thelma's to have creature comforts like lovely warm baths. Schools were so backward about hygiene back then. At High Trees we'd have a bath once a week and a hair wash only once every two weeks. Imagine that! And then they didn't have a hair dryer so we'd be sat, dripping wet and shivering in front of a fire. It was straight out of a Dickens novel.

I missed Mum and Dad terribly. We had to write letters back home every Sunday. I hated Sundays with a passion – they were so boring. There was literally nothing to do after we'd been to church. You weren't allowed off campus and there were no activities and no TV, of course. I can remember just sitting in the school field feeling really depressed but not knowing I was depressed. It was quite a sad little life really. I don't like Sundays to this day. I'd know if it was a Sunday if I was dropped down from another planet.

Before this sounds too much like a misery memoir there were some good times at school as well. I was a tomboy so I loved climbing trees right to the top and I was good at traditional sports like netball, rounders and hockey. I liked reading and art, especially drawing, and I was good at ballet. I made some friends, too, like the twins whose parents lived in the Far East and who taught me how to play Mahjong. They had these beautiful sets carved out of ivory. I loved that because it passed the time and it was something no one else could do.

In terms of our education, even though it was strict and regimented I know it was excellent. I just hated playing by the rules, which is probably how I came to rebel eventually. But that happened when we moved back to England, to Guildford, the soon-to-be centre of my new and exciting world.

2

THRILLS AND PILLS

The year was 1960 and a new dawn was upon us – both in my little world and the world as we knew it. But for now, life mainly revolved around school, travelling to and from England and climate/culture adjustment depending on where I was calling home. I had a warped view of the seasons and their associated traditions. At the grand old age of ten I had still never seen snow and I equated Christmas with the beach. Kind of backwards. Christmas on the beach is probably my lasting memory of our life in Africa because it was one of the final things we still did there. We'd swim in the seawater pool at Winneba that flanked the ocean, and eat our dinner on the sand – hot sausages from the thermos, rice and groundnut curry (Dad's speciality), fresh fruits and ice-cold beer and drinks. I think this early exposure to a tropical climate and all its otherness explains why I hate

England's grey and cold so much and adore the sun and its skin-tingling effects.

We had started to spend more time in the UK. Mum was getting more and more homesick; she had bad fibrositis in her neck and shoulders from the tropical climate, and decided that we needed a family home in England. So Mum and Dad bought a beautiful house in Guildford, Surrey to use as their British base. Beechway Corner in Merrow was a lovely four-bedroom Thirties build with a large garden, a very upper-middle-class house. The area was pleasant and there were loads of interesting things to do. Chris loved it and had his friends Paul and James to kick about with him. The house had a quarter of an acre of land, with beautiful beech and apple trees in the back and a huge weeping willow in the front. It meant we had somewhere to go in the holidays. Previously we'd stay at people's houses or even in hotels. I remember we stayed in a hotel in Godalming one summer. That was pretty awful for us because hotels in those days were quite staid and you had to be quiet all the time. We were always being told to 'shhh'. My mum realised we needed a home and somewhere for them to retire to.

I moved schools from High Trees to become a boarder at a school in Guildford called Tormead. The house was literally a ten-minute walk from school and often my mum was there so when the school took us on walks past my house I'd run through a gap in the hedge and say 'Hi, Mum!' Chris went to Milner Court, a boys' prep school in Kent, so we were separated. I think Chris, who was only seven when he started there, was quite prepared to go; he was boarding-school-experienced if a little wary (or a 'tough little fucker' as he likes to call himself now, looking back). We were still based in Africa for a while – Dad was still working there, but Mum was spending more and more time at the house in England. Dad had really long breaks during the summer and would come to our new home for the entire school holidays.

I do vividly remember 1957 and independence day for Ghana – the new President Kwame Nkrumah, the dancers, the black star gate, the fireworks, the drums, the colour, the excitement and the knowledge that our baby days were gone forever. The Royals (The Duchess of Kent) flew out to hand over our old Gold Coast, in the first of many ceremonies like this in Africa. 'Freedom and Justice' following the winds of change.

We liked it in Guildford but it wasn't Africa. We loved Africa; it was so much more exotic than dreary old England. Also, as we got older, the trips became more interesting for us because we could appreciate them more, and relish the bragging possibilities. The other kids at school were in awe that we'd get to go to this far-flung tropical place and come back looking tanned, full of life and healthy. When you're younger you think it's normal but as you get older you realise you were quite privileged.

When I was twelve we made the move completely. Mum had been pushing my dad to get out for a while and then she became pregnant with my youngest brother Michael, which is when she really put her foot down.

She said she wasn't willing to bring up another kid in Africa. It was too much for her; she just wanted to enjoy England's green and pleasant land. Looking back, moving to England wasn't the best move for my dad financially because he had been very well paid over there. He took a decent gratuity pay-off rather than a pension and then came back to the UK to look for a business to start. He had two options. He could either buy a petrol station with flats above it on the very-groovy-at-the-time King's Road in Chelsea, *or* a post office with a flat above it in Guildford. What did he choose? The post office! Oh dear. He made a good living but he could've made a fortune. It was almost certainly my mum's influence; he was a talented businessman and entrepreneur but he would have done anything to keep her happy, and he did sacrifice a lot for a real family life. She would have wanted him to stay closer to us in Guildford to spend more time with the family, but having a post office you had to be up at 5 a.m. Like some kind of prison sentence! It was a newsagent's too so he had to do all the papers. What a culture shock it must have been for him – from *Out of Africa* to *Postman Pat* in a flash.

Because we now lived full-time in Guildford, I became a daygirl at Tormead. There was a huge difference between being a daygirl and a boarder in that the daygirls hated the boarders and vice versa. I'd suddenly become the enemy within my own peer group and in need of friends, fast. In stepped Liz, my soon-to-be partner-in-mischief.

We were like the odd couple, Liz and I, because I was

so tall and she was so short. I always wanted to be her height because she was so petite and pretty. I felt gangly and awkward next to her gamine waif. I ended up being 5' 8" so I was always the tallest in the class. She grew to 5' 3" so she was titchy but very cute. We hit it off immediately when she sat next to me in class. Her father worked on one of the newspapers on Fleet Street. They had quite a lot of money but they weren't what you'd call posh. She was fastidiously stylish, really neat, with an elfin mousy blonde crop. I don't know why we hit it off really, we just did. I was the naughty one, whereas she was calm but quietly up for it, which was a killer combination. We used to cook up plots together.

I had been doing well academically at this point – top marks in all my exams – but this friendship came at a time when, number one, I started to have more interest in boys; and number two, I had more freedom. A potent combination. The big plus of being a daygirl was the fact you could walk home, either on your own or with your friend. So on these languid strolls home during the summer term of '63, Liz and I would daydream and plan our adventures. Adventures that were certainly not parent-approved. I was moved down from the A stream to the B stream due to a chronic case of not caring. I was pretty bright but I was a lazy little sod and hopeless at arithmetic. I suffered from a severe lack of willingness to actually understand it. I never learned my tables.

By age thirteen, I'd discovered music in a big way. I was suddenly mad about Tamla Motown, this intoxicating soul music coming through the airwaves from

Detroit. The Four Tops, Smokey Robinson and the Miracles, the Temptations, Martha and the Vandellas . . . I loved it all. To our absolute glee and amazement Liz and I discovered a club in Guildford called the Harvest Moon that played this music and somehow we managed to get in. We were the coolest dudes in town!

We'd go after school, claiming that we were going for coffee in town, but really we'd go there – this cavernous warehouse space, throbbing with boys and dancing bodies. It seemed to be open at the oddest times, bang in the middle of the day, but it was always packed. Of course we were lying about our age and we certainly weren't going in our school uniforms. The trick was to wear your clubbing clothes under your uniform and carry shitloads of make-up at all times.

We used this brand called Miners Makeup and the look was the blackest painted eyes with 'A Touch of Pink' lipstick – a frosted rose so light it made your teeth look yellow but we still thought we were so cool. I'd wear black spotty bell-bottoms with a tiny T-shirt. The trousers were hipsters so really low cut. My mum hated them but I loved them. I also had a little white coat with a Peter Pan collar that I'd pair with super-short skirts and flat Mary Janes. I was quite imaginative with fashion, good at improvising, so I'd buy kilts from the kids' department, which I'd wear with long white knee socks and French loafers. I was whip thin so I got away with it. All the dresses were A-line or empire line and short short short. Slingback shoes, false eyelashes, hairpieces – we did it all. Even though I didn't like them at the time I'd buy cigarettes out of the machine. I'd sometimes buy those brightly coloured ones that were hugely expensive but they were all for effect; for fashion.

Then there were the boys. The Mods and Rockers. You liked one or the other and we liked the Mods with their scooters and parkas with fur hoods. They were cool in sharp suits. Some of the Mod girls used to wear really bright chintzy trouser suits. They looked like sofas, looking back, but that was the fashion.

We started going dancing at the weekends, too. I'd tell my parents I was going shopping. From hanging out at the Harvest Moon with all our cool cat friends we discovered that there were other clubs too, like the Shoreliner Club in Bognor, near Brighton, which was open for the whole weekend. All day, all night – imagine that! We were like, how do we get *there*? Simple: I'd tell my mum I was going to stay with Liz, she'd tell her mum she was staying with me, and they were so dim they never checked.

So one weekend, off we trot to Bognor. It was so exciting. Everyone was taking Black Bombers and Purple Hearts, which are basically speed, not that we knew what they were. We were free! It was like being at a rave. We stayed up dancing all night. Then we had to get home – not as fun. It's Sunday teatime and I'm on the train back to Guildford, basically off my head – eyes popping. To my horror, when I got home the vicar and his wife were having lunch with my parents. I even remember the exact meal to this day, it was that hard for me to eat: hot ham, parsley sauce, potatoes and beans.

I'm staggering in there, trying to be normal, sitting down and being told that I had to eat this food. Of course, they wouldn't have known. They had no clue about drugs. Nor did we: as far as we were concerned, we were just taking slimming pills that some people had stolen from their mothers.

It's not like we were popping pills all the time but if we did we'd get them from one of the boys we were with. It was more friendly than anything else but I did have a snog once at the all-nighter. That was a pretty new experience. And then I had a bit of a thing with this beautiful Mod boy who took me home one day. But it wasn't that sexual, it was all about dancing and being part of this scene. Liz had a boyfriend that used to find these Purple Hearts so it was probably Liz who got me into that. Mum and Dad thought she was a bad influence. We couldn't afford them most of the time because we were only on pocket money. I did occasionally nick money out of my mum's purse. Naughty girl.

At school we were like the cool kids and we felt like we knew more than anyone else because we were doing these naughty things and they weren't. Not everyone knew about it – just the cool gang. Everyone was so into dancing and the latest sounds. The music scene seemed to be really concentrated around our area too, which was handy. Occasionally we went to clubs in Woking and Eel Pie Island but we didn't really go into London. We thought we were cooler than the Londoners and that we knew what the next big thing was. I remember seeing the Beatles at Guildford Odeon and screaming all the way through the show. Music and the dance scene all seemed to come from that area. A lot of the gigs were in Woking, Godalming and Guildford.

We got away with it for quite a long time. I was clever about it – I'd make sure I wasn't coming home late every time or anything. Even when I wasn't staying at Liz's, I'd say I was going shopping and then get in at about 7 p.m. I used to marvel at how they didn't find out for so long. But the penny finally dropped. I got caught because I used to climb out of my window or creep down the stairs once my parents were in bed and one day I was spotted.

What would become of me? After thinking it over and leaving me to stew for a while, Mum and Dad decided the best thing to do was to send me away to convent school. In Belgium! But of course. The Ursuline Convent in the Flemish village of Tildonk would be my new home. They may as well have sent me to Mars, so far was it removed from the Harvest Moon Club and all its sins. Of course I was wailing and begging for them not to send me but to no avail. I was going, whether I liked it or not. The deal: get all your exams, and then you can leave.

* * *

Phase One of Operation Belgian Convent involved getting my uniform, which didn't disappoint in the weirdness stakes as it turned out to be a 1930s sailor's outfit. Very Coco Chanel, thinking back. The funniest thing about it was the stipulations that came with each garment, such as the blue pleated skirt that 'must be long enough for kneeling and praying'. For winter we had a navy blouson with a removable white starched nautical collar. The top was V-shaped and came with an uncomfortable boob-flattening device, called a plastron. Again, this hailed from the Thirties when the fashion was all about not having a bosom. In summer we swapped the blue blouson for a white blouse. Then came the white gloves. Instead of being obsessed with hats like the British, they were obsessed with gloves. You had to wear them all the time and if you didn't you were stuffed, as I would later discover.

So I've got the uniform and I've finally accepted that I'm going to this convent school. I've also somehow managed to make the leap in my head that it might be quite glamorous – going to school in a foreign place and all that. I'm thinking, ooh, I hope it's hot. Little do I know.

The day arrives and all the new recruits have been told to meet at Victoria Station. There I was, with my giant new trunk and my mother shoving me on the train, Dover-bound, to catch the ferry. It looked like some kind of cult – all these teenagers dressed in starched sailors' outfits assembled on the concourse.

It's all going fine until we get on the boat. It was September and the sea was really rough, throwing the ferry all over the place. We're told to go out on the deck in an attempt to combat the mounting feeling of nausea. It doesn't work. Suddenly 100 sailor girls are vomiting on the deck and – here's the punchline – standing the wrong way so we're covered in the sticky storm of puke.

We hasten below deck to lie down, slipping and sliding

on this steady stream of vomit and choking on the diesel fumes. There was sick *everywhere* and *everyone* was sick. Finally we get off, green and stinking, to board another train. I'm tired, sick as a dog and also petrified as to what lies ahead. I hadn't been to visit the school with my parents so it's all new to me. I arrive and *oh my God*. It was like arriving at Colditz.

It really was like a prison, or maybe a religious cult, with all these nuns wandering around on a mission to turn you into a good Catholic girl or, even better, a nun. We had to gather every morning in this room, the *salon*, for assembly. This was really scary on the first day when you didn't have a clue what the nuns were saying because they all spoke in French. I remember sitting on these carved wooden seats and burning my legs on the pipes that were concealed beneath the pews. We all got third-degree burns!

What a culture shock. Everything was in French for a start. It was quite a bizarre school. The English girls were separated from the French girls and the French girls were separated from the Flemish. The Flemish girls – and their language – were seen as inferior to the French, as if they were peasants. There was a bit of apartheid going on there. English girls weren't allowed to speak to the Flemish girls at all but we were allowed to speak to the French girls because we would learn French. But of course we hated them so we never spoke to them. Confused? I know I was. All the classes were taught to us in French. I got there and I hadn't a clue. Then there was the constant praying. Because it was a convent you had to go to chapel, not just in the morning but also at lunchtime and evenings. That was a big culture shock, too, because the services were Roman Catholic and all in Latin.

The dormitories were even weirder. They were like nuns' cubicles, separated with curtains. There was no running water so you had a Victorian bowl and jug. There's me, Miss Fashionable, with my fringe and my hair all ironed and cool, thinking how the fuck will I wash my hair every day with cold water? It was a trauma. I worked out I could just wash my fringe so that I'd keep that straight and just suffer wiggly hair elsewhere: a compromise. Sometimes the nuns made me tie my hair up into bunches, which didn't really work for my look. And every night we'd have to kneel outside our cubicle and pray. Talk about repenting for my sins.

I had to learn French very quickly. Within a month I was managing fine and within two months I was fluent. I've forgotten it all now – I can only speak it when I'm drunk or if I'm in a panic and it's a crisis at work. I remember vividly the moment when I realised I could properly speak French and that was when I started to dream in it. That was my breakthrough.

We were constantly monitored like we were in prison. The nuns read every letter that came in and out and we were only allowed to read religious books. On Sundays, though, we'd get a film to watch, like *The Sound of Music* or something. Any film with nuns in it, basically. If you were naughty then you couldn't watch the film. And sometimes if the whole school was naughty that was it – back to boring Sundays again for me.

On the plus side there was the food. The nuns made this amazing fresh bread so we lived for baking day. The delicious aroma would drift through the school – *yum yum yum*. We ate it for breakfast with marmalade, jam and Nutella, which was frozen so hard you could cut it. We'd buy Golden Delicious apples and sweets from the tuck shop. If we saved coupons we could get a giant bar of Côte d'Or chocolate. They'd take us to Brussels occasionally and we'd go to this giant store called Le Bon Marché, which was quite exciting and full of foreign delights to eat.

On Sundays, because we were English, we got bacon. The school's speciality, though, was horse meat! Can you imagine? All the English girls with ponies were up in arms. *How can you do this?!* It was actually quite nice. We had to eat it and I didn't care for horses so I wasn't that bothered. It was quite good to eat one – if only those driver ants could see me now! It made life interesting, put it that way.

Despite missing Liz and my clubbing gang from back home, I actually made a lot of friends so I wasn't lonely. I found a couple of really cool girls called Jane and Caroline, or maybe they found me. We all had fringes; we were like a cult. Most of these kids were from army families and their parents were stationed in Germany so they had all travelled a lot, like me. Jane had beautiful hair and a boyfriend, which none of us did. She was cool. We all pretended we had boyfriends but we never really did. We probably knew a boy. Once. Jane was quite respected in school because it was almost certain she'd bonked. It was real love. Her boyfriend used to write these letters that we'd all drool over. I think he wrote songs and played the guitar. Double swoon! Looking back, he was probably a complete drip but Jane was really in love with him.

Once I'd settled in it was really only the nuns and the constant praying that bothered me about the school. It was full on. If a nun died we had to go and view the body, which was an experience. The priest would come too. Us girls were always sure he was shagging some of the younger nuns. There were lots of rumours going around. As well as the sermons and daily prayers we'd have religious lessons too, also in French, with the nuns talking down to us from a pulpit. It was like brain-washing, no, it *was* brainwashing. Because most of us English kids were Church of England they'd teach us that we were heretics and that we'd burn in hell. We used to get all riled up about that. Quite a lot of the girls got sucked in and wanted to become nuns. Luckily I wasn't one of them though I can see why the Roman Catholic religion might seem quite attractive with all its rituals, guilt and gold. The Church of England is much more staid in comparison.

At Lent we'd have to take part in this ritual called Retreat, which involved a mammoth four visits to church on Ash Wednesday followed by two days of silence. What fun! The entire school would queue up to have the priest daub a big, black charcoal cross onto our heads, which we weren't allowed to wash off. So there was everyone walking around the school grounds with these ridiculous symbols on their heads for the duration of the retreat. Hilarious. There were no classes but we could read religious books. Of course we all used to read rude books wrapped in a religious cover – St John the Baptist or something. I also remember kneeling on the netball court to be blessed by the priest, which was really painful!

We weren't allowed out on our own but we did have some trips. We went to Salzburg once with the nuns. They were very excited because we were visiting some churches. *I* was excited to be finally getting out of the school but I was banned from leaving the hotel because I'd lost my gloves. Can you believe it? I was left behind in the hotel, which we were convinced was a brothel. I wasn't always so unlucky, though. We took a trip to an amusement park once and had the most amazing Belgian waffles: nothing like you get in the UK. They were incredible. Hot waffles and chips with mayonnaise, which I'd never had before. That was such an exciting experience.

One half term my parents decided it wasn't worth me coming home because it wasn't long enough, but I thought, sod that, so I decided to sneak out of school. I'd saved up some money. I don't know how I got away with it but I left with girls who were going with their parents and went to the bus stop. I was shitting myself because there was a nun standing there but she didn't recognise me because I was dressed in my own clothes. I had got changed in a hedge.

I got the bus to the station, the train to the ferry, bought a ticket, got on the ferry, arrived in Dover, took a train to London, then another to Guildford and just walked into my house. My parents were gobsmacked.

Them: 'My God, what are you doing here?'
Me: 'I just wanted to come home.'

I don't think they quite understood the possible ramifications of my having gone AWOL but I totally got away with it. The school never found out so I did it all again the next half term. I probably bullshitted my parents and told them I'd asked a nun otherwise I would've been in deep shit but I could be very determined when I put my mind to it.

Which brings me to exams: crunch time. I learned that I have an incredible memory but that it's very short term. I never did very much work during term times, I'd just be farting around, but then I discovered if I read something I could memorise it word for word. And that went for diagrams and maps, too. I had a very visual memory. So I worked out, if I went to the loos with my textbooks the night before an exam when everyone else was sleeping, I could remember everything I'd seen. Just as long as I didn't speak to anyone – I mustn't be distracted. Guess what? I passed every single exam. My parents fell over. They couldn't believe it. I left the convent triumphant with my Bs and Cs and headed back to my old stomping ground in Guildford. I was about to turn seventeen and dreamed of becoming a model.

3

MUM, I WANNA BE A MODEL

It's 1967; I am seventeen and heavily obsessed with:

- Mini skirts
- Tights (essential for mini skirts)
- Motown
- The Beatles
- Ironing my hair straight
- The Rolling Stones

The problem with my interests, as with teens the world over, is that they bear absolutely no resemblance to my parents', or even fit a vague frame of reference. So when I'm kicking around, bored, back home in Guildford after the Convent School Exam Triumph, and say, 'Mum, Dad, I want to be a model,' you can imagine how well it goes down. Not well.

I don't let that stop me, of course; as I've said, I can be very determined (stubborn) when I want to be. Plus, my parents and I have already proved – with the afore-mentioned Convent School Exam Triumph – that we are able to strike a deal when the need arises. The need has very much arisen. The deal? I can go to modelling school (yes, they had schools for it in those days) but only if I do a secretarial course too. Done!

Before the modelling idea came into my head I don't remember having a burning ambition to do anything else *per se*. Girls weren't really encouraged to pursue careers in those days. I certainly wasn't wetting my pants at the thought of being a secretary, though, that's for sure. In terms of interests, I know I was very good at ballet and art at school but it's not like they presented any real 'job' opportunities, not in my parents' eyes anyway.

When I was boarding in Guildford there was a Russian ballet teacher who saw my potential and gave me the lead in a few school productions. She told my mum I was really good and that maybe I should go to ballet school but Mum didn't really take it that seriously. I think she was sort of proud that I was good at it but didn't push it any further. Then when I went to the convent in Belgium there was a French teacher who also recognised that I was quite good and who gave me the lead in a Gershwin number, but ballet and I parted company once school was over. I was probably too tall for it anyway.

I was also very good at art – I definitely had an eye for it, in fact so did Chris, but ours wasn't the sort of family that gave credence to something as wishy-washy as going to art school. Mum and Dad associated artists with being dropouts. You wouldn't make any money so what was the point? They thought it much better to pass the Pitman Shorthand Course and get a solid (boring) job.

I'm not entirely sure where the modelling idea came from but I was 5' 8", which was considered tall in those days, reasonably good looking and really into fashion. It kind of made sense. I also thought it would be easy and fun – meeting lots of swinging people and being part of that whole London fashion scene which was the bees' bollocks at the time.

I was really turned on to fashion through music – that was my first love. It had started with the Motown clubs and the Beatles when I was a young teenager, and then came the Stones, who my father absolutely hated which of course made me even more interested. Immediately I thought, *ooh I'm gonna love them*! There was also a singer called Twinkle who sang something about her boyfriend dying on a motorbike. Perfect! And later, Marianne Faithfull with 'As Tears Go By'. I loved those girls and that look – all platinum blonde hair and smoky eyes.

The mid to late Sixties were all about cool rock stars and their model girlfriends. Chrissie Shrimpton, Jean's younger sister, went out with Mick Jagger before Marianne came along. Then there was Pattie Boyd who married George Harrison. She was a bit older than me but, weirdly, there were some parallels. She had also spent time as a kid in Africa (Nairobi) before moving to Guildford with her mum and sisters, one of whom, 'Jenny' (her real name was Helen), went on to sing in Fleetwood Mac and marry Mick Fleetwood. Jean Shrimpton of course did all those iconic *Vogue* shoots with her boyfriend David Bailey that were really influential in terms of defining a new, almost documentary-style aesthetic. I would later go on to work with Bailey myself though I'm sure if my seventeen-year-old self had been privy to that information she would have fainted on the spot. Jean Shrimpton was also a graduate of the Lucie Clayton Modelling School, which is where I had my sights set.

First, though, came the secretarial course. I was really good at shorthand but couldn't type, which isn't ideal for a budding secretary. I did the course with my friend Liz and she was good at everything. Liz and I had stayed in touch since our earlier all-nighter misdemeanours and continued going out to the clubs and doing exactly what our parents didn't want us to. I think they'd given up by then. I was very headstrong and I already had a mouth on me. We'd have fierce rows to the point where I caused a lot of trouble in my family – I made Mum and Dad cry on some occasions. I was an awfully disruptive teenager but our worlds were just so far apart.

That's how it was, though; the gap between the generations then was less of a gap than a canyon. We were on completely different planets. For our parents, now they were back in England it was all about austerity – both had lived through the Second World War – and kids were 'seen but not heard'. There was still rationing in the Fifties and then – bang! – the Sixties exploded with a ton of new and exciting stuff. My dad was born in 1912 so his upbringing was Edwardian and very staid. My youth was all about the invention of these thrilling new sounds. Everything was about freedom. It was amazing and the fact your parents didn't understand it made it even more amazing. All Mum and Dad wanted was for me to marry an accountant and become a housewife. All I wanted to do was become a model and shag a Rolling Stone.

They were very conservative, British stiff upper lip and all that. It was most noticeable with my mum. It's like she'd become old overnight. She was a good-looking woman and always quite fashion-conscious but when she got to her late thirties I can remember vividly her taking her beautiful dresses and stilettos from Rome and giving them to charity, replacing them with tweed suits. She looked so drab. I always thought it was awful but that's what women did at that age. They sort of buckled down. She felt she was old at thirty-six. Imagine that now!

It was the most powerful of eras because of the sheer acceleration of modernity and freedom. It was a time of revolution: both politically and culturally. All the while you're looking at your parents thinking, there's no way I'll ever be like you, I'd rather die. The drugs were frightening for Mum and Dad and, as a mother, I can appreciate that now. It was when the Stones and the Beatles were being arrested all the time and there were definitely various pills being necked in the clubs that I'd frequent. Occasionally, friends would steal their mothers' slimming pills – called Black Bombers – and we'd all get high on them. But my focus wasn't on drugs – I was much more interested in dancing and the music. There was this incredible music explosion, led by the Beatles and the Stones, Hendrix and the Doors, the like of which I believe we'll never see again.

It was also a time for innovation and fabulous new inventions, like the pill, that really affected women for the good. And there were snazzy new fabrics. Lycra and nylon were a big deal! I remember Mum and Dad getting nylon sheets – they were awful but we thought they were the best thing ever because you didn't have to iron them. Plus it was trendy to have them. Well, about as trendy as your parents could get. Everyone got burn marks from them, particularly if you were shagging. Hilarious. With Lycra came tights, which is what paved the way for mini skirts to get shorter and shorter. You'd go out and all the old ladies would *tut tut* because your skirt was practically up your arse. And fringes! We would literally get the ironing board and brown paper out and iron our hair. If you got it wrong you got a ridge and that just wouldn't do; oh my God, you'd go into a blind panic. As for anyone with curly hair, well, they were fucked in those days. I remember rituals like going to Woolworths and buying little stiletto shoes with slingbacks and dogtooth tights. And getting my first packet of fags – Senior Service. They were disgusting. They made me cough but I persevered because it looked cool.

I'd constantly be buying things and hiding them from my mum.

Periods of social change like this are, of course, when people get creative. I was lucky to be born in that era. There was a real feeling that anything was possible. To dream big. That's what fashion does, too, it creates a dream – a world to escape and aspire to. I definitely had a feel for it. I'd look at magazines and see something and think, 'I've got to have that' and maybe adapt it for myself. And there were models I admired, like Donyale Luna, this amazingly avant-garde black woman who might as well have been from outer space she was that extraordinary-looking. I loved her look. Fashion and the pages of my favourite magazines just all seemed so glamorous and exciting. Lucie Clayton here I come.

The Lucie Clayton Charm School, as it was first called, was based in Bond Street. It was founded by Sylvia Lucie Goiledge in 1928 as a finishing school and expanded into modelling two years later, becoming Britain's top modelling agency during the Fifties and Sixties. It was super famous – everyone had heard of Lucie Clayton. The funny thing was, it was only Lucie Clayton in name. By the time I was there it was owned by a guy called Leslie Kark whose wife Evelyn became the public face of the establishment. As well as modelling, you could also learn cookery, flower arranging, make-up, deportment, dressmaking and 'style of dress' (what to wear with what, which would be called styling now, of course).

Modelling then was like a cottage industry; not like

it is now. Lucie Clayton practically held a monopoly. If you were a model, the chances were you'd be at Lucie Clayton. Back then you had to do your own hair and make-up. There'd be no entourage to doll you up. This was a big part of what we learned on the course – how to apply make-up and style your hair. We all had this Max Factor Pan Stick, and this brown cheek thing and we learned how to put on false eyelashes and do black eyeliner and put our hair in a bun. Shit like that. Then you learned how to walk (the book on head trick), how to get into an E-Type without showing your knickers, 'etiquette' . . . it was all very fabulous, if slightly ridiculous. It seemed like a sort of madness to learn how to walk and talk but I do think it was helpful for those that did go on to become models because it built confidence. I remember Jean Shrimpton recalling her time at the school as being useful because it helped to bring her out of her awkward teenage self and gave her the confidence to do her hair and make-up and interact with different sorts of people. All of these were essential skills for models then and in some ways now but now they don't learn it.

The next step, if you were deemed half-decent and tall enough, was to join the Lucie Clayton Modelling Agency. This was a shrewd move on their part. It's a bit like when somebody wins *X Factor* and gets a record contract at the end of it. You think you've hit the jackpot! I remember thinking, right, it's all gonna happen now. Any minute somebody will call up and say, 'Wow, Carole Owen, you're amazing, come and do a *Vogue* cover!' But of course it doesn't work like that. In those days you had to work in a showroom. A deathly place where you were basically a human mannequin, parading the clothes as buyers looked on. Bitchy people might be inclined to say, *well isn't that what fashion shows are now*? But it really wasn't the same thing at all. There was no drama, no actual show. It was literally just being gawked at wearing some usually very uninspiring outfits. It was awful.

So the reality of modelling wasn't nearly as glamorous as I'd imagined. I didn't like it at all. I didn't realise you had to be a certain sort of person to be good at it. I just felt silly and self-conscious. You'd meet photographers too who were full of innuendo so you'd think, I need to get away from him. It was quite nerve-wracking in that respect.

Sometimes girls got massive long seasons where it was weeks of work but mostly it was just the odd day. I was the odd-day girl. And then I did a bit of the photographic stuff – test shoots and the occasional brochure – but I just wasn't very good. I think I was scared of it. I didn't get that buzz, which made it really difficult. And I wasn't confident. Modelling's a funny thing because it's about you and you only. I had one girlfriend, Vivienne, who also did the course and did quite well out of it, but I didn't last more than six months.

In hindsight, what those six months gave me was a genuine insight into how it feels for the models, even now, all these years on. Particularly how I felt in front of the camera – so self-conscious! I'm sure most of my girls feel like that at the beginning. Maybe if I'd clicked with a photographer I might have been good at it but I wasn't about to find out. It's scary in front of a camera. I think I would have been good at shows but they weren't important then.

I understand the insecurities models feel. It starts from an early age, being the freaky tall girl; being 'different'. A lot of models have low self-esteem thanks to a childhood spent hunching over in a desperate attempt to fit in. But you'll never fit in; you'll always be the tall gangle. Then suddenly you go into this world where everyone's tall too and you do fit in! That's great, of course, but not if you're not cut out for it. There are a lot of girls like that – they're beautiful and they should be models but you can't get them to like one thing about it. They'll try it but hate it and you know they'll leave, like I did. I gave up on modelling and had to come up with a Plan B. Luckily I had my secretarial skills (thanks Mum and Dad!) so I followed Liz to the City, to do an actual proper job. *I know* . . .

4.

TEMPING AND FRENCH ADVENTURING

After the modelling hadn't worked out my main goal was money, i.e. earning some. Also, it was a matter of some urgency to get me out of the house and doing something. Me bored and penniless at home would have been the death of my parents. Liz was earning £14 a week at this City brokers and she managed to wangle me a job too, also at a whopping £14 a week. I remember my father being really impressed – that was good money in those days.

Unfortunately, the job was hideous. I could do my shorthand but I couldn't type quickly enough and they really wanted you to churn it out – Liz could do about 130 words per minute. Then if you were asked to do invoicing you had to set the margins on the typewriters and all that. It was really difficult – I could *never* do it. I hated it. Nah, not for me.

I got fired eventually which was so humiliating even though I knew it was coming. I got fired because I was crap. I knew I wasn't keeping up and my boss was trying to persevere with me, help me even, but it just wasn't working. Liz stayed on there and kept making a fortune and I'm like, shit, I need a job.

This is how I became a temp, which, by the way, is brilliant. Or at least it was for me then when I had no clue what I wanted to do with my life. Most of the time I wasn't asked to do much work. Somebody would go on holiday or they were in between jobs so they'd say they needed a temp but half of the time they didn't need one at all. Half of the time I'd just sit on my arse and read a book. It was fantastic.

I temped all over the place – a week here, a week there – but then I ended up landing a dream gig: they needed somebody at Apple, the Beatles' record company in Savile Row. Scream! I was mainly just answering the phone, typing a bit, and – the rest of the time – pretty much just acting fabulous. You know, BECAUSE I WORKED FOR THE BEATLES! Scream!

I managed to hang on in there for about four months, which is quite a long stint for a temp. I couldn't believe my luck – it was such a cool place to work. I remember a lady would come around at lunchtime and ask what we'd like to eat. Sometimes we'd have lobsters and other really posh things. George Harrison would come in occasionally which, as you can imagine, was very exciting. I was a huge fan. The whole scene was just very groovy. Everyone who worked there was young and hip and I loved it. I ended up seeing a French guy who was also working there. I think he was called Daniel, though I can't remember because I had quite a few lovers around that time. That might sound a little cold-hearted but at that time I was really just focused on having fun, being free and having adventures, which is how I came to accept an invite to go and live in France for a bit.

*   *   *

My temp job at Apple came to an end at the beginning of the summer in '68. My friend Jackie, who I'd met previously in Guildford, had upped sticks and gone to the Riviera to be with this French guy who she'd met in London but who had gone back home. She called me up and said: 'You have to come out here, you'll love it.' I had a bit of money saved up from the temping and didn't have anything lined up so I thought, why not? The only problem, which I didn't really consider, was that Jackie was living on a campsite. In a tent! I turn up with a massive green aluminium suitcase which is not really the done thing in the camping world. It wouldn't even fit in the tent. I'm sure I must've looked ridiculous. So I'm living in a tent and it's hot. Jesus, is it hot. I can remember waking up at five or six every morning dripping in sweat. Not a good look.

Jackie's boyfriend's family lived in a place called Les Arcs, which was out in the hills above Saint-Raphaël, where our campsite was. They were farmers with a smallholding and a vineyard. She went out there to be with him but didn't want to be presumptuous and expect to have her feet *sous la table* immediately, hence the tent. After a while she did move in with the family and, more often than not, was staying at their house on the lavender-hued hill while I slummed it in the tent. At least now I had the tent to myself. Small blessings.

As I got more settled and started to find my way around I began to meet people on the beach between Saint-Raphaël and Cannes. There were lots of bars and clubs all the way along that stretch of the coast and it was easy for me to get waitressing jobs. I'd also wised up with my suitcase and put it in a locker at the train station. That was my wardrobe. I used to go to the station, get all my clothes out, work out what I was going to wear and put it back. Bit of a drag but hey, you make it work.

I just had a ball out there. I met lots of great people. Where possible I'd try to avoid having to sleep in my sweaty tent in favour of staying at a friend's place. I always had my tent to fall back on but I really didn't like it and it wasn't exactly conducive to looking fabulous. I became quite well known as the local English girl on the scene. I probably stood out because I was on my own in foreign climes, which was quite unusual for a girl in those days.

I was in the local paper once because one of my bosses entered me into this ridiculous competition: 'Miss Wonderful Legs of Saint-Raphaël'. I only went and won it! I was a bum, really; this was my equivalent of a gap (part) year, I suppose. I'd get an impromptu job, stop working, then get another job. And I'd be out dancing every night.

In spite of my below-par facilities for grooming I didn't have any trouble attracting attention from the opposite sex. I was naughty really, thinking back. I even dated twins once! They were hot and seemed to really like me; they used to fight over me, which I secretly loved. I remember walking past them and thinking, ooh they're quite cute, and we started talking. They earned money by selling these paintings made by dropping paint on a sort of spinning top to create splashy designs. They were a bit shit but you do what you've got to do to get by, I suppose. I admire that. I met another French guy who was quite wealthy. His mum had a holiday villa so I would stay there with him a lot. It was my eighteenth birthday whilst I was there (17th July, 1968) and he invited me on his small yacht to celebrate. It was supposed to be this fabulously romantic jaunt through Cannes and St Tropez but, true to my seafaring form, I was terribly sick. I think he was very disappointed. I was mortified. Not exactly how it had played out in my head.

I didn't see much of Jackie – she had a different crowd and spent a lot of time with her boyfriend. She was in love with the vineyard guy in the hills whereas I was desperate to know where all the beautiful people went and plonk myself right in the middle of it. The French Riviera towards the end of the Sixties really was the place to be – it was when Brigitte Bardot was at the height of her seductive powers and the resorts from Cannes to Nice were a total playground for millionaires, models and rock stars. I suppose it still is but in a more showy-giant-yacht-way than it seemed then.

I used to hang out with this pop star called Sheila who I met through her manager in Juan-les-Pins. She was a huge star in France at the time. She had a pony-tail and played a lot of tennis. We'd go to restaurants in St Tropez or I'd stay at her place in Juan-les-Pins. I tended to flit between the workers, like the twins, and the richer playboy/scenester types. I was drawn to both sides of the track. Sometimes I'd go to the big casinos in Cannes, not that I knew what I was doing playing blackjack and roulette but I had a go. There was a lot of money down there and really wealthy older men but I wasn't up for hooking up with the older ones like some girls did. That particular cliché was not for me. Some of my flings might've been wealthy but the ones I liked also happened to be young and fit. I've never been into the Sugar Daddy thing. Nor was I into settling down. There was one boy who said he loved me but I was too into having fun and going out dancing every night. He wanted to come back with me to London but I was like 'no no no'. I suppose I was quite promiscuous in a way but everyone was doing the same thing – we didn't live under the shadow of AIDS. It was all about having the most fun possible.

Then at the end of August it suddenly all just stopped. I remember it quite vividly. There's a wind that sweeps along the coast called *le Mistral* – this infamous Sahara wind that blows and blows and gets quite violent and sandy. All of a sudden the Parisians bugger off back to

Paris and everyone starts packing up and leaving. It's quite strange; the Riviera becomes ghostly, a chilly shadow of its sunny former self. You kind of hope it hasn't finished but it has: time to face the music and go back to England. What happened next would have a huge and lasting impact on my life – for good and bad. His name was Don.

5

MARRIAGE AND BABIES (NOT IN THAT ORDER)

I came back to Guildford all tanned and fab . . . and absolutely full of it. My Riviera adventures had certainly put a jaunty spring in my step. The problem with having *too* much of a good time, though, as any hedonist will tell you, is that you develop a taste for it. You have to maintain it – feed it – or life gets very dull. You need more fun, more thrills and, in my case, more trouble. Enter Don – the best worst man I ever met.

I was in a pub with a friend and he started eyeing me up: this super-confident guy all suited and booted, with a twinkle in his eye. I'd seen him around. He was hard to miss, mainly because he was so handsome, in a Warren Beatty kind of way. But he also had a twin brother, so it was double trouble. I obviously had a thing for twins! They were like the naughty boys of Guildford – all the girls fancied them and they were always having affairs that went wrong. He was the bad boy you should stay away from which for me was total moth-to-flame territory. I'd had lovers, probably five or six by then, which wasn't bad for a convent girl, but I suppose I saw Don as a challenge.

It didn't take long for us to become an item. He took me for a drink and then we pretty much started seeing each other. It was exciting because it sort of felt forbidden and naughty. It was around this time that my parents moved to Kent. They'd bought this beautiful old rectory and I was supposed to move with them but by then I was Miss Independent who knew everything so I said: 'No, I'm going to move to London.' I told them I was going to go live at Jackie's flat in Marylebone but I didn't do that, I moved in with Don. My parents had met Don once and not taken to him at all so from then I kept him hidden – out of sight, out of mind. He wasn't exactly take-home-to-the-parents material. He was a graphic designer but when I met him he wasn't working that much so he'd help his brother cutting hair at the shop. He'd basically been drifting so I encouraged him to go back to being a graphic designer. He got a job and then we got a flat together in East London, in Forest Gate. We were having a good time – he was great fun though he was a lot older than me. I always went for men older than me but because he was really good-looking and I'd managed to 'hook' him, that was the satisfaction for me. I thought I was in love with him.

Don and I had been seeing each other for about a year when I fell pregnant in the December of '69. I'd been on the pill but I'd also been neglectful. I was only nine-teen and didn't have a clue what to do despite thinking I was Miss Worldly. Eventually I made a decision. I thought, I'm with this guy and I love him (or I thought I did), I'm already living with him so it will be fine. I started imagining this rose-tinted domestic scene with the baby, flowers in the garden and all that, and it seemed OK.

The problem was, he'd had such a past with women and he already had a child, with a girl in Guildford. He'd split up with her when I met him but he had this reputation as a bit of a ladies' man. He saw his son from time to time but, as far as I knew and given the distance to Guildford, not that often. Then the saddest thing happened; when we'd been in London a while the little boy died. Don went to the funeral and I think it was really traumatic for him. I remember him coming back and saying, 'Maybe I'll get back with the child's mother.' I was going bananas, saying, 'But I'm pregnant!' and he backtracked and said, 'No no, it was just so sad.' I guess that was my first red flag.

I didn't tell anyone that I was pregnant. Not a soul. I knew Mum and Dad didn't like Don so I certainly didn't hammer their door down with the news. Looking back, though, it was obviously ridiculous to keep such massive news to myself because I was actually quite alone. And scared.

By the end of the summer in 1970 I was getting really close to my due date. I had still not told anyone I was pregnant. I'd been working in a shop in Marylebone and eventually I had to leave. Don's job was quite well paid then, he was making money which he'd never really done before, so he owed me quite a lot. The doctor I was seeing was a German woman who suggested I have my baby at home. Ask me that now and I'd laugh you out of the house but then I thought *what a great idea!* because I'd never been in hospital before. To recap, I'm hidden away in the arse end of London, I've lost touch with Jackie and Liz since I've been nesting with Don, my mum and dad don't even know I'm pregnant and I've elected to have a home birth! A catalogue of dumb moves.

A week before I was due I panicked at the sheer enormity of everything that was going on and rang my godmother, the gorgeous Thelma, for advice. I told her my news and asked her if she'd tell my parents for me. She said no, it was something I had to do myself. I decided to wait until after the baby was born.

The big day came and I had this horrendous birth, because believe me there's nothing more painful than childbirth unaided at home. The somewhat archaic requirements for having your baby at home in those days were as follows: four bricks, newspaper, towels and sheets. The four bricks were to prop up the bed so that you were in the right position. I had a midwife who delivered the baby but it was the most painful experience ever. No painkillers. Absolutely nothing! I was quite lucky because it was short but I didn't feel lucky. My baby girl was born on 12 September 1970. I called her Simone, after Nina Simone. She was beautiful.

My parents came to see me in that awful flat two days after she was born and were so upset. Mum told me that dad cried in his sleep that night. It was awful.

* * *

Things got very real very quickly. My reality wasn't even close to the rose-tinted scenario I'd made up in my head. I had just turned twenty and I had a tiny little baby in a shitty flat with no clue what to do. I had no help – no nurse, no nothing. The midwife would come and visit occasionally but essentially you were on your own. Don, of course, was hopeless. He was always 'working late'. I felt so alone because I'd cut myself off from my friends and family. I was stranded and the baby cried and cried. All the time. At some point I gathered myself and came up with a plan. I got it in my head that if we moved house, to a nicer place, that would make everything better.

We moved to Gants Hill in Essex to a maisonette with two bedrooms. It was a 1940s build and really quite nice I suppose, roomy with a garden. I naively thought it would be a lovely fresh start for us, thinking *he'll be home every night and I'll cook him dinner*, but of course it wasn't like that. Instead he would come home late, drunk, and I realised what I'd let myself in for. It was a situation that was becoming unbearable for me.

Sheila and Hack insisted on Simone being christened and their old vicar from Ghana, the Reverend David, did the honours. My friend Barbara took on godmother duties because Jackie was away. My twenty-first birthday the following July signalled the beginning of the end for Don and me. My parents had gone away so we had a party at their house in Kent, the Old Rectory (probably without informing them that we were doing so). We'd gone there for the weekend and I was really ill, like properly suffering. I had these massive blood clots coming out of me. I didn't know what it was but it felt like my liver was dropping out. I was incredibly thin and I remember telling Don how worried I was. But I don't think he gave a toss. Here I was, suffering and vulnerable and he didn't seem to bat one eyelid. I thought then with absolute clarity, this guy's not right. He wasn't right all along, of course, but I'd just not seen it or wanted to admit my mistake. Soon after, back in Essex, I rang my brother Chris and said: 'I can't do this any more. Can you come and get me?' He jumped in his car immediately.

My family all hated Don. They thought he'd taken advantage of me and led me into this trap – although, and as I have already said, on that point they were wrong – so there was no hesitation on their part in staging a rescue mission. They were horrified as to how I was living. Chris was living in London in a tiny bedsit in the Elephant and Castle working as a trainee sales rep for Pan Books. He had an estate car, so we packed up all my stuff and my little baby Simone and, looking over our shoulders, we fled. I just left Don a note. I went down to the beautiful house in Kent and my parents were incredible. Well, my whole family was – so supportive. There I was, in this tiny village between Ashford and Canterbury, a single mother with an illegitimate child – a terrible embarrassment for people of my parents' generation – but they did what they felt was right. My parents opened their arms to me. They were wonderful.

Don then decided he wanted to see the baby but it was too little, too late in my eyes. I didn't even care if he'd been having affairs by that point. I knew that I'd made my mistake and he wasn't the man I thought he would be. I don't think he ever gave a shit about me; he was incredibly selfish as far as the baby and I were concerned. My father didn't want us to have any contact with him. We allowed him to come and see Simone once but the atmosphere was so bad that we rowed and he hit me when I had Simone in my arms, in front of Chris, who immediately decked him and dragged him kicking and screaming out of the house. He didn't make a return visit. He had said, with such false pride, that he'd pay money towards Simone, but he never did. He was very cruel really, looking back. It did feel like I was being rescued.

* * *

I spent some time regrouping at the beautiful Old Rectory in Stowting, getting some much needed love and support from my parents and family, who were totally amazing during this time. The rectory was the family's HQ, our castle: it had nine bedrooms, three staircases, a real country kitchen and a stunning garden in two acres of land. The walks and bicycle rides around the village were so relaxing and therapeutic.

It was a total refuge for me then and in the future. For many years, Chris and I came down every weekend and holiday, often with a bunch of friends, and lapped up the local village life, mostly centred around pubs like the Gate, the George, the Anchor (now the Tiger), the Black Horse and occasionally the village hall.

Hack and Sheila were, as ever, hugely popular and highly respected in the village, and we all made some truly wonderful, lifelong friends in Kent. The Hollises at Park Farm were very close to us: Simon (Chris's best friend at school), Mark (who later became Premier's financial controller), Jeremy and Matthew were the four brothers, all of whom were ex-colonial kids (they grew up in Nigeria) as well. Les and Carol Boothright and the wonderful Carol Macdonald-Bell became our very special friends, with whom we all had many fun adventures and truly great times. Our village culture was so stabilising and unquestionably helped bring my health and confidence back.

After a few months it became very apparent that I needed to get a job. I've always been a restless person so you can imagine what I was like aged twenty. I have such a low boredom threshold so I was driving my parents mad because I had nothing to do, well, apart from looking after my baby! To be frank that just bored the pants off me. Mothering isn't my strong point – I really don't have much of a flare for it. In spite of this,

I've somehow managed to raise three wonderful kids. My kid was lovely, a brilliant, brilliant child, but I needed something else to do as well. Eventually my parents said: 'OK, you've got to get a job in London and commute.' So that's what I did, I went back to my temping agency and started working, coming home every evening and being with Simone at the weekends.

I remember that time as being really fun. I got into the routine of temping, being a bit independent and enjoying some time with my friends. I'd neglected my pals during the Don years so I had some catching up to do. I guess I wanted to make up for lost time. There was so much happening: the music was great, it was sunny all the time (as I remember it!) and I was young and free, or certainly acting that way anyway. It felt like a huge burden had been lifted and having Mum and Dad there caring for Simone really took the pressure off. I know now that I abused their generosity at this time but I was still so young and immature. I wanted to live!

I was hanging out a lot with Vivienne, who I had met at Lucie Clayton's modelling school. She was still modelling and doing OK. I was also friendly with a girl called Annie McNab. I'd met her because she worked in a local insurance place and I'd gone in there one day. We became really good friends. We'd go to the pub a lot or out dancing at gigs and clubs. We frequented the Baracuda and the Bag of Nails, and other places mainly around Carnaby Street and Baker Street. This time was really about having fun with my friends, and not so much about boys. I was really off men for a while. I'm sure I had a few flirtations but nothing serious.

Then, after six months or so I met a guy called Ricky on the commuter train back to Kent. Ricky was the managing director of a company in Soho that did film production. He was a handsome, older guy with dark, wavy hair and a prominent moustache. He had a wife and son but his marriage had broken up. They still lived together in Ashford whilst they were trying to work out what should happen next. He asked me out for dinner after a couple of weeks chatting on the train. The aftermath of that date was quite hilarious because after the meal he had to drive me back to my parents' village and because I had never driven there myself I didn't know the way. He was going mad because we were going round and round these tiny country lanes and getting nowhere. Exasperated, he said to me, 'Don't you know where you live?' All I could say was 'no'!

I went out with Ricky for quite a while. He was a really good cook so he often used to make dinner for my parents and stay at the Old Rectory for a few days before going back to his house in Ashford. He was grown up and kind, and would buy me clothes and presents. It was nice to have someone who was very attentive after Don. I guess I was looking for some security.

It got to a point where it got difficult for Ricky at home so he took on a flat in London. He got this little two-bedroom Victorian terrace on the Fulham Road. It was pretty dark and dingy but quite a good deal. I'd sometimes spend the night there after work, maybe once or twice a week, and we'd both be in Kent at the weekends.

Ricky was quite a powerful player in the film production industry, and his wife, Sandra, was a fashion editor at IPC. But he hadn't been at the flat that long before he started having money troubles with his company and ended up having to declare himself bankrupt. He lost everything. It was very sad. He was quite extravagant but in a nice way, very generous. You know what people are like in business if you've suddenly failed: it's like you've got a disease, so there was nothing left for him in London. He decided to emigrate to Canada and offered me the flat. My mum and dad seemed to think it was a good idea for me to have a place in London during the week so I took it with Annie because we could both afford it together. The flat was so near to Stamford Bridge I could watch Chelsea playing football out of my bedroom window.

I was a bit of a hippie chick at this time. I used to wear floaty dresses by a designer called Van der Fransen that were amazing. They were made out of vintage fabrics and fashioned into hip new shapes and pattern combinations. Lots of different prints and colours. Kaftans were all the rage then too so I had quite a few of those and we'd always layer up lots of long beads. I'd henna my hair a rich, dark brown and wear red lipstick. I was still really into my Tamla Motown and then I got into the Phil Spector stuff. I also used to like Jimi Hendrix and Marc Bolan from T. Rex. I hung out with Marc a bit. My friend used to date him. He was beautiful. Guys were quite feminine at that time. They'd started to wear make-up, which I always thought was quite cool.

Annie and I loved this pub in St Christopher's Place called Pontefract Castle, which was one of the hip hangouts at the time. And we used to go to a Greek restaurant in Charlotte Street called Anemos. We'd go there and throw plates at the wall. Literally hundreds of plates – it was fantastic! You'd get in trouble with health and safety nowadays for doing that. We used to get absolutely smashed. I remember once getting so drunk I ended up in a dustbin. Somebody threw me in it. I was meant to go home straight after work on a Friday, of course, to see my parents and Simone but sometimes on Friday – pay day – I'd get completely wasted and then have to go home on the last train. Or sneak in really early on Saturday morning. That definitely didn't impress my mum and dad.

Most weekends, though, I would be back at the Old Rectory. Chris and I had really grown to love having this house in the country. It was actually very cool so we'd often invite friends from London down for a weekend away to this fabulous house. We'd have delicious lunches outside in the gardens and barbecues and things. My dad loved young people so he welcomed our friends with open arms. In summer, we'd drink Pimm's in the garden and in winter, rum and blackcurrant in front of a log fire. This carried on as a bit of a tradition, so once we'd set up the agency Chris and I would invite models and photographers down for a relaxing break. My parents would go away occasionally and we'd have these sneaky parties, sometimes inviting as many as 200 people and putting up about eighty people too. Full English for eighty hangovers was quite a logistical challenge.

In the summer of '72 I stopped temping because I found a permanent job at a graphic design studio called Face in Wells Street. It was here that I met the next man in my life, Mick, who would become my husband. My job was to liaise between the Face client art directors of ad agencies and the graphic designers. There were no computers in those days so it was very much a cutting and pasting job using cow gum and scalpels.

Mick was the top graphic designer at Face. He was very talented and sought after. In that business he was the top guy. He was also a bit mad and monosyllabic – very odd – but I was quite fascinated by him. He was one of the cool creatives coming out of the East End at that time, like Bailey, Duffy, Donovan and Michael Caine, and he spoke in rhyming slang and riddles. He was also self-taught – confident, extremely well read and knowledgeable. He had long blond hair and a beard, and was very athletic. I thought he was quite attractive but he wasn't my usual type because he was blond. He used to fluster me with one-liners. He was very perceptive, too, so he'd say things about me that were quite accurate and sharp. I'd not really experienced anyone like him before. One day I think he found my diary and read it and then couldn't resist telling me about it. I'd written things in it about Don and how unhappy I was. He realised he knew Don because they were in the same business and wasn't a big fan. Then he started to take the piss out of me. I was horrified that he might have read my diary but sort of impressed by his audacity too. It was a strange sort of attraction.

I first kissed him in the corridor outside the studio after we'd been out for lunch. Then we started to date. We kept it secret for a long time but people cottoned on soon enough; it's kind of hard to keep these things quiet when you work together. I think people were surprised because everyone thought he was a bit of an oddball. He was very talented and intelligent and quick-witted but he could also be very quiet and non-communicative. He was a bit of a loner, I suppose. When he had the hump at work everybody would get me to try and bring him out of it.

I took him to meet my parents. At first, they were convinced that he wasn't right for me because he was East End and we were very middle class, but they did get used to him quickly and after a while really took to him. They knew he treated me well, especially after Don, and he was stable, with a good job and plenty of money – that ticked lots of boxes for them. He was also fantastic with Simone. He started coming with me to the country most weekends so they got to know him very well and we all got into quite a nice routine.

We decided to get married. I think my parents were torn, because they really liked Mick and marrying him was the respectable thing for me to do – with a fatherless kid and no home of my own – but they still weren't fully convinced that I could make it work with him because perhaps we weren't quite the right match. I loved Mick though and he was brilliant with me and Simone.

Despite this bubbling under the surface, I remember my wedding as being a happy day. We got married in the church opposite the Old Rectory and had the reception in the garden at home, which was so lovely – really pretty. It was all quite avant-garde, which was totally my style, *very* Seventies. I wore a long tunic-style dress with long flowing sleeves designed by Janice Wainwright. Janice was the only other designer apart from Ossie Clark permitted to use Celia Birtwell's printed textiles from the Sixties, so she was a name known in fashion circles. I hennaed my hair, so it was a glossy brown with a hint of red and I wore it long with a centre parting. My friend Oli, who I'd met through Don, was my bridesmaid. She was my best friend; I was very close to her and we went out together all the time. She worked for Janice Wainwright as a house model and office manager for years. I always got beautiful suits from them and everything she did was appliqué. Oli worked there for years until she met Philippe Nault, a brilliant French artist, and went to live in Paris, where she became an agent for various designers.

We were sitting in the bathroom at the Old Rectory the night before the wedding and she said, 'Carole, you haven't got anything for your hair.' Nightmare! So she found a headband and stitched flowers on to it. Like I say, very trend setting! I carried a bunch of red roses that matched my ruby lips. When I see the photo of Dad and me at the church it gives me happy memories because we both look quite content. I'm glad Dad was by my side because I loved him so much.

For our honeymoon, we went on a driving tour of Scotland. It was the most beautiful weather and we drove all the way up the west coast staying in really nice hotels. We went to the Isle of Skye and Oban. I liked it because we were moving all the time so I didn't get bored and Mick had bought a red Alfa Romeo and I *really* liked that. I was a wife and a mother and we three were a family – it was all fab.

Simone and I moved into Mick's place in Mitcham. He had a two-bedroom flat. It was horrible actually. Well, the flat was OK – a really modern Sixties flat above a row of shops – but Mitcham was *awful*. It was too far away from the action in London; too suburban. I'd given up work because I didn't have a babysitter for Simone so I was attempting the housewife role. Mick would go to work and as it was my choice, I would get up and attempt to do homemaker things. I was okay at cooking but found it really boring just being at home. It was a disaster for me because I can't not work. I went into a real depression. Mitcham was not rocking at all and to make it worse I was prescribed Valium by the doctor, which flatlined me even more. I had it on repeat prescription so I was just eating Valium all the time, not realising it was bad for you. I can remember one day realising that I'd never even got dressed. I was like a zombie and spent a lot of time spaced out in the flat wearing a blue dressing gown.

Once again, work would be the saving of me: I had to work to stay sane. Being a stay-at-home mum was not for me. I went back to Alfred Marks to get another temp job – I wasn't fussy what, I just needed to work. Temping suited me because it was usually quite easy work and the money was good. It panned out a little differently this time around, though. Instead of offering me temp work as they had in the past, they asked me to work in their promotions department. I didn't have a clue what the role entailed but I said yes anyway. The job involved booking pretty girls for the Motor Show or to spray perfume on unsuspecting shoppers in Selfridges, that kind of thing. I'd unwittingly taken my first steps into what would be the making of me. I didn't know it yet, but I was learning how to become a booker.

6

GIRLS! GIRLS! GIRLS! STARTING AT THE BOTTOM

I shrugged off the blue dressing gown and got my groove back, thanks to the promotions job at Alfred Marks. I'd found something – admittedly by accident – that I was good at and really enjoyed. We did a lot of bookings for department stores like Harrods and the big trade shows such as the Ideal Home Exhibition, which was founded in 1908 by the *Daily Mail* and a really big deal. Over a million wide-eyed homeowners would go to Olympia to witness the unveiling of fabulous new inventions like the first microwave oven in 1947 or the first hover mower in 1965! The girls would just be there to be pretty. They'd be draped over the bonnet of a car in a bikini at the Motor Show or handing out leaflets at the Ideal Home show. They were eye candy – blokes would go and ogle them. It was all quite different then.

Essentially, this role was really similar to what a model booker does, just with different raw materials – the criteria (i.e. height, measurements) for promotions girls aren't as strict as they are with fashion models. In a nutshell, it was about finding pretty young ladies with personalities. Personality was key because often the jobs required interaction with the general public. The girls we hired were always very glamorous and well-groomed – pretty young women who either didn't want to be models or perhaps weren't tall enough. I realised that as long as you 'got' what the client wanted – professional girls who looked good, and were happy and jolly – you were onto a winner. A badly trained booker will throw everyone at the brief but it's wrong and it's just wasting the client's time. You have to always make sure you stick to what you know they would like. I learned this early on.

The office was on Oxford Street, at the corner of New Bond Street. I found childcare for Simone at this little school in the crypt of St Martin-in-the-Fields church in Trafalgar Square. It was brilliant. They accepted really young children there, even babies. Simone was three and they looked after her all day while I worked. Janice the head teacher was genius, a really great lady who became a friend. We saw a lot of her and she was very fond of my little girl. I'd get the train into town from Mitcham, drop off Simone and then make a mad dash to the office on Oxford Street.

Mick and I had got into a routine with Simone and were trundling along nicely. We'd become a little family.

We took a holiday to Hydra, the beautiful, tiny Greek island that's been a refuge for artists and intellectuals over the years. The American writer Henry Miller lived there in the 1930s and Leonard Cohen bought a house in the Sixties, prompting a raft of other creative types to follow him. I can see why it would be inspiring because it's so pretty, with the small fishing port and tiny winding streets flanked with open-air tavernas. It's also very peaceful because they don't allow cars on the island; donkeys are the mode of transport du jour! It's very other-worldly. There's a brilliant photograph of us getting off the boat taken by one of those snappers that lie in wait ready to pounce on all the unsuspecting tourists. Mick looked really cool then with his mop of blond hair, aviator shades and Seventies beard. He's wearing an all-white ensemble with these tiny tennis shorts – very Björn Borg! I'm working the St Tropez look in a jersey T-shirt that I've fashioned as a thigh-skimming dress and teamed with wedge sandals and this straw bucket bag that I picked up at one of the little artisanal stalls. I wore my hair long (still hennaed) with a fringe and I'm holding Simone's hand in the picture. She looks so cute wearing her floppy sunhat. I have fond memories of that trip.

There are certain people who help to shape you in your career, and life too. My boss at Alfred Marks was one of those people. She was this fantastic older woman who was very strong and driven, which was very inspiring to me. I admired her and learned a lot whilst I was there. She'd done really well to build up all these prestigious clients such as Selfridges and Harrods. She taught me about dealing with clients, learning what they want and finding the right girl for their needs. It was all about establishing and nurturing good relationships and then being able to sell the girl to them. I also learned how to interview the girls, to see if they had the requisite personality for all that small talk they would have to make on the job. My boss could see that I was good at it so she really encouraged me. She actually came to see my parents in Kent to tell them how wonderful she thought I was. It's the first time anyone had told me I was good at anything work-wise so it gave me a lot of confidence. I hadn't exactly been winning gold medals in my career up until this point.

I'd been there about a year when I saw a job advert for a model booker at Lucie Clayton. I decided to apply, more out of curiosity than anything else. My friend Jackie said to me, 'Oh, you'll never get it, you'll never get it,' but to my great surprise I did. And then I had a dilemma because it wasn't like I *had* to have this job, I was just seeing if I could get it. I ummed and ahhed for a while and then decided to take it. I felt that it was a good step forward for me so I had to tell my lovely boss that I was leaving, which was hard. She was devastated. She wanted to keep me but I was adamant this new job was what I wanted.

Off I trotted down the road to Bond Street and the famous Lucie Clayton Model Agency – my dream job! I thought it would be glamorous but of course it wasn't. I basically learned how to be a dogsbody; I was the lowest of the low in there. The first thing I had to do was get all the model cards (with a picture and vital statistics for each model), and lay them out on a big table in alphabetical order, then repeat, repeat, repeat, like dealing playing cards. Then I had to address envelopes to every single client ready for a mail-out. I was like a one-woman factory production line. That was my job. In its entirety.

It wasn't the high-flying, glamorous scenario I'd imagined. I hated it because I thought I was going to be a booker, but looking back it was actually a good grounding. Know your place! You have to start with the basics while you're learning the ropes and sometimes it's the simple/menial things that really matter. I've carried what I learned at Lucie Clayton with me throughout my working life, and that is still how I teach trainee bookers today (and they don't like it any more than I did). Even in the digital age, I expect my bookers to send cards out to clients. Some of them (a few) really get it, whereas others consider themselves far too fabulous for such menial tasks and I literally have to force them to do it. Then they're gobsmacked when they get phone calls back from it.

Bookers who've left me and gone elsewhere have said afterwards, 'What you've taught me about doing that is it really works!' and they've passed it on. Maybe that will be my legacy. It seems quite old-fashioned but it does yield results. That's one of my key pet hates with everyone being so reliant on email. This is a visual industry and it's just not the same sending electronic images. With an actual physical card, an art director or photographer can stick it up on their wall and next time they're planning a shoot it's there and they'll think, *oh yes, I really liked that girl* and call us up. I know clients do that, because I ask them and they say, 'yes, we love receiving cards', which I then relay to my bookers all the time with the add-on, 'See, I am always right.'

Eventually I was allowed to answer the phone and, in a very controlled way, shown how to organise go-sees and castings. One of the first times I was tasked with getting models to a casting, I misread the address because everything was handwritten in those days. It was in Davis Street but I'd read it as Dover Street so the models went to the wrong place. I got in so much trouble for that and had to dash to the wrong street to apologise to all the girls and redirect them. I never made that mistake again.

There were four of us on the booking table along with the boss, Leslie Kark. He'd bought the company and retained its name. His wife Evelyn would sometimes masquerade as Lucie Clayton in her role. Every month there was a graduation ceremony for the new modelling hopefuls who'd done the course that I had taken, and Evelyn (a.k.a. Lucie) would present them with their awards. Bit weird really. Anyway, Leslie really developed the business and it was a time of growth for the industry. Modelling had started to get cool in the Sixties. Before then, it was very staid and models were usually debutantes or posh girls who'd taken the finishing-school route. Now it was getting more diverse, with an influx of middle- and working-class girls who forged working (and often other) relationships with the hot photographers at the time. These relationships paved the way for a greater intimacy in the images. It was an exciting time.

The roster at Lucie Clayton in the Sixties and early Seventies was like a who's who of swinging London. Famous alumni include Sandra Paul, a *Vogue* cover girl both here and in the States who worked a lot with Bailey and Norman Parkinson. She's Sandra Howard now, a novelist and wife to Michael, former leader of the Conservative Party. Celia Hammond was Terence Donovan's muse. They did some fantastic work, a lot of it shot on location with a really candid feel. Celia was very versatile. She could be very sex-kitteny, reminiscent of Brigitte Bardot, or more refined, a bit Grace Kelly. She went out with the musician Jeff Beck for many years and another Donovan, the folk singer, penned the song 'Celia of the Seals' in tribute to her animal welfare work. There was Tania Mallet who was one of the Bond girls in *Goldfinger* and Paulene Stone, who married the actor Laurence Harvey and worked a lot with Brian Duffy, the third photographer to make up 'Black Trinity' with Bailey and Donovan, a term coined by Norman Parkinson.

Those three photographers (also sometimes called 'the terrible trio') really changed everything. They were like superstars and became as well known as the models and actors they worked with. All three were Sixties working-class East Enders in contrast to the so-called 'gentleman' photographers of the Thirties, Forties and Fifties such as Cecil Beaton, Norman Parkinson and Anthony Armstrong-Jones. Fashion photography became about selling a mood; there was more movement in the pictures and the girls became personalities. In the Fifties, fashion photography was about selling the fantasy of upper-class life. Models tended to be socialites and they'd always be photographed in the grandest places in London, like the Ritz and the Savoy. The Art historian Sir Roy Strong puts it very well in Bailey's brilliant Channel 4 documentary, *Models Close Up*. He says, 'It was a time when models were actually ladies, not tarts like David Bailey made them. They were inaccessible goddesses clutching a glass of champagne or elegantly deploying an umbrella.'

How hysterical is that?! Bailey wasn't at all interested in the stiff, almost still-life set-ups favoured in the Fifties. As he puts it: 'Models were beautiful objects rather than a personality. I was always interested in the personality more than I was the model.' He certainly did have a weakness for their 'personalities', yes!

In those days, the different types of modelling were very segregated. When you started out, for the first two years you weren't allowed to do any photographic work at all and even then it was only a very small pool that would do editorial. There were showgirls who did showroom work at certain times of the year. For editorial, the big names were *Woman*, *Woman's Own* and *Good Housekeeping*. If you did *Vogue* or *Harpers & Queen* (as it was known then) it was like, *ooh la la*. At the more homely end of the scale I booked girls for catalogues and knitting patterns, too. That was huge because a lot of women still made their own clothes back then. The core business was catalogues and advertising. Cigarettes, alcohol and chocolate. Three of my favourite things!

83

There were a lot of drinks ads, like Lamb's Navy Rum, and then Bounty and Turkish Delight and the notorious Cadbury's Flake ads.

When they started to trust me and give me more responsibility as a booker I felt like I was just where I was meant to be. I loved going to work. Lucie Clayton moved offices from Bond Street to Brompton Road in Knightsbridge and I found this fantastic Irish lady called Annie to look after Simone. She started at the Lycée Français school on the Cromwell Road opposite the Natural History Museum in South Kensington. Annie would collect her from school then I'd pick her up after work and drive back to Mitcham. I'd learned to drive by then. I must've been tired – it was really quite a busy and frantic time.

Mick was great but he didn't talk a lot and he could be grumpy at times, which didn't gel with me. I know that he really loved me and he'd do anything for me but occasionally we'd have a row and he wouldn't talk for days. I can't stand that. I can have a row with anyone but I always forget it, I never hold grudges. I once got a bucket of water and threw it over his head in the sitting room to make him talk. It got a reaction anyway – he thought it was quite funny. I guess we had quite a fiery relationship but I do with most of my men. In the autumn of '75 my husband went to South Africa for two weeks on a work trip and, unbeknownst to him (and me), my next chapter was about to begin. His name was Richard Best.

7

MICK AND RICK

I'd been told to go and collect some photographs of one of our models from the photographer Richard Best at his studio in Primrose Hill. We'd already chatted on the phone to arrange the pick-up and I must say I was intrigued to meet him because he'd been such a flirt on the phone, as had I! I always flirted on the phone; it was one of my tricks to snag clients. So I was already feeling intrigued when I tentatively knocked on his door. He appeared and it was like *boing*! – eyes-out-on-stalks territory. I couldn't believe it – I was left temporarily dumbstruck by how good-looking he was. He looked a bit like Brian Jones (before he died) or maybe Mick Jagger, as Brian was blonde – one of those rock stars who can just glance at a woman and her knickers fall down. I was in trouble and I knew it.

Rick, as he prefers to be called, invited me in to peruse

the contact sheets and before we even had chance to properly look he locked eyes with me and said, 'Come for a drink,' which was definitely more command than question. I didn't say no. We went to the pub opposite his studio, the Queens, and I sort of forgot to go back to work. It was all so intoxicating – the afternoon flew by in a blur of drinks and flirting, neither of us wanting it to end but I had Simone to think about. Somehow I managed to collect her from school as normal and then persuade my friend Vivienne to look after her that evening. Baaad.

I knew that I was playing with fire but I couldn't help myself – I was so instantly drawn to Rick. We didn't sleep together straight away because I can't cope with two men at the same time. I knew that as soon as I crossed that line my marriage would be over. But to be honest I think I knew it was over anyway. It was the thunderbolt thing. I saw Rick as much as I could while my husband was away which meant begging favours from people to look after Simone. It was a big affair and I was just falling deeper and deeper in love (infatuation?) with Rick.

When Mick came back from South Africa it didn't take long for things to unravel. I was still seeing Rick, which was a juggling nightmare, not to mention emotionally distressing. I was getting more and more reckless, coming home late after seeing Rick and being increasingly distant with my husband. It careered along like this for a week or two before Mick knew something was definitely wrong. It was difficult but I told him it wasn't working. He was really in love with me so he was distraught. Poor Mick – he goes away for two weeks and he hasn't got a wife when he comes back. I had to leave.

It was all a bit too familiar – the moonlight flit back to Kent. I gathered Simone and all my stuff, piled into the car and off we went back to Mum and Dad's. They thought they'd got rid of us but here we were, back again, shouting 'heeeeelp!' They were really upset because by then they'd got to know Mick and he had stepped up to the role of Simone's father. We'd been operating quite nicely as a family unit up until then and were pretty settled but here I was, messing it all up. This signalled the start of my very irresponsible years. I was so in love with Rick but he wasn't at all interested in my kid so my parents once again came to the rescue.

We had to come up with a plan for Simone. It wasn't going to work with her at the school in Kensington so my parents suggested we move her into the local primary in their village. It was a really good school and right opposite the house so very handy. I still had to go to work at Lucie Clayton so I fell back into the routine of travelling back and forth to London just as I had previously after splitting from Don. I was commuting and supposed to be getting back to the Old Rectory to see Simone in the evenings but I kept getting home later and later because I was so wrapped up in seeing Rick. I was madly in love with him and desperately trying to bat away his other girlfriends, which didn't exactly fit in with my mothering schedule. He was out all the time, the eternal bachelor, which meant I was out a lot, too.

I was pushing my luck, big time. I kept asking my parents if I could stay out later, or if I could stay with a friend. It was becoming more and more clear that I wasn't going home to look after my kid but my reasoning was, she's asleep! Then in the morning she was getting up to go to school and I was saying bye and heading to work, so I didn't get to see much of my poor little Simone at that time. My parents struggled with that and I struggled with it too, the guilt of not going home. Eventually my dad suggested I take up a flat in London again and just make sure I came home at the weekends. So that's what I did. Annie was still renting Ricky's flat in Stamford Bridge so I lodged there during the week, when I wasn't staying with Rick.

Life with Rick at this point was a hedonistic roller coaster – we were out most of the time, at pubs or clubs. The Queens in Primrose Hill was like his office. If I wanted to get hold of him I'd call the pub. He'd hold work meetings there with retouchers and clients. Primrose Hill was a genuine bohemian enclave then, not like it is now with all the yummy mummies. It was a little more scuffed around the edges, which I prefer, and there were lots of colourful, artistic characters in residence that gave the place a ramshackle buzz. Rick lived near to the actors Robert Stephens and Denholm Elliot, David Bailey lived at the end of the Regent's Park Road and John Swannell, another big photographer, was close by, too. It was sort of a secret, happening place that you didn't want to tell anyone about. I'd never heard of it until I met Rick. It's not on a tube line so you have

Top left: Harold 'Hack' Pinnington Owen – my lovely dad.

Top right: Sheila Mary Moorhouse – my lovely mum.

Left: With Hack, Sheila and Chris at the University of Legon, Ghana.

Above: The *Accra.*

The Asantehene
honours Hack as
an Asante Chief
in Kumasi.

We loved
Winneba beach.

Colonial kids with
classic cars.

Top: Convent girls — Tildonk, Belgium.

Above right: My first test shoot.

Above left: My first modelling job.

Right: In St Raphael, South of France.

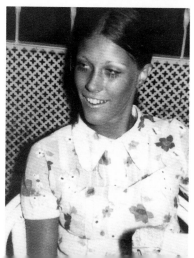

Top: On the beach in the South of France.

Above: The Old Rectory, Stowting, Kent.

Top left: Simone's christening, St John's Wood.

Above: Hack giving me away.

Left: My beautiful Simone.

Below: Mick, Simone and me, on a Greek island holiday.

SF Airport - to Dallas
Big Food!

Top: Sunday lunch at the Rectory.

Above left: With Rick in Florida.

Above: Rick and the gas guzzler.

Left: On the road, scouting in the USA.

Clockwise from top left: Rick in Menorca; my brother Michael; Simone with Sissy; Rick at a party; Simone and me in the fields behind the Old Rectory.

66 New Bond Street London W1Y OAT   01-629 0667

LUCIE CLAYTON

9th May 1974

Miss C. Owen
Flat 7
337 London Road
Mitcham
Surrey

Dear Miss Owen

This letter confirms your appointment to the staff of Lucie Clayton Ltd,

I am required to give you details which are as follows. Your appointment started on Monday 6th May and your hours are from 9.20 a.m. – 5.30 p.m. Your salary will be paid monthly at the rate of £1,750 per annum. If however during your first few weeks you would like an advance do please tell Accounts.

One months' written notice may be given by either side and you will be entitled to 3 weeks holiday. Please note that holidays not taken in one year do not accumulate to the next.

It is a basic condition of this contract that you do not work within one miles radius of this agency during three months

ope you will be

FOUNDED 1928

Above: Lucie Clayton letter.

Left: First test shoot.

to go to Chalk Farm and walk over the bridge, which is why it felt so hidden away.

There was a real sense of community so you'd see the same faces around. Odette's, an Italian restaurant opposite the Queens, was a big local hangout that became something of a Primrose Hill institution. Bailey was often in Odette's. It was opened by Peter Langan who also owned the (rather swish) Langan's Brasserie in Mayfair, just off Piccadilly. Peter was a real character. He was a big drinker so you'd go into Odette's and he'd often be there, holding court or propping up the bar.

Rick and I were both into our music so we'd go to gigs quite a lot at dingy music venues like Dingwalls and Monkberry's in Camden, or the Camden Palace. Rick was friendly with a lot of muso types who I slowly got to know and who, by the time we came to live together, I would see quite regularly at the flat. He knew a lot of people associated with Queen, like Mike Stone who produced most of their albums. We didn't much like Queen at the beginning and Mike would always invite us to gigs or give us their albums but we weren't that fussed – though I love them now. I was probably a bit influenced by Rick who liked his more traditional rockers like Joe Walsh and Nils Lofgren. Roger Taylor from Queen came to Rick's flat with Mike once but we didn't really bat an eyelid! There were a lot of Elton John's guys around too, his roadies and so on, and I remember seeing Keith Moon, the drummer from the Who, at some of our hangouts.

We used to have a lot of poker nights at Rick's place

and the same faces would gather. There was Len Worker, who was a fantastic artist who lives in France now, Andy Barr and James Fraser, whose family owned Fraser Cards. James always had money so everyone wanted him to come play and lose it because he always lost! My friend Robbie would come over a lot, too. She was married to Dave who was the most particular guy. He was highly intelligent. If you asked him, 'How do you make the hydrogen bomb?' he could tell you. He used to have an antique and props shop in England's Lane.

Rick and I gravitated towards trouble. We'd stay up playing poker till five and then I'd get up and go to work. There's a pill for everything, I suppose! I used to work really hard but also be hedonistic and self-indulgent, bearing in mind I had a child as well, although she wasn't living with me. We used to sit around and smoke, drink tequila, stuff like that. Sometimes we'd stay up all night.

There were a lot of late nights/early mornings but I still managed to drag myself in to work at Lucie Clayton. I've never been one for pulling sickies. If you're going to party and have fun then you have to be prepared to put up with the consequences. That's not to say I didn't suffer with terrible hangovers – everyone did.

Although I was going out a lot, my life at this time was actually pretty stressful. It was exhausting trying to keep up with Rick and, more importantly, keep the other women at bay. I remember having massive arguments with him every Thursday, regular as clockwork. I'm jumping ahead in the timeline a little now but it got to the point where I was virtually living at his house but playing this game where he mustn't notice that I lived there! There was no suitcase, it was just: 'I'm here!' I kept my stuff at the flat in Stamford Bridge or in the boot of my car. Anyway, every Thursday we managed to have a fight. Without fail. I think he did it on purpose so that he could get rid of me for a bit. Thursday would come around and sure enough we'd have a giant row and I'd storm off in my car. I was good friends with Mike Stone's live-in girlfriend who we called Susie 'Boobs'. They had a place in Mill Hill and we got on brilliantly; she was fantastic. She also understood the quirks of my relationship so every Thursday I'd call her up and say, 'It's Thursday, I'll probably be round,' and she'd get a bed ready for me.

I can laugh about it now, but not knowing where I stood with Rick was actually very stressful, which started to take its toll on my health, and I lost so much weight. I also felt like I'd let my daughter and my parents down, which I suppose I had. Mum and Dad were full-time parents again: raising Simone while I selfishly went off gallivanting. They realised she needed stability, which she wasn't going to get from me so she lived with them in that beautiful house. Simone would come and see me sometimes at Rick's. There's a cute picture of her stood next to Rick's car, a green Chevy Nova, outside the Primrose Hill flat.

Eventually we settled into more of a relationship and I finally took Rick down to the country to meet my parents in the summer of '77. Unsurprisingly, they weren't all that thrilled to meet this marriage-wrecker guy with long hair and a fondness for booze. And there was also the issue of Mick. He was incredibly close to Simone – he was her dad now – so he was still going to the Old Rectory to see her. He'd also become close to my family, too, particularly my brother Chris.

It was quite awkward sometimes because obviously Rick couldn't come when Mick was there which meant I was often there with Mick. At one point there was a chance that we might try to repair our marriage but it didn't work. When you're married I think you should try and make it work, at least once. But it didn't – he was too shy or scared to really give it a go but, more to the point, I'm sure my heart wasn't in it. In reality I wasn't ever going to pull myself away from Rick. He was so dangerous and difficult to pin down and, I know it's a cliché, but I found that so attractive. I like dangerous men. He was a challenge. I had to be quite clever about it but I did break him eventually and I was right to persevere because we're still together now, nearly forty years later. Rick's the love of my life.

Looking back, you would never have put Mick and me together. I'd fallen in love with him and he absolutely adored me but we were probably a bit too different to be fully compatible. He was a big loner and difficult to talk to sometimes but I was incredibly attracted to his talent and wit. I loved being married, though, up until I met Rick. Mick made me feel very safe and secure and in those days it was the 'right' thing to do. What you tend to do in life is you have a dangerous relationship and then you follow it with a secure one. You do that thing that your mum tells you: 'You must settle down.' I went from Dangerous Don to safe Mick and then to Rick, who was far from safe. Don was a similar kind of guy to Rick in a way. He was also very good looking with loads of girls after him, and that to me is a challenge. I have to get rid of them.

When I met Mick, he was really hard working, he was at the top of his game and he really looked after me. We were in love and I think social pressure certainly played its part but because the social boundaries really shifted in that era, I didn't go for who I was programmed to marry because I was quite rebellious. I was probably expected to marry a boring lawyer or accountant, that's what my parents would've loved. Instead I went for a talented, intelligent man from a working-class background who had made good. I went away from the established route because that's really what I was about. Of course because my parents were from another generation they would have much preferred if he was an accountant but they really liked Mick and got on very well with him and he's a brilliant, kind man who loved me and my daughter, who became his daughter.

In hindsight it wasn't the right match, which is a real shame because it could have been so great. I think my dad felt that. He knew me best of all. Mick had a very different upbringing to me. I'd had a very privileged lifestyle with a private education; he came from a working-class background – his parents were East Enders. He was highly intelligent, as was his father – he's one of those people who knows everything, like an encyclopaedia. I like a brain but it was a mismatch in a way because our cultures were so different. He was quite fascinated by mine. Ultimately, though, it was meeting Rick that changed things – I felt differently about him and I couldn't deny that. It wasn't that Mick did anything wrong.

Soon after we'd become an item Mick had opened his own design studio called Mushroom Studios in Tottenham Court Road. When Annie and I were living in Stamford Bridge we used to clean his studio for him for extra money. It was hilarious – we were the worst cleaners on the planet. When Mick and I split up, Mushroom did really well for a while but then it went downhill during the three-day week and the winter of discontent bad times so he founded another company, South Side Studios, with a small loan from Hack which became a big success, with offices in London and Sydney, Australia.

Life rumbled on for a couple of years with me running around with Rick during the week and spending weekends at the Old Rectory. Relations improved between my parents and Rick. He actually enjoyed going to the country and he'd help out my dad with manual tasks like chopping wood for the fires or decorating and doing odd jobs. It got to a stage too where Rick and Mick would tolerate each other if they happened to be there at the same time. Being full-time carers for Simone though was still a huge pressure for my parents so when she hit seven, in 1977, we decided the best thing would be to put her in boarding school. It was always on the cards because Chris, Michael and I had done the same;

it was what we knew. Sibton Park was a lovely school in Kent – no more than five miles from the Old Rectory – so she could come home at the weekends and see us all. Everyone chipped in – my parents, my brother Chris, even my wonderful husband Mick, which was very noble of him. We managed to remain close friends.

Flashing forward to now, Simone still sees Mick as her dad and they both live close to each other in Kent. He gave her away at her wedding to Steve in 2002 so he's a very special person in my life even if he didn't turn out to be the man for me. Looking back, I'm proud of the way we all – Simone, my parents, Mick, Rick and I – adjusted to what were really quite stressful circumstances. But life moves on – it has to.

* * *

Rick and I travelled a lot in the early years of our relationship. I have a ton of great memories, and photographs, from the road trips we shared. Our adventures really helped to cement us as a couple and we had *a lot* of fun. In those first few years we went to, coincidentally, a lot of places beginning with M – Majorca, Minorca, Mykonos, Morocco and Miami. In Mykonos, we had an apartment up this massive great hill. At night we'd go out and get absolutely pissed, dance till dawn and then we'd have to walk all the way back up this bloody hill! In the end we decided we liked the hill because it kept us fit. For breakfast we'd have honey and yoghurt and these amazing eggs that had really yellow yolks.

In Morocco and Majorca we hired a motorbike to get around – our very own *Easy Rider* experience! It feels very free, and romantic, to make your way around a foreign land on two wheels, like you're really living. We went to Morocco in the second year of our relationship and we were totally loved up. We were also firmly still in our naughty phase so when we arrived in Marrakesh, the first thing Rick said was, 'We have to get some dope.' So we were wandering around, asking people for dope, as you do, and we ended up meeting a guy who went off and came back with a bag of brown 'stuff'. Rick gave him the money – it was really cheap but still, money – and suddenly realised it was henna. Henna with twigs in it! He shouted 'Oi!', threw the bag in the air and chased him down the alley but then decided it wasn't worth it. It was a bit dodgy us running around the tiny back streets of Marrakesh on some half-baked dope mission.

At the souk, we were warned not to carry a bag because apparently there were some women who carried razor blades and split your bag. Because they were women and didn't look like thieves no one noticed them. I hated it. I just felt on edge all the time. Marrakesh is an intoxicating sort of place but not exactly relaxing, especially when you're with Rick, who's always looking for mischief. We went to Agadir, which was better because we could hang out at the beach and it was less crowded. It was a bit of a hippie haven and there weren't as many hustlers. Rick decided we needed some protection though after our experiences in Marrakesh so he befriended this guy who looked after us. For some unknown reason, Rick told him he was a boxer and that he wanted to buy a gun to protect himself! He couldn't get Rick a gun, but he was all right, this bloke, and we felt better when he was there, not so green. We rode horses on the beach in Agadir. That was fun, especially when Rick's would only trot backwards. Stubborn mule.

We travelled to Miami in the summer of 1980, smack bang in the middle of the race riots. Like I've said, we had a habit of walking into trouble. We wanted to check out an area called Coconut Grove that was meant to be all groovy, so we'd hired a Cadillac and were driving around this part of town but it was dead, there was literally nothing going on, so we kept on driving, got lost and ended up in the ghetto, which was quite dangerous in those days. We stopped the car and nervously asked a guy on the street how to get out. He was fine and directed us back to our hotel in downtown Miami, a Holiday Inn.

At the time the Holiday Inn was considered to be the bee's bollocks: if you were a rock star you'd stay at the Holiday Inn. They had a pool, which was just luxury! There's no way I'd stay there now but that was then. The riots started in Miami that night and we were so close we could hear it. It was frightening – there was banging, police sirens, screaming and shouting. We watched the news and realised it was quite serious. We needed to get out of there.

It didn't just go on for an hour or two; it went on for *days*. We jumped into our Cadillac, which Rick loved driving, and headed out of Miami onto 'Alligator Alley' to cross Florida. Even though we'd been warned not to stop we did anyway, in a lay-by. Next thing we know these two pick-up trucks stopped next to us filled with a load of rednecks and, to our horror, a shitload of rifles and shotguns in the back. We were scared, especially since we'd been warned that it wasn't safe. Luckily Rick was thinking on his feet – he was good at getting out of hairy situations should the need arise. He got out his Polaroid camera and said, 'Carole, I'll take a picture of you,' like he was tempting them to come over to us. Sure enough, they came to see what we were doing and Rick said: 'Would you like us to take a picture of you?' They nodded, so he took their picture, gave them the Polaroids and immediately got rid of any tension. They were our best friends then! We got out of it by taking their picture. A camera can be a very powerful tool.

We got back on the road and ended up in a place on the Gulf of Mexico called Naples. I couldn't believe my eyes, it was like a tropical paradise. So different from where we'd been. The beach was a mass of pink sand dotted with shells and pelicans. It was like, wow, we like it here! Off we stumbled to find a bar. First things first! I remember it being so dark going into this bar after being in the bright sunlight I fell over the table. We started talking to this barmaid, Brenda, who had a funny accent – they all talk like hillbillies around those parts but we loved it. We just drank bourbon and chatted away. The barmaid suggested we stay at Howard Johnson, which is a motel chain that you have all over America.

We thought it was fantastic, nothing like you have in England and so cheap. We were thinking, ooh, we could stay here quite a while! Even though we were still paying for our Holiday Inn back in Miami.

Brenda got really friendly with us and said, 'You've got to come to this Bluegrass bar.' She was really really nice so we went with her and she was trying to give us the lay of the land. She told us there was a bunch of regulars who played pool there and that the sheriff played in the Bluegrass band. Then she said: 'There's one thing about the people who play pool – don't play them. If you beat them, there'll be a problem. They're all rednecks.' We're both nodding and listening.

Next thing, I'm sitting drinking and Rick has vanished. 'Where's Rick?' I say to the barmaid, already having a very good idea where he'll be. Sure enough, there he is, in the pool room beating everyone at pool. Eek! I got really nervous, as did the barmaid. She was like, 'This can't happen.' Anyway, it got to the last table and it was a girl he was playing and she beat him. Thank God! But still, all the guys who he did beat were getting a bit antsy. We were drinking and wondering how we were going to get out of there. The barmaid told us the sheriff was due to turn up soon to play in the band. She yelled at us, 'There's going to be a raid, we need to get out of here!' We're walking out and suddenly all these guys who Rick had beaten at pool were lined up to prevent us leaving. What did Rick do? He shook all of their hands and said, chipper as anything: 'If you're ever in London, get a red number 79 bus to London Zoo and ask for Rick. They all know where I live!' So, unbeliev-ably, they all shook his hand and said they'd come and see us. We got out of it but it was so scary. I'll never forget that trip and I think it shows why Rick and I have been such a good match – we're both daft enough to get ourselves into some pretty hairy situations but clever enough to get back out of them too!

8.

DEVELOPING AN EYE

I learned the ropes of the modelling business at Lucie Clayton but I developed my eye – a crucial skill – at the next place I worked: Bobtons. I'd been at Lucie Clayton for about two years; I was twenty-six and getting itchy feet. I'd become a good agent – I learned the rudiments of how to book there – but there wasn't really room for me to grow. Plus it was a bit old-fashioned.

I decided to look elsewhere and applied to Models 1 and Bobtons, which were two of the main agencies at that time. I was looking to broaden my experiences and both agencies worked internationally whereas Lucie Clayton didn't – it was quite parochial. Other agencies included Gavin Robinson, which was quite commercial; Cherry Marshall, a similar enterprise to Lucie Clayton with a finishing school attached; and Nevs, a men's agency. The modelling business was still very much a cottage industry at that time and Models 1 and Bobtons were the most progressive and modern. Both seemed to be going places and were definitely the cooler options.

Models 1 was the bigger of the two and it's still going strong now. Jose Fonseca and April Ducksbury founded it in 1968 and it was they who interviewed me for the job. I went to their offices on the King's Road and felt pretty nervous because they were already quite established figures in the business and they had really good girls. I liked them, too; we got on. Soon after our chat they offered me a job but I still had my interview at Bobtons to do.

At Bobtons I was interviewed by one of the co-owners, Gillian Bobroff. My first impression of Gillian was that she seemed completely nutty. She was very of the time: a glamorous hippie chick, jingling with jewellery and flamboyant energy. She was really open and friendly – lots of 'darlings' – which I liked. I decided to go with Gillian, it was a gut feeling so I went with it – something I've done throughout my career when it comes to people. She's the same sign as me too and I really click with Cancereans. I also got the sense there'd be more movement at Bobtons, I thought I could really do something there, so I said yes to the job of booker. Models 1 were quite shocked that I turned them down but I just preferred the energy at Bobtons. It felt right.

The offices were tiny, literally just a couple of small rooms above a clothes shop called Sidney Smith at the Sloane Square end of the King's Road. There was a winding little staircase leading up to the office where the models would perch like birds waiting for castings. I was right about movement because on my first day Gillian was there but her partner, Laraine Ashton, wasn't and it was chaos. Laraine was definitely the organiser of the two whereas Gillian was the creative brain, the visionary – she didn't concern herself with anything as dull as the day-to-day running of a business. This meant I was thrown in at the deep end and had to start booking, even though I didn't know a single girl. I bluffed my way through it because they had a book with all the models' pictures and essential info in it, so I sort of blagged it and kept saying 'it's my first day' to whoever called. The phone just didn't stop ringing. As it turned out that was the beginning of the end of the Bobtons partnership. Laraine left soon after to set up on her own. I think she and Gillian were unable to see eye to eye.

We were a small booking team. There was Suzanne Stone, the booker, who I became very friendly with but who looked at me like I was an alien for at least the first two weeks. I think she was wary of me stepping on her turf; bookers are territorial like that. She celebrated her twenty-first birthday soon after I started so she was younger than me but super-organised and really good at her job. She was on the scene too, always out with one of the models or a musician boyfriend (she dated Phil Collen from Def Leppard for a while). She had a really strong look – a mass of wildly curly long hair with vigilantly painted red lips and she usually dressed in a short skirt with cowboy boots. John was another booker – a little Scottish boy who was great fun. He had a partner called Charlie who was a partner at a big ad agency but I think John was quite promiscuous and Charlie got pissed off. They had quite a long-term relationship but split up eventually, probably because of John's wild ways. He'd go cruising on his lunch hour to Sydney Street swimming baths with a hanky sticking out of his back pocket to indicate to potential suitors that he was available. So there we were, munching on our sandwiches, while he merrily nipped off for a shag with a complete stranger. Suzanne and I were horrified! He was so lovely but we couldn't quite believe what he was up to. He'd come back after an hour and sit down perfectly normally as if nothing had happened.

David Mainman, another gay gentleman, ran the men's department. He was older than the rest of us – kind, well-spoken and always impeccably dressed. He wasn't as wild and out as John because his family background was very old money and conservative. I think he struggled with reconciling his sexuality with his more conventional past. It would have been considered taboo. He was an amazing cook and he'd have fantastic dinner parties around at his house in Shepherd's Bush that always turned a little crazy. As everyone got drunker all the gays would go upstairs and then come down the spiral staircase with feather boas sticking out of their arses. It was hysterical. He was also a very good booker but probably a bit too nice, not ruthless enough. Really he should have run the agency when it came to it but I got it in the end. Suzanne and I would socialise a lot with David and John – they'd take us to the Coleherne in Earls Court, a famous gay pub full of the leather and moustache crowd. It was crazy.

It was an exciting time to be stationed on the King's Road. Unlike now where it all feels a bit sterile and gentrified, in the Sixties and Seventies it was a real centre for counter-culture. Independent boutiques like Mary Quant's Bazaar and Granny Takes a Trip kicked things off in the Sixties, then it became the headquarters of punk, with Vivienne Westwood and Malcolm McLaren's infamous 'Sex' boutique at World's End and the controversial clothing store Boy, which was wild. I remember tentatively going into Boy and all the assis-tants were punk and that was a bit nerve-wracking. It was all a new thing; a new look. There were all these boys stomping down the street with their Mohicans and ripped denims. I found the whole scene really intriguing and a bit scary because it was quite aggressive. I didn't get into the look myself, I stuck with variations on my hippie-chick thing, but Suzanne nodded to it a bit with skin-tight leather jeans and little kilts. I think it looked particularly good on women. Fashion girls adapted it and made it sexy.

Cool London is no longer concentrated in one or two areas like it was then. Now there are several areas in London that are legitimate – Shoreditch, Dalston and Hackney in the east, Camden and Kentish Town in the north, or Covent Garden or Notting Hill, but it was pretty much just the King's Road and Carnaby Street in the late Seventies. They were certainly epicentres for fashion. A lot of photographers had their studios there too, or there were others dotted around Bond Street and Wigmore Street, more centrally. In the Eighties that all changed when central London rents skyrocketed and people started to migrate east. Now agents, designers and photographers are dotted all over the city which makes it a lot less personal than when I was at Bobtons and photographers could easily drop in for a chat and models wouldn't have miles to schlep across the city to castings. These days they're going south, east, north and west. It's all to do with rent. They'll probably be in bloody Scotland soon. It's not as spread out in New York or Paris.

I cherish that time when there was such a buzz around the King's Road and our little agency was a social hub. We'd always have models draped on the stairs chatting or a photographer swinging by to chat to Gillian. The office was so tiny that we didn't even have a meeting room. When clients came in we'd have to take them to this private club that was underneath Sidney Smith called the Alibi. It was in a basement so there was no natural light. This was extremely handy when you were feeling hungover, as we often were. Not exactly conventional but that's what it was like in those days, a bit rock 'n' roll.

Gillian was the living embodiment of this hedonistic spirit. She was always partying or entertaining. She was a really attractive woman – blonde with piercing blue eyes and her own distinctive style. She'd take trips to Ibiza several times a year, staying for a couple of months in the summer, and come back really tanned, dressed all in white and accessorised with loads of glittery hippie scarves and bangles. She was married to David Charkham who'd been a child actor and was very good friends with the composer Lionel Bart who created the music for *Oliver!* They used to call his Chelsea mansion the 'Fun Palace' in the Sixties and Bart would party with everyone from John Lennon to Noël Coward. He was a big scenester. David was Gillian's second husband and a lovely man. He used to help in the agency but I think he got fed up with that.

Gillian was about thirty-six when I started and she was a confident businesswoman but she had a wild side too. I love dangerous women so that's probably part of the reason I liked her. I can't be doing with boring people – I'd rather you were difficult than dull, a preference that probably made it easier for me to work with some of the supermodels, but we'll come to that later. Laraine Ashton and Gillian Bobroff were totally different types. Laraine, who later married the photographer Terry O'Neill, was very feminine – one of those women that men want to look after, whereas Gillian was very much in the *I don't give a fuck about anyone, I'll do what I want* camp, which was refreshing and exciting. I met Harvey Goldsmith through her, who I'd go on to work with and who became a good friend.

Gillian was an excellent networker, very good at matching people together which is essential in this business. I definitely learned that from her. She had masses of friends, often famous actors and musicians or the cooler aristos. She'd trip off for the weekend to this giant mansion house in the country owned by Lord Montagu of Beaulieu. He had a huge collection of classic cars and another property on his estate that looked like a gingerbread cottage, called the Gate House, which was like Gillian's second home. It was all very fabulous.

She liked the grittier end of the social spectrum too – she was a close friend of Donovan, who was a proper East End lad. Then there was Keith Moon, the drummer from the Who, who she adored and who was a complete nutcase! He was dating one of our models, Annette, and would often swing by the office and make us all laugh. She also loved the wealthy set like Rothschild and property tycoon Jack Dellal, known as 'Black' Jack Dellal, allegedly because he was a big gambler. He was certainly a big character, which is probably why Gillian liked him so much. He was always at Annabel's and Tramp and other hotspots of the time.

It was Gillian who really helped me develop my eye. She had an amazing skill for identifying unusual beauty and spotting the next look. We might not realise it but our eye adapts to accept new forms of beauty. It takes somebody showing you how to do this in the beginning and even then you might not 'get' it. You almost have to retrain your brain to dismiss any conventional ideas of beauty. We often couldn't see it when Gillian brought in new girls. She'd say, 'I really like this girl I met at a dinner party, she's coming in.' Then Camilla showed up and I was horrified, I thought, *that's not a model*. The entire booking table agreed with me. Then she went on a trip somewhere, the photographer took extra pictures on location, I saw the pictures and I got it. She was strange-looking in person but on film she was amazing. I really remember that point: I made the connection. Then I started to hone it myself. I guess my second brain kicked in and said, you need to watch this woman because she knows what she's doing.

I learned a lot from Rick at this time, too. He was a photographer so he also had a good eye. He knew how to transform a mediocre picture simply by how you crop it. I'm really good at this even to this day. I know that cropping can change a dull picture and make it special so I really try to impress this on the new generation of bookers as they come through the agency.

In terms of jobs, I was booking a lot of catalogue and TV commercials. TV ads then were huge projects with great directors and some have become iconic: Turkish Delight, Bounty and Flake. Every year there was a new Flake campaign. Ridley Scott and Tony Scott were both prolific directors of TV commercials, as were Alan Parker and Adrian Lyne – all of whom went on to have very successful careers in Hollywood. Adrian directed *Flashdance*, *9½ Weeks* and *Fatal Attraction*. TV commercial directors were gods in those days and the ads were so creative – these guys were major artists, using commercials as a stepping stone to directing feature films. If you were working with Ridley or Adrian it was a privilege so the girls loved it. It could be tricky to book though because the models had to be Equity members in those days. If you knew you had a girl who was going to be good at TV commercials then somehow you had to get them an Equity card which meant they had to do some dancing or something like that to get it. It was a closed-shop union. Equity loathed models and did everything they possibly could to stop them getting a card.

Turkish Delight was one of the last jobs I booked at Bobtons and I got a day rate for the model of £300, which was unheard of – studio fees were normally kept notoriously low thanks to the union. The good thing about TV ads in those days, though, was that models would generally get repeat fees every time the ad was played and would make money when it got sold to other territories. Now studio rates are still low and they tend to offer buy-outs rather than repeat fees.

We also used to do a lot of press advertising, and the main magazines for that were *Honey*, *Woman*, *Woman's Own* and *Woman's Journal*, which were your day-to-day bread and butter. They tended to be horrible pictures with horrible photographers and horrible clothes but they brought in good money for the girls and for us. Catalogues were also a big deal then. The models would do these long trips to tropical places like Barbados for about ten days and often have affairs with the photographer, but keep that to yourself! It was the Seventies, *everybody shagged everybody.*

We had a lot of great models at Bobtons and the height requirement wasn't as strict as it is now. We had plenty of models who were under 5' 8" whereas you would rarely get that now. One day Roger Daltrey from the Who came into the office (he was friendly with Gillian) with some pictures he'd taken of these twin sisters, Jennifer and Susie McLean. They were really young when they first came in, maybe sixteen, but we took them on and they did really well. They weren't so tall but they were sweet, dainty girls with big personalities and they just zoomed. They worked with Barry Lategan, who is one of my favourite photographers. He used to shoot all the time for Italian *Vogue*, and I always thought his work was very painterly: beautiful, beautiful pictures. There was always talk about the twins: one of them was rumoured to have been hanging out with Roger Daltrey, but it might have been just that: talk. And Dustin Hoffman was another name that came up in conversation. Suzanne saw them socially more than me; I think she stayed with them for a while. That's how it was; we were all quite friendly with each other. Like Desiree, a Bobtons model who became my pal. She lives in Belsize Park and we're still great friends. She used to do a lot of Italian bookings and was a good show girl because she was 5' 10". She was from the US but lived in London most of her life. She was quite wild! She had dark blonde hair, wavy, and she actually had quite a strong nose which she later had changed to help her get more work.

Another big name from that time was Vivienne Lynn. She was tiny, probably 5' 4", but she was stunning – half Japanese and half English – so she had something that nobody else at that time had. She was very exotic. She wore beautiful Japanese clothes and she was so feminine and elegant, almost bird-like. Vivienne was huge in Japan and never stopped working so she'd divide her time between Japan, Paris and London. Japan was all new to me but at Bobtons I learned how important that territory is for developing models, which would come in useful later. Vivienne was mainly a beauty girl and a born performer – she recorded a single that became a number one hit in Japan! She was also very much a New Romantic scenester, hanging out at the Blitz Club with the likes of Boy George, Marilyn and Philip Sallon, and she dated fellow fashion chameleon David Bowie for a while. Her look was very avant-garde; she was wildly experimental like all those Eighties club kids. It was a real creative hub and she'd work with her friends, such as Zandra Rhodes, whose campaigns she modelled for. Zandra and Vivienne were a riotous match made in heaven. She also did a lot of British and Italian *Vogue* and was a Flake girl. Years later she got engaged to Tony Curtis, which was weird. I remember her telling me: 'He's amazing, he's lovely, and we met him at dinner,' but it was quite a strange combination because he was so much older than her. She was absolutely potty about him but then it all fizzled out.

The musician-model alliance was still going strong, which Gillian loved, of course. She was always a fan of the cool rock types. I looked after Jo Howard who had just started dating Ronnie Wood from the Stones and later went on to marry him. She came into the office the day after she'd met Ron at a party and he'd told her he worked in a supermarket! Hysterical. Jo did a lot of catalogue work, Freemans mainly. Then we had a model called Lil Wenglass Green who dated Keith Richards for a while. Lil was a very cool girl and wouldn't look out of place now with her Debbie Harry-ish blonde rock chic look. Along with Ronnie and Jo they became a bit of a foursome. I can only imagine the stuff they got up to with those boys on tour. I only met Keith once – he seemed like a cool guy.

Lil was Swedish. In those days there were a lot of Swedish models working in London. She was one of those hip girls on the scene and totally bonkers, which I think you'd probably need to be in order to date 'Keef'. Swedish girls have a habit of speaking English with a strange cockney accent, which amped up the crazy factor even more. Lil stayed with Gillian for a bit and Keith Richards would call up the house all the time. Then there was Annette Walter-Lax, also a Swede, who went out with another wild rocker called Keith – Keith Moon. Annette was a lovely girl but sadly unlucky with men. My Rick was very friendly with Keith so we'd often hang out with him and Annette at Tramp, one of the super-cool members' clubs in London at that time. Annette was going to marry Keith but then he died, in 1978, which was so tragic. Apparently he was all set for proposing to her but he overdosed on the medication he was taking to help him get off the booze. She went on to marry Gareth Hunt from *The Avengers*. He was quite a big actor at the time.

I remember this time as being really fun and packed full of larger-than-life characters. There was never a dull moment. We had Amanda Lear on our books – she was once Salvador Dali's muse. Alexandra Bastedo was an actress who was in a big TV series in the Sixties a bit like *The Avengers* called *The Champions*. She was one of those real bombshell types. Deborah Vaughan was a really top model who worked loads in Italy and she lived with this guy who was some sort of a prince but didn't have any money. She committed fraud and ended up in Holloway Prison. Jane Goddard was another one who found herself in trouble. She was a brilliant model – very cool, with amazing blonde curly hair. She did *Vogue* and a lot of catalogue. They weren't as snobby then about mixing the high- and low-profile stuff. In the Eighties she got more and more trendy. Her husband was a really good photographer called David Anthony. He photographed her a lot for *Vogue*. In the end, her husband started dealing Colombian coke with this guy called Mark Turner, who was another model's (Sue Purdy's) husband, and eventually they got busted. The police found a mountain of coke on the kitchen table at David's.

We were friendly with them and Mark used to come around to drink tequila slammers – tequila with dry ginger ale. He and Rick would take cling film to the pub with them, pour the tequila, pour the ginger ale and then slam it on the table. It would froth up like a soufflé. It was a great drink but not for the faint-hearted!

One Saturday we were asleep and David's brother came round and told us the police had been following them. David and Mark had both been arrested, and he thought he should tell us since we were friends of both men. Eek! We got out of bed, drove to the Old Rectory and lay low for a while. It turned out they'd been followed and the police discovered everybody who was involved. David went to jail for three years and I think Mark got a year. It was all very dramatic.

There was a lot more variety with bookings in those days and all these characters with quite crazy lives. I guess a lot of models used to be actresses too, or dancers, or they'd be able to do the whole gamut of different kinds of modelling. It wasn't as regimented. We used to book hand models then, too. Anne Ford was tiny but made loads of money from her exquisite hands and feet. She did a lot of TV commercials and beauty ads. She made a fortune, she was one of our top billers. Susan Mayer was the biggest hand model of all time – imagine that! – but always yearned to be a 'normal' model. She had a really squeaky voice so when she rang up the office it was hard to not laugh. You thought she was taking the piss but she wasn't. She made a bomb. We also had Caroline Munro, all legs and long brown hair, who was a Bond Girl and quite a celeb. She did the Lamb's Navy Rum campaign, which at that time was a huge contract and just ran and ran so she made a pile of money from that.

What strikes me when I look at the models' cards from back then was how old they all looked when they were actually quite young. The fashion was so conservative and they were always caked in make-up; no one was fresh. Some of them were really quite cool girls, like Lil, who you could fit in now, but they had to wear this mask. They were all trying to appear older, I suppose because the buying power was very much with middle-to upper-class women who had money. It wasn't so much focused on youth like in the Sixties.

Models were still doing their own hair and make-up at this time, too. Everyone was taught to put on this really thick layer of pan stick, which looked so unnatural. Catalogues would expect you to have a basic wardrobe of nude underwear, the right coloured tights – black and tan – and court shoes. Later, in the Eighties, it started to get more professional and models started to demand hair and make-up, which opened up a whole new industry. There was more prestige to catalogue work then, certainly for the photographers, because they could make so much money. David Stanford was a photographer I worked with at this time who only really shot catalogue and was probably the wealthiest photographer ever. He was good but he was a catalogue photographer so he'd just churn it out and go on wonderful trips to Mexico or wherever. He's probably retired to a palace in the South of France somewhere now.

I was getting more and more responsibility at work, especially as Gillian spent an increasing amount of time away from the office. I had to step up to wining and dining with clients, which could sometimes be quite scary, especially if you didn't know the right protocol. I remember going to a sushi restaurant for the first time with some Japanese clients. It was in St James's and was one of the only Japanese restaurants in London at that time. It was so posh! The client was Twining's Tea who wanted to use a model we had called Angela. So it was

Suzanne and I, Sayo, a Japanese agent who'd hooked up the deal, and these bigwigs from Twining's Tea Japan. We got there and had to take our shoes off and sit on the floor, which was a first for me.

You couldn't get sushi on your lunch break at M&S in those days so we didn't have a clue what we were doing. We played it like Follow Your Leader and just watched what they did. Here we were, these two really green English girls, pretending we were worldly. It was a massive culture shock – all the women bowing down subserviently to these quite scary Japanese men. I can't imagine we were very good. We were negotiating a contract, quite a big one, but we didn't know how to deal with these men because they seemed like warlords or something. The food was delicious, though, despite the fact we had no clue what we were eating. After that experience we started to go quite regularly to another Japanese restaurant that had opened in Hanover Square. We loved it.

I'd started to become a good negotiator. Once you know what you're doing you can start planning, which is so much better for the model. You can decide what to take and what to leave. And because there weren't that many models around you had a lot of power. If you could get a girl that everyone wanted, particularly for the higher-end stuff, you were in a position of strength because they wanted that model and couldn't replace her with anyone else. It's not like now where the choice is infinite and the work is not as creative as a result. I'd just hold my nose and guess a figure, knowing that if they didn't go for it there was always someone else wanting this girl anyway. It was like playing poker, which I loved. Sometimes you lost, of course, but you've got to be in it to win it.

I was working hard and playing hard. Socially it was very exciting. Rick and I used to go to Tramp on Jermyn Street a lot. Tramp was a bit of a muso hangout – Bowie was there sometimes and we'd bump into Rod Stewart occasionally. He used to date one of my girlfriends. He was good fun, but very short! All the action was centred around W1 and then it moved out towards Camden in the late Seventies/early Eighties.

We'd go to Camden Palace quite a lot for gigs and they held the annual Models Ball there a few years running. It was to raise money for the Association of Model Agents (AMA). Sometimes they were quite posh, sit-down dinners and the tickets sold like hotcakes because anyone could go as long as you paid up. As you can imagine, it was extremely popular with men. One year all the girls had to dress up in lingerie – that was the theme. All these hapless men couldn't believe their luck – tall, tall girls swanning around in stockings with suspenders and heels. I was keeping my beady eye on Rick to make sure he didn't wander off with anyone!

We went to quite a few parties at Gillian's place, too. Rick really liked Gillian; they got on well and knew some of the same people such as Keith and Annette. We met Gareth Hunt at one of Gillian's gatherings. He'd just got that Nescafé coffee ad and he was obviously cele-brating because he was plastered. You were always pretty much guaranteed to bump into a random celebrity at Gillian's. The Hollywood actor Ryan O'Neal, who starred in *Love Story*, was at her fortieth. Suzanne and I were in hysterics at these parties because Gillian wasn't the tidiest of people. In fact, she was a right mess. Her mews house was tiny and she had these little yappy dogs that would shit everywhere and Gillian wouldn't notice or be bothered enough to clean it up. So there'd be all these celebs squished onto a sofa and, more than likely, sitting in a pile of shit. Sometimes we'd be nice and attempt to move it but there was shit everywhere. You'd have to look before you sat down and wherever you put your feet. It was gross! They were Yorkies and they used to bite as well. We hated them.

The dog shit piling up at Gillian's home was becoming a metaphor for her life. She often didn't come in to work. The more I learned, the more she relied on me, then she'd just disappear on these holidays to her 'health farms'. She was painful when she was in the office so secretly we were glad when she was off. When she was good she was good but when she was farting around she was annoying. As time went on, her good moments became few and far between and we ended up knowing more than her, which is a dangerous situation for an employer to be in.

When she was incapacitated I used to drive from Rick's place in Primrose Hill to Marylebone to pick her up or I'd just catch her up on work stuff and then leave, all the while trying to dodge those fucking dogs. We'd basically pretend to have meetings, looking through magazines and saying, 'Ooh yeah, that's lovely' and so on. As Gillian got more reliant on me she didn't feel the need to come in. I'd say, 'No, I don't wanna come over today,' but she'd persuade me. She was very demanding – like a supermodel.

It got to the point where I was running the agency for her. I'm quite organised and I always think ahead so I was doing a pretty good job. I wasn't that experienced when I went in but I'd really gained in confidence. I'd had to learn a lot about international bookings and dealing with big clients. I was basically shouldering a lot of the responsibility. We'd moved from the tiny offices at the bottom end of the King's Road to these giant posh offices at the Sydney Street end, which I really think was Gillian's downfall. They were far too grand. The décor was really expensive and over the top – all silver painted wallpaper and peacock tails. She had her own little office which was decorated like some kind of Moroccan harem and if any of her fabulous friends came in the blinds would go down and vast plumes of smoke would come seeping out from under the door.

Everything caught up with her after a while – the wild living and even wilder spending. The money ran out and her backer wanted me to take over but it all went wrong. It had gone too far. In the end, the company got wound down. I called Chris and said, 'The company's being liquidated, what does that mean?' and he said, 'That means you're in deep fucking shit,' which is when the plan was hatched to set up on our own.

I'll never forget meeting Gillian in the Chelsea Arts

Club on the last day and she started crying and asking me if she could have a job. It was horrible. Gillian was special to me, she was so charismatic and a really nice lady. She was talented and generous but the business had clearly come to an end. It was the end of an era but an exciting new chapter lay ahead and its name was Premier.

9.

GOING PLACES

I came up with the name Premier pissed as a rat at a friend's house, while playing poker. I could see the letters spelled out in front of me like a fateful, albeit fuzzy, apparition. It's kind of apt that I arrived at the name during a gambling stint because that's what starting your own business is, isn't it? A great big, white-knuckle gamble.

Rick and I played poker with our merry group of misfits quite often and I'd become very good at it. We'd be up for hours playing, drinking tequila, smoking those Thai sticks. The stakes got a bit too high one night. There was two grand in the pot and one of our friends wanted to keep playing but didn't have the money to put in, so threw in their Mini as collateral. They lost. Because they didn't have anything to drive home in they took the car with them and I never heard from them again. That taught me a big lesson: never play poker with close friends because you might lose them. They were quite prepared to take two grand off me but not ready to lose their car. Very awkward.

It was 18 December 1981 when we all assembled in Chris's flat – me, Suzanne (from the now-defunct Bobtons), Chris and about twenty worry-faced models currently without representation. This was it: sink or swim. It was Chris's idea to set up on my own, to which I replied: 'I haven't got any money.' His matter-of-fact reply? 'We'll find some.' So here we were, a week before Christmas, seriously blagging it. We told all the girls to go away and have a great Christmas and that we would be open at the beginning of January. Because it was Christmas everyone had shut down so I was able to keep all the models from tinkering off to other agencies. With Chris by my side, I had the confidence to convince them to trust me and that all was under control.

But it wasn't really – not quite. We still needed to actually find that money. True to his word, Chris came up with £7,000 of his own cash. He was doing really well for himself as a freelance publishing rep, travelling all over the world on behalf of various different publishers. My younger brother Michael invested £3,000. The resulting £10,000 was a lot of money in those days, but it wasn't going to be enough, so I went to see my friend Martin Stainton to ask him to invest in us. Martin was a chartered accountant and very well connected in the music business. His clients included Pink Floyd and Chris Blackwell, who founded Island Records. Martin agreed to invest £7,500 on behalf of his clients, and Mum and Dad, supportive as ever, put up the Old Rectory as a guarantee. With £17,500 in cash, and a bank overdraft facility of a further £50,000, I was able to keep my promise to the models and officially open for business on Monday, 4 January 1982.

But Suzanne and I started to make bookings straight after that December meeting with the models and, by the time the New Year came, we'd already booked about £25,000-worth of catalogue jobs. We'd been working from Chris's living room, and it quickly became obvious that we needed an office, so we found some serviced offices in Regent Street and moved in just before Christmas. Now we were legit. Everything just happened so quickly, which was probably a good thing, because if I'd thought about it too much I might have hesitated. And hesitation can be fatal.

We'd been in this tiny serviced office space about a week when who should walk through the door but Eileen Ford, the matriarch of the modelling world! The woman who, along with her husband Jerry, founded Ford Models. She was Goliath to my David and had flown in basically because she was nosey – she wanted to know what was going on with all the Bobtons girls and to see if we were kosher. The upstarts that we were. How did she even know where we were? In this industry bad news travels fast. She was wearing a skirt suit and a smart coat – very classic, not trendy at all. She looked like a well-coiffed mum. Actually she was scarier than the nuns at Tildonk; it was more like meeting Maggie

Thatcher. Her hair was honey blonde and stiff and she was very straight-talking.

We had a chat and it transpired there were a couple of girls she wanted in New York, so I said, 'OK, but I want two girls in return.'

'But I'm Ford, I will make your girls,' was her answer, as she stood firm in front of me, all skirt suit and rock-hard hair. I thought, *two can play at that game*, so I held eye contact with this scary woman and repeated, 'I need two girls back – I have to pay the rent.'

And I got them. Wow! The Eileen Ford seal of approval! We were officially on our way.

It's weird thinking back on that meeting with Eileen now, because I actually wasn't intimidated at all. I had the balls to stand up to her. I could tell Chris was impressed. When Eileen left, he said to me: 'You were so good, born to it.'

One of my first big challenges in the beginning was to visit the main fashion cities during show season. This was a daunting prospect because I'd never done it before. To me, that was what the boss did. I'd been to New York once, when I was at Bobtons, but it wasn't on official business, not at first anyway. Josephine, one of our models, bought me a plane ticket to go and visit her as a thank you for taking care of her in London and getting her lots of jobs. Gillian, ever the opportunist, suggested I go when she was there too so that I could lend her a hand with business stuff. Josephine lived on Staten Island in one of those white clapperboard houses, which I thought was so lovely and American. She met me at the airport and I was so clueless about New York that I hadn't even heard of Staten Island and I certainly didn't know you had to catch a ferry to get there. It was all very novel to me. I don't know if I was there during show season that time but show season wasn't like it is now; no one really cared about it.

Gillian was staying in Joey Hunter's apartment. Joey was a big agent for Ford New York. He was very New York – Italian and really charming. He was married to Debbie Dickinson, Janice's younger sister, who was also a model and actress. He kept two beautiful love birds in his apartment, which was suitably oddball for my naïve eyes. I was there one night wanting to get back to Staten Island but it was too late to catch the ferry, so I ended up sleeping on the sofa and I remember feeling so homesick. New York was a bit overwhelming, and I think my jetlag had kicked in.

It was on this trip that I met Eileen Ford for the first time, before she rocked up to our tiny office in London. I accompanied Gillian to visit the main New York agencies – Ford, Elite and Wilhelmina. Travelling wasn't as frequent as it is now. You probably went to the US once every two years and you didn't trade girls in the same way we do now. If you got an American girl you were lucky. It wasn't how it is now where it's like a running race to get a girl and so competitive; it was a very parochial business, a series of self-contained cottage industries in each country. No one – except John Casablancas of Elite – quite understood just how big the modelling industry could become and there wasn't the abundance of girls that we have today.

I can remember going into those powerhouse agencies with Gillian and they weren't at the peak of their powers but they were the names everybody knew. I went to Ford and met Eileen for the first time. I don't even think we spoke but she saw me from behind her giant desk. Gillian did the talking. We went to Elite and I met John Casablancas, father of the now-rather-famous Strokes singer Julian, and soon-to-be king of a worldwide Elite network of twenty-nine agencies that spawned the super-model phenomenon. Not quite yet, though. I was terrified because I was just a little oik running behind Gillian who was a bigger oik but still an oik. And they probably thought, who are these oiks?! I was only twenty-seven at that point and still very green.

We also went to see Wilhelmina, founded in 1967 by former Dutch model Wilhelmina Cooper and her husband Bruce. She was alive and well then, holding court in a big corner office flanked by skyscrapers. It was all very awesome to me. They were the big players of the day so if Wilhelmina, Ford or Elite asked for your girl you just fainted.

Gillian was there trying to get some interest in a girl and to get some girls to come over to London, which in those days was quite a big deal. Models did travel but you had to really entice them. Then when you did get a really good American girl, like my friend Josephine, they did extremely well. Word spread and we'd book the girl on London jobs. Occasionally Ford or Elite would come over to London and we'd give them a casting and they'd pick one or two girls. The look was very different then because Americans were very classical. They wanted girls that looked like Americans: long hair, great teeth and tall. Not as tall as we like them now but still tall.

On that first trip we all went to Studio 54, which was such a big club – literally and metaphorically. I was wearing this insane outfit – a leopardskin dress with leopardskin leggings and very high heels. I always wore very high heels then. And off I trotted into this chasm of a club and promptly got lost – I couldn't find anybody. I went to the loos and the lesbians decided they liked me so I had to run away! I was a bit scared because it wasn't like you had mobile phones then so you could just meet up with your friends again. I found them all eventually, though, and had a dance. It was *very* disco, totally mad. I'm glad I had the opportunity to go to such an iconic venue. I probably didn't appreciate it enough at the time.

Joey Hunter took us to Little Italy and we had the most incredible meal. I found it fascinating all around there; we kept thinking there were Mafia everywhere. I remember thinking why did Joey keep his back to the wall? He loved to make out he was 'connected'. Joey could easily have been cast as a Soprano rather than a model agent. New York was very exciting but also frightening. I can remember walking down Broadway with Josephine and feeling utterly terrified that we'd get shot. We were two frightened women and if anyone swerved towards us we'd freak out. It was like the Wild West. The murder rate in Seventies New York was so high in those days that you really worried that you might get shot.

So that was my first visit. I was pretty much gobsmacked the whole time I was there – in awe of all these big people that were like modelling royalty. I felt like I knew nothing, I was a newbie, but that was my learning experience.

On my second trip to New York, now substantially promoted to founder of Premier Model Management, Eileen Ford invited me to go to the Museum of Modern Art with her husband Jerry. Bearing in mind that compared to her I was still an oik, this was a huge honour. I had the sense to recognise the networking opportunity and graciously accepted the invitation but, of course, museums bore the pants off me. It was definitely an 'I'm going to show you something amazing and you're very privileged' invite. So she took me around this exhibition and I had to pretend I was interested, which I wasn't. On another visit, a bit later on in 1983, she took me to the Trump Tower, which had just been built. It had water cascading down from the top into the atrium, which was pretty special and so Eighties. They were quite odd, these excursions that we'd take together doing things that had nothing to do with modelling, but ultimately a nice thing. I felt like I was being accepted into the bosom of the industry. We got quite friendly over the years with her son Billy, who also worked in the family business and took over once his parents retired. He was nice but I always got the sense he was slightly ill at ease with his inherited career, like it wouldn't have been his first choice. Chris and I would often go and see him or he'd come and see us in London. Chris even went to play golf with him at the RAC club in Ewell (Billy travelled with his own golf clubs).

As well as Ford, on that first Premier trip back to the Big Apple I went to Wilhelmina, Elite and a men's agency called Zoli that was founded by the eponymous Hungarian designer, who was such a lovely man. The agency folded eventually, soon after he died. This time I had to visit the agencies on my own, which was a bit nerve-wracking. It had definitely helped me having that initial foot in the door with Gillian though and I was very grateful for that, but I was still pretty inexperienced and I had to pretend I knew everything which I didn't. I had to pretend I was on their level, but I wasn't yet.

I travelled with Chris the first few times – he was doing his book stuff so that kept our costs down because we bunked in the same room together. We stayed at the Mayfair, just off Broadway and with an almost-view of Central Park. It was a bit of a rock 'n' roll hotel, full of musicians – Billy Joel was a regular drinker in the bar. It had the biggest rooms. In those days New York hotels always had huge bedrooms and even if you booked on your own you always had two double beds. And it was peanuts! I was still a tourist on those early trips – I remember taking one of those horse and carts around Central Park.

I definitely didn't feel safe, though, not for a number of years. I'd visit models who lived in these huge apartments hidden behind giant doors that were like the doors of a bank vault. They were so heavy with four deadlocks, tons of chains and this big iron bar that came from the floor and stuck into the door so even if someone managed to get through the deadlocks and the chains, the door still wouldn't open. But they all had fire escapes so you'd be thinking, what's the point? Anyone could get up there!

As well as feeling a bit scary to the likes of me, I also recognised that New York was a very exciting place. Popular culture was moving and changing so quickly and there was a genuine underground arts scene, fuelled by the music scene and a hip set of influential individuals that were passionate about new sounds, fashions and an edgier aesthetic. I visited an agency called Click that was in Carnegie Hall and the trendiest agency in Manhattan. It was started in 1980 by a woman called Frances Grill who was working as a photographic agent for the young-and-talented Steven Meisel and Bruce Weber. She decided to open up a model agency. Click stood for the noise a camera makes when it captures the shot.

The office had a big neon-pink 'Click' sign and every girl had a black T-shirt with the same logo. If you managed to get hold of one of those T-shirts you were really quite cool! We gave Click a beautiful model called Sophie Horenz and she eventually went to live out there. She stayed and never came back. They were a very trendy agency compared to, say, Ford, which was the brand name that everybody knew but who weren't so cool. Another very hip agency called Name was opened soon after by a French lady called Louise Despont. Suddenly coolness was becoming very important. Before it was about stability and a brand that everyone knew, that mums and dads knew and trusted, then suddenly the girls didn't want that. I really picked up on the importance of cool on those first trips to New York. I took it all in like a sponge, ready to drip-feed my own business back in London.

There wasn't a massive fashion culture in New York then, though, not in the mainstream anyway. The main reason for a model to go and work there was to earn the big bucks. New York was where you'd go if you wanted to really make big money. So for some models that's where it would end. I was forging those relationships for my models to get work over there and generally they wouldn't come back. Big campaigns at the time were mainly for beauty brands such as Revlon, Maybelline and Helena Rubinstein. Ralph Lauren, Calvin Klein and then Donna Karan came into prominence later in the decade.

The order of the shows was different when I started out. It used to go London first then Milan, then Paris, which was big, then New York. Milan and Paris were the really important show cities – New York and London shows weren't a big deal then. There might just be a couple of days when the shows were on and it wasn't the heavy pressure that you have now. It didn't have other connotations, it didn't lead anywhere. Some girls just did shows for a living but it didn't lead to campaigns or anything at that time.

I was even more nervous about visiting Milan than New York because, number one, I'd never been there before, and two, I didn't speak the language. It was daunting, too, because that's where a lot of the big, grand fashion houses were. I borrowed a whole load of clothes from Chris's girlfriend at the time in order to posh up. I tended to wear jeans and stripy leggings, which wasn't going to cut it. I asked somebody to recommend me a hotel that wasn't ridiculously expensive and I ended up in this awful B&B. The room was like a cell, with putrid green walls, a slit for a window and a TV on one of those arms on the wall. It was hideous. That was a lonely first night in Italy's fashion capital.

On the second day I met my printer friend Peter Marlowe for lunch and I think he realised I was completely out of my depth. He was there with his wife and he offered to take me round all the agencies. Peter used to print model cards and do the portfolio books for all the model agencies. They were the big yearbooks that featured all the models from all the agencies in one place. Quite handy really for clients. It's not how it's done now: there'd be way too many models! Peter owned the company that did this and I'd first got to know him at Bobtons when I'd inevitably be calling him up last minute to add in an extra shot of a girl, or tweak her biog or whatever. Peter's website still has all the old model agency books and model cards going back to the year dot. A really interesting walk down memory lane.

The first agency he took me to was Riccardo Gay,

which is a big agency in Milan and had all the top girls. That's where I first met David Brown, a lovely, Australian-born booker who I'd go on to work with for years with Naomi Campbell. They took me out for lunch with the agency and welcomed me into the clan. Peter was known throughout the world by every agent so he was a really good, not to mention generous, friend to have. I also visited Why Not?, another big agency. In those days I managed to catch a few shows, too – I remember seeing Armani and Gianfranco Ferré.

I loved Milan because I adored the food. It's a funny city; everyone whinges about it because it's quite grey and industrial-looking but hiding behind the boring office facades often there will be a beautiful courtyard filled with plants and flowers, like a secret garden. Its beauty is tucked away and I love that. Also, the people are really nice – so friendly, which is a massive help when you're starting out. And did I mention the food?!

There aren't many Italian models so the girls would tend to be from the States, Germany and sometimes Sweden. Because you were in Milan and they were doing all this high fashion you found yourself a bit in awe of the girls as well. They were proper models! Milan was a real fashion city. It was home to Gucci, Pucci, Fendi and Ferragamo, versus the relatively new scene in New York and London's creative-but-broke design community. There's a certain opulence to Milan.

Then we came to Paris, which is so much more difficult than Milan, especially as a newbie. The people are difficult, bordering on rude, and – don't shoot me for saying this – the food is often horrid. I much prefer the beautiful Italian food. Chris was with me on the maiden voyage to Paris. Ever cost-conscious, he made me go on the Metro, which I didn't like one bit. We went to this really trendy agency called City and Paris Planning where I met Gérald Marie for the first time, the guy who would go on to head up Elite with John Casablancas and be disgraced in the controversial MacIntyre exposé of our industry, but that comes later. Gérald used to wear the most extraordinary clothes when he was at Paris Planning. He'd rock leggings with T-shirts and jumpers layered over the top and he was quite a stocky guy. He also had really long curly hair. We got on well; he's got a great sense of humour.

We stayed in a funny little place in the Marais where we'd be woken up by market traders in the morning. Chris was still doing his publishing work but I needed him because he was not scared of anyone. He was very confident. I wasn't as much – not like I am now. I was quite timid. I'd never thought of myself as anything other than a worker. I was totally blagging the agency boss thing. I could do the booking part no problem but that other side of it I really had to learn. Chris was a natural schmoozer, very charismatic. He was almost like my boss at that time, though I wouldn't admit that to him! I had to learn confidence, it didn't just come to me. I think this is partly because women weren't necessarily in top positions at that time, we didn't have that many role models. Chris and I made a strong double act and managed to make a good impression quickly.

I met a big booker named Dominic Gallas who worked for an agency called Metropolitan. His claim to fame was discovering Claudia Schiffer in a disco in Dusseldorf. Metropolitan was run by Aline Souliers, who would become Claudia's head agent (and caused me no end of grief). There was an agency there called Pauline's, run by Paul Hagneault, and Glamour, owned by Jerome Bonnouvrier, who later founded the New York agency DNA, with his son, David. Many agencies then were a bit of a mess in a way. They weren't modern and stream-lined like they are now until Elite changed all that and everyone had to become more businesslike. We gradually got to grips with the agencies and names to know, we placed our girls and met new girls, did the networking thing, ate and drank and generally made ourselves known in the right places.

After a few months in our temporary, rented office space we found some premises in Goodge Street, above a hardware shop of all places. They were small – initially just two little rooms on one floor, with the accounts department operating from the spare bedroom at Chris's home, but they were adequate and a decent location, just off Tottenham Court Road. We did very well very quickly. Most agencies don't do very well at the start because they don't have any models but I had loads and thanks to my travels I'd begun trading girls with my new foreign agent contacts. Chris was also travelling a lot, too, with his publishing work, but he always called in to see the agencies, so our name became known very quickly. This was invaluable in terms of PR and making

those important contacts and not something we could
have afforded ordinarily.

After about a year we'd become quite established and
it was fun. I started to enjoy working for myself although
it took a while for it to sink in that Premier was mine.
To celebrate a good first year in business we decided to
host the first of what would become our legendary
Premier parties. Never underestimate the power of a
good party! It does wonders for business. Janice King,
one of our models, was dating this Mexican guy, Danny,
who opened Café Pacifico, a Mexican restaurant and
lounge bar in what used to be a banana factory on Langley
Street in Covent Garden. No one had ever heard of
Mexican food at that time so it was like, *oh my god!
The coolest place on the planet!* There were people
queuing to get in. It felt exciting, like we were really
going places. The next step was to build on our cool
factor and we did this with two very important models
for us: Kate Hatch and Susie Bick.

10.

COOL GIRLS

In order to survive, an agency needs not just commercial work that brings in the money, but cutting-edge editorial too, which means cool girls. In the early to mid Eighties the fashion landscape was really quite commercial and we were doing well with it, booking lots of catalogue and mid-market magazines, but I was aware that we needed to start addressing the high end if we were going to keep momentum and grow the business. Plus, that's where my personal passions lie too. I love the artistic, more creative end of the spectrum where models, photographers and stylists collaborate to produce something spectacular and possibly game-changing. In order to do this I needed some high-end (or 'editorial' girls) to work on the new wave of edgier, street-inspired fashion magazines that were emerging, like *Blitz*, *The Face* and *i-D*, so we started looking for that special girl.

One day we found her: she was called Kate Hatch and she literally just walked in off the street, aged seventeen. She was very English looking – like a Burberry model looks now. She was so elegant, with cropped hair, a bit like Stella Tennant. She started doing *Vogue* and working with some of the top photographers, like Martin Brading and Neil Kirk, pretty much straight away. We worked really hard to build her career. Then, after about a year, because we were neither established nor cool enough, photographers – big photographers – started whispering in her ear: 'Why are you with a funny little agency like Premier? You should be with Models 1.'

To our great sadness we lost her – to Models 1. We were really gutted because we'd put a lot of effort into her – we'd made her, which sounds vaguely Mafioso but so be it! She decided to trip off somewhere else, thinking, *maybe they can do better*. This episode taught me three big lessons:

1. Build relationships with all the top photographers and make them like you.
2. Watch your girls, because some of them get big heads at the first whiff of success and will drop you like last season's trends.
3. Other agents are predatory and always ready to pounce.

Even though Kate had flown our nest, her special magic dust had done its thing and we were starting to be viewed as a cool agency. Soon after, another girl walked into the office with her parents and I knew immediately she was rock-your-world amazing. Her name was Susie Bick. She was fourteen, from Bromley, and her parents were quite wealthy so money wasn't the prime motivation for them. I gathered that their daughter was a bit of a handful. They were keen for her to become a model – perhaps channel some of her alternative energies – and, although she was very young, she was into the idea too.

We agreed to take her on and, to begin with, we would work around school. She wasn't into school but it was important that she finished. Now it's quite common to scout girls younger than fourteen but then it was unusual. With Susie, though, it was a no-brainer – she was extraordinary, we just knew that she was going to be an extraordinary model. I think she was the best I ever found. With skin like pure white marble, raven hair and pale green eyes, she was straight out of a pre-Raphaelite painting. And more than that, she was the most natural model. When they're really special like that, they're like thoroughbred horses. They sort of quiver.

We started working on Susie slowly, but she just zoomed. Everyone wanted her – every top photographer, magazine and stylist. She bypassed catalogue work and sailed straight into the high-end/avant-garde stuff. She did *The Face* and started to work with Nick Knight, who was a hot young photographer then. She did a Christian Dior campaign – we just started rocking with her. Even for one so young, Susie knew instinctively what was naff and what was cool. She had this incredible ability to understand the clothes and know how to model them.

As well as her ethereal looks, Susie was gifted with

natural style. She knew what the trend was before it happened. Kate Moss has this gift too, and I love Kate, but for me Susie was more special. She was only about 5' 8" but all her proportions were there. You can have a girl of 5' 8" who's got short legs and short arms or you can have one whose limbs are long, and she's quite bird-like and spindly. That really works. Girls like that photograph taller than they are.

Susie was like something from another planet. In a way, she knew more than me, even from day one. It's like she was born to do it. She was a chameleon too, transforming her look in an instant and never playing it safe. She'd pop into the office sometimes and suddenly have no hair – she'd just have chopped it all off! With some models that would be career suicide but with her it worked. She was radical and she knew what looked good. You'd change her entire book so that it was up to date and then she'd go and change her look again! That's what was so exciting about her and those very rare models that bring the extra magic – it's as much about them as it is about the clothes.

'The cool girl', and Susie in particular, opened my eyes to a lot of the challenges/predicaments that came with caring for her. Often, these really special girls – the 'thoroughbreds' – are difficult to tame. Part of what makes them so special is the fact that they're highly strung. You only have to jump forward a few years to the supermodel era to realise that. For me, though, I see it as a challenge – it's exciting and I love dangerous girls. Probably because I was one! It's in the DNA.

We sometimes couldn't control Susie; she was so naughty. She wouldn't turn up for work if she didn't want to be there and, if she did turn up she wasn't guaranteed to stick around. She did a lot of work with a great photographer called Neil Kirk, who shot a lot of editorial for *Vogue* and *Elle,* amongst others. One day, she was working with him, and it had taken us about three hours to get her up and to the venue (all training for the supers . . .). Then, suddenly Neil calls me and says, 'Susie's disappeared.' Not only had she turned up several hours late, she'd now gone and done a vanishing act with no explanation. She'd climbed out of the toilet window and gone home. He was going bananas! I suspected she'd been up all night and needed to sleep but, whatever the reason, it was extraordinary behaviour. The thing with Susie, and a select few that followed in her wake, is that she was so incredibly special, and nice too, that people put up with it. On that occasion, she dragged herself back when she'd had some kip, they finished the shoot and all was forgiven. All she said to me about it, casual as you like, was: 'I needed a lie down.'

To me, she was just the most incredible girl. She was – and still is – my favourite model but I don't think she ever really fulfilled her potential. It was through her own choice, though; she didn't care for fame, and money held no meaning for her. She was too into her lifestyle, and her boyfriends and staying in London. If she'd gone to America at the right time she would have been one of the supermodels. Her name is huge still – at least within the industry – but the public don't know her so much.

Susie was probably the first girl that I really took under my wing and made my personal project. I think she was searching for something, which I can relate to. She had that sense of adventure, mischief and, dare I say, a 'fuck it' attitude. Like a lot of people during this hedonistic time in the mid Eighties, she partied a lot and did some crazy things. London's club scene was very exciting so there was always something going on and no shortage of characters to share in the fun. I'd go out with her sometimes, to clubs and concerts. We'd go to the Wag Club in Soho, which was ultra cool. I was her friend but I was also her mentor and trying to keep an eye on her.

I'd try and teach her to be responsible, but as a younger girl's agent you sometimes just have to go with the flow, rather than become a surrogate parent (which can rebound on you). We work with girls' parents, but try to leave the parenting to them. Our job is to build a girl's career, so we focus on teaching her professionalism rather than lecturing her too often on her private life. Having said that, we are often *in loco parentis*, and we do take that responsibility very seriously. More on this later.

With Susie, I had to learn new tricks: don't tell her the real time she has to be at a shoot, make it earlier, or go and physically collect her for a job; acquire a key to her apartment so you can get in if needs be!

When you start making vast amounts of cash from a young age it can be quite dangerous – mainly because you don't ever really learn the value of money. Susie was always extravagant. She'd go to clubs and pay one of the other models that were floating around, and probably broke, to hold her bag for her. Not in a grand way: just so she knew where it was. She'd always have a protégée that looked up to her but could never catch her up. They'd try and emulate her but they couldn't.

We can't tell models what to do with their money, but we do try to guide them because modelling is often a short career. You have to make provision for your future. In Susie's case, we would invoice her fees, collect them and try to persuade her to save some. It was tough because all she wanted to do was spend it. In the early years, we had a deal with her: she could come into the agency every day and collect some pocket money but the rest was invested – this often worked better in theory than in practice, but we did manage to put away some money for her.

When Susie was sixteen, we sent her to Japan. In those days, Tokyo was the perfect place for models to start their careers: they'd work every day, which taught them timekeeping and professionalism, and they would make really good money. Japan was booming and the yen was very strong. This was the time when designers like Kenzo Takada, Yohji Yamamoto, Issey Miyake and Rei Kawakubo (of Comme des Garçons) were riding high and Japanese fashion was really innovative. Japanese designers were always experimenting with new technology and techniques but there was also a massive catalogue industry, churning out modelling work.

Japan had a huge appetite for European girls and Japanese agents were constantly coming to London, searching for new talent. We placed Susie with a Japanese agent and she went to Tokyo on what's called a guarantee: her agent guaranteed her a minimum amount of money for eight weeks. Susie did catalogue and a lot of magazines. Over there, editorial work paid really well, and the Japanese editors and photographers were fascinated by her. They loved her pale skin and she wasn't too tall – they didn't like lanky girls there. Susie loved Japan so much that she returned several times. Models who were successful in Japan could earn as much as £25,000 a week (remember, this was nearly thirty years ago, and well before the supermodel era).

Even Susie couldn't spend that kind of money on clothes, and she used some of her Japanese income as a deposit to buy her first place with a mortgage that we arranged for her with our bank. I've always encouraged models to buy property – a mortgage is a really effective way of disciplining people with fluctuating earnings to save their surplus income. Emboldened by our success with the mortgage, we tried to get her subsequent Japanese earnings into a savings account for her, but it was hard because Azzedine Alaïa often got to her first, tempting her with those amazing leather coats and beautiful furs and God knows what. It was part of Susie's magic that she completely changed her look on an almost weekly basis – but that came at a price.

Ultimately, Susie always did what Susie wanted to do, which I respect, but I do feel a bit sad that she didn't quite fulfil her enormous potential. I used to push her and push her. She had an agent in New York but she would never stay there long enough to establish herself. She'd fly in, do her jobs and come back to London. To get the kind of success the supermodels and those other girls later had, you had to live there — at least have an apartment there. That's what I wanted her to do, have a New York base. But it was not to be — it just wasn't Susie. There was huge money to be made in New York — far more than in London — and Susie could have become an international star, but the creativity wasn't there and that's what she craved.

London was so cool then and she was the epitome of that, whereas New York wasn't — it was just a money-making machine, and Susie wasn't driven by that: it was the aesthetics of the job that she loved and doing the best things with the best people. Susie would work for nothing if it was going to produce the picture she wanted with the right person. She'd pick up photographers that weren't well known if she thought that they were talented and work with them.

I don't think she liked the American way. She was more punk in her outlook — a game changer. There's never been anyone like her and I don't think there ever will. Susie epitomised Premier for me and where I wanted to be.

11

BOYS! AND NEW BOND STREET

After Kate and Susie, things just zoomed for us. Then one day Susie brought in this guy she'd been dating called Ralph Parsons. The best word to describe him was beautiful. He had these amazingly sculpted cheekbones, a great pout and a Wham! haircut. Suzanne and I both thought he was gorgeous so we signed him up on the spot, despite the fact we'd never done men before. I remember saying to him, 'We'd like to work for you. We don't usually represent men but we can do it.' He wasn't at all concerned and just shrugged and said: 'Ah, cool, I'll be the only man.' So that was that. We figured, how difficult can it be?

Suzanne and I rang around everyone we knew and said, 'You've got to meet this guy,' and he just took off. Because he was really special it was easy to get him work and he got big really quickly. Then we took on another guy called Justin Allen, who looked like James Dean but more boyish. He also thrived. Our men's division consisted of just these two guys for a while and did really well because they both had such a fresh look. We booked them nearly every day and for a while we ticked along nicely. They really added to the agency's overall cool factor too because everyone wanted them.

Then, about a year later, another hot guy turned up at the office. He was called John Pearson and silly-handsome. It turned out that one of our clients, an editor called Becky Bain, had suggested he come in and see us, telling him I was 'the best in the business'. Not bad! It was really funny because Justin happened to be in the office on the same day and he and John were both wearing matching 'jazz' caps and were kind of sussing each other out. Then, as if on cue, they both pulled out a pack of Winston fags and a Zippo lighter. They were like peas in a pod! We took on John immediately and Justin moved into his flat that afternoon! For them it was the beginning of a thirty-year friendship and for us, we'd found our diamond.

With those men it wasn't that different to booking women because they were so special so we basically just booked them as if they were women, as in we'd ask for the same money. Now this is unheard of because modelling is, of course, one of the very few industries where women get paid more than men (aside from prostitution – sad but true). These boys were so in demand, though, they could command big bucks. We'd be showing them to the top photographers and saying, 'you've got to shoot this guy' – and they did! So we were forging contacts with the very best in the business and they'd do high-end editorial before moving on to shoot major ad campaigns. John became a big international model very quickly and started working with photographers like Herb Ritts who shot him for the Drakkar Noir campaign. Then we set about getting him an agent in Italy and the US and so on.

John was from Hull and a really grounded kid for one so young – he was only eighteen when we first took him on. He also had a mischievous side that could get him in trouble. I'll never forget him coming in to the office one day and saying to me, 'I've got to go to court.' When I asked why, he sort of shuffled around on the spot a bit and said: 'Well, I was sort of caught firing a gun out of a car.' I was speechless. I'm thinking, fuck – a drive-by shooting, this is bad. Turned out it was a starting pistol and he was just messing about. As he put it, there were lots of 'near-lethal' car races on the back streets of rural Yorkshire. John and his mates shot the pistol out of the window at a chasing car. Big problem for them was the car had two police officers in it who'd just finished their shift! Suddenly, they became surrounded by vans and cop cars with guns aimed at them. There had been an armed gang in the town holding up post offices all around the county so the police thought they were that gang! Of course they weren't but I was still nervous when the court date came around. I really wasn't sure which way it would go. We needn't have worried, though, because the court let him off with a stiff warning.

He is back on our men's division now, thirty years

later. Men get better with age. John's had such an amazing career. He's worked with all the top designers and photographers, jetted all over the world. The *Sunday Times* heralded him the first male supermodel. I got him the Belstaff campaign when he rejoined Premier after a period with Select. Recently he walked for Prada for Spring '13 and was just shot for Italian *Vogue* by Steven Meisel with Linda Evangelista at age forty-eight! John lives in LA with his lovely wife, *Harper's Bazaar*'s fashion editor Alison Edmond and their three kids. It's crazy to think I knew him when he was just eighteen.

With the men doing so well and our commercial bookings thriving, the agency just kept on growing. It became apparent, *we were gonna need a bigger boat.* Our friend Martin Stainton put us on to the perfect place in New Bond Street, the first and second floors of a beautiful Georgian mansion house. The room on the first floor had previously been the ballroom of the house so it was vast with this beautiful arched window. It was really ornate with carved red brickwork and gargoyles – the whole nine yards. I took the carpet up and found a parquet wooden floor beneath it. It was stunning. It also happened to be the former HQ of Pink Floyd – the house that Prog Rock built! Moving into swish new premises really helped us because it showed that we'd traded up and image is everything in this business. The only downside to being there was the extortionately priced children's clothes shop below us called 'Please Mum'. We didn't much care for the owners who were also our landlords, or the wealthy Mayfair set and their ungrateful sprogs!

To go with our snazzy new offices, in 1985 we also commissioned the artist and photographer Edward Bell to design our model book and cards. Edward is an artist and photographer who had designed the album cover for Bowie's *Scary Monsters* in 1980 and he had also done photographs and illustrations for *Vogue*, *Tatler* and *Elle*. In those days, model cards were always a standard A5 size, but these were square and had a street-art feel to the design, with paint-effect frames around the models' pictures and brush-stroke handwriting. It was all very groundbreaking and fabulous. We were culti-vating a more edgy image.

Our roster of models was getting more international thanks to the contacts we'd forged overseas. We had a lot of Canadian and American girls in particular at this time. We took on this model called Alice Gee who was Canadian and of Chinese descent. We thought she was a bit of a gamble when we first signed her but she never stopped working. She was incredibly elegant and her oriental features were beautiful. She soared with high-fashion stuff and was a great mover. She did so well in London that she came to live here. We were so happily surprised. Stacey Wagner was from Idaho and absolutely bonkers – a bit of a wild child. She started to work with a photographer called Roger Eaton who was very cool at the time. She was not conventionally beautiful (she had quite a prominent nose) but she was attractive and she photographed well. She was quite edgy.

Stacey would come with us to the Old Rectory some weekends and was always good fun. She got quite friendly with my brother Michael, and my dad loved young people so he was enthralled by her. One weekend she came down with some hash and made some hash cakes. She was always baking so this was nothing out of the ordinary. She baked these little buns and had two trays cooling on the table, one with hash and one without. My mother came in and put them all together on a plate so we didn't know which was which. My parents ate them! And so did our friend Carol MacDonald-Bell's dog! He was an Airedale Terrier called O'Sullivan and he ended up on his back on the lawn with his legs in the air. We practically died with laughter it was that hysterical. Chris had to put Mum and Dad to bed; they just seemed a bit bewildered by the whole experience.

I remember a lot of happy and hysterical times during weekends spent at the Old Rectory. We used to have loads of barbecues and parties in the garden. We asked busloads of people down – mainly photographers and models we knew. Sometimes my parents were there, sometimes they'd go away. The only thing I was good at cooking was chilli con carne. I couldn't do rice but I'd do baguettes with garlic on them. It was fantastic.

At that time, the immigration system hadn't caught up with the appetite of English magazines for foreign models and you couldn't get work permits for the US and Canadian girls, so they had to come in as tourists. Stacey came into Heathrow so much that the tourist story wore a bit thin and she ended up having to travel via Ireland, arriving in England on the ferry to Holyhead. Where there's a will there's a way!

Another big name at that time was Mimi Potworowska, who was a brilliant show girl and went on to become John Galliano's muse. She was of Polish heritage and quite strange looking, also with a big nose (it must have been a trend!). When John was just starting out I used to help him out by giving him the girls he wanted for nothing or next to nothing. He used Mimi all the time and of course she loved working with him because he was so talented and creative. He was a lovely man too though I did have a bit of a fight with him when he moved on to Paris in the '90s and suddenly stopped using our models. They were distraught but I think he was being leaned on by the French to book in that country. I was still cross with him for a while. I think it's important to look out for friends who've helped you along the way.

The eccentric French designer Jean Paul Gaultier loved a couple of our girls at that time, too. Christine Bergstrom was a really statuesque blonde from Sweden. I'd describe her as handsome more than pretty – she was striking and worked with him a lot in Paris. Then there was Amanda Cazalet, another Gaultier muse and fantastic show girl. She was amazing. She did really strong pictures and appeared in Madonna's *Sex* book. She was a bit of a scenester at the time. Famke Janssen, Clare Forlani, Saffron Burrows and Alison Doody were all beautiful girls we had on our books who went on to have successful acting careers. They were all with us when they were babies. Saffron had a crush on Chris, which was quite hysterical because he had no idea. We also looked after Lisa Snowdon and Lisa Faulkner around this time – both are now big TV and radio presenters. Lisa Snowdon came to us from the glamour agency Samantha Bond, looking to change direction. She did really well, made a fortune and then went on to work at MTV and so on.

Another big name to cross the Premier threshold around this time in the mid Eighties was Corinne Day. You've probably heard of her now as the controversial 'Heroin Chic' photographer who did those iconic shots of Kate Moss as a teenager, but first Corinne was a model, with me! She came into the office with her grandmother, who had brought her up, and she was so pretty with fabulous long blonde hair. Unfortunately, she was a tiny bit short and by this time height was becoming more of a thing. We still took her on though and she was a pretty successful commercial model, but she hated it. We tried really hard to make Corinne more editorial but she mainly did catalogue and magazines. She told me that this was how she learned to take pictures: observing photographers that she didn't like and doing the opposite of them.

In 1987, Gérald Marie asked me to represent his latest girlfriend (and soon-to-be wife), another Canadian called Linda Evangelista. She ended up doing quite well, but more on that soon. Gérald always placed his girls with me in London. Before Linda it was Christine Bolster, who'd previously lived with him in Paris. Linda's first job in London was a cover story for *Company* magazine, which was considered quite a cool magazine then. She stayed on Chris's sofa bed sometimes when she was in town doing jobs and they became good friends. She was very Canadian, which is to say that Canadian girls are very self-disciplined. They have really good manners and they can cook.

Once we'd settled in at New Bond Street, we decided to throw a huge party at the Wag Club in Soho, which was the coolest place on the planet at that time. We invited all the agents from Paris, Milan and New York and basically all the coolest people we knew. It had capacity for 500 people and, using the rule that you always invite double to get a full party, we invited 1,000. But it didn't quite work like that with the Wag because *everyone* came. Oops. It got so full and the management were freaking out about fire risk and so on. The fire brigade actually turned up and forbid anybody else to enter. At some point, I fell down the stairs; let's just say it was all very dramatic.

There was a massive queue of people snaking down the road and around the corner; people were throwing their invites out of the toilet windows to their friends on the street and the crowd got so big it stopped the traffic in Wardour Street. Imagine! Management told us that they couldn't let any more people in and I remember going to the door to see if there was anyone I absolutely had to let in and seeing all these people I knew screaming to get in: important agents like Gérald who'd come from Paris, and the photographer Peter Lindbergh! I just shut the door and thought, *oh my God, what am I gonna do?!* So it was a big success but we also pissed off a lot of people. As a PR exercise (not that it was planned) it really made a statement that we were cool. We were ice cool!

We kept on expanding and taking on more models until we needed to take the other two floors in the building. It was around this time that we decided to establish a hair and make-up division too, followed by photographers. I had this vision of running a sort of one-stop shop, with hair, make-up and photographers and even a studio under the one roof. It was very successful for a time and definitely a good concept because we had the girls, we had the boys, we had the photographers. I always thought it was clever that people didn't have to go elsewhere for everything they'd need for a shoot – book everything in one go and boom! The end goal was to have a photographic studio on site too but we didn't have the space in Bond Street.

We made some mistakes with these expansions because the separate departments were all in different rooms and a small business like ours couldn't control it. I was booking, Chris was travelling much of the time, and we didn't have time to oversee it properly. There were some big fashion names working with us: Jess Hallett ran the photography department, and another big casting agent – probably the biggest now – who cut his teeth at Premier was Russell Marsh, who does Christopher Kane, Marni and Céline (he spent ten prolific years at Prada before that). Russell had been working for a guy called Michael Rosen who was a show producer and Michael had obviously taught him everything he knew. Russell was very talented but there wasn't any money then for casting. He was really good friends with me and Vicky, my head booker, and we always needed extra staff so he'd come in and help out with the models' portfolios. We were helping him out because he was always broke but obviously a major talent – he has a brilliant eye.

* * *

On the home front, Rick and I were still living in his beloved rented flat in Primrose Hill. I feel like we became a much more solid unit when I finally managed to convince him to part with some cash and buy our own flat. It still took a bit of persuading and ten years together to finally tame him!

As I've mentioned before, in Primrose Hill we'd have these poker games and I used to win vast amounts of money. I could win my month's salary in a night so we often had loads of money in cash just lying around the flat. One day a friend of ours rang up and said one of the villa houses in Maida Vale was up for sale for £11,000 and at that very moment we had £12,000 in cash under the bed. I said, 'Rick, Rick, let's get it,' and he said: 'No, I'm not moving to Maida Vale, it's full of prostitutes.' I mean, what an idiot! What are they worth now? Millions? It was on Warwick Avenue, for God's sake. We did a lot of very un-smart things in those days. I still think about what a wasted opportunity that was.

A little later another opportunity came along. I had a

client who worked for Levi's and she had a two-bedroom Edwardian flat on Castellain Road in Maida Vale that she wanted to sell. It was on the ground floor, there were wooden floors throughout and it was a really gorgeous place. I managed to get Rick to agree this time and we got it for a song. We loved that flat, it was really bright and airy with beautiful bay windows and we'd often have guests to come and stay for the weekends, like my friend Marion Foale, a knitwear designer. Her very upscale label was called Foale and Tuffin. It felt like we were properly settled now; we even got pets, which is very domesticated! We bought two British Blue cats – a boy cat called Tom and a girl cat called Blue. She was the runt of the litter and, bless her, a bit thick. Tom was the hero. We loved those cats and everyone knows that once you're a couple and you have cats then you have kids, which was the next thing that happened.

It wasn't planned but I fell pregnant. I knew I wanted more children but Rick wasn't all that enamoured with the idea though he sort of warmed to it in stages. When we found out that I was pregnant I think he was hoping for a boy, then of course I ended up expecting a girl which threw him a bit. He was probably nervous at the prospect of another female on his hands! I was just focused on making the birth experience a whole lot more civilised than my previous home-birth nightmare. There would be no bricks and wet towels at the Wellington, a lovely private hospital in St John's Wood.

I sailed through my pregnancy – literally loved it. I love how total strangers want to help you and are so much nicer to you when they can see that you're pregnant. I love the fact you can just eat whatever you want. Then, the Wellington experience was just so civilised from start to finish. I remember going for an appointment and the doctor asked me, 'When would you like to have your baby?' I didn't realise there was a choice in the matter but certainly wasn't complaining since, at this point in my life, a schedule was what was needed. She was due in February so I said: 'Well I'd really like her on my dad's birthday, February 13th,' which was a Saturday. He said, 'OK,' and jotted it down. I thought to myself, *that's fantastic, this means I can work till Friday*, which is what I did. I went to work with my little suitcase and then waved to everyone at the end of the day: 'Bye bye, I'm going to have my baby!'

I checked in to the hospital that Friday night and a nurse came to my room very early the next morning with a pill to induce me, and a lunch menu. I ordered a huge meal of steak and mashed potatoes for one o'clock and said to the nurse, 'I'd like to have my baby before lunch please,' which is exactly what I did. I had a major epidural, couldn't feel a thing and even managed to watch a cowboy film during the birth because it was so easy compared to the last time. My little girl was born on 13 February 1988 and we called her Sissy.

I adored the Wellington. They had this cute thing where they gave parents a candlelit dinner after the birth so Rick came for that and everybody else came by to visit me too. I think I was in the hospital for about three nights but I could've stayed there for ever. It was like a hotel with the bonus that somebody would come and help you with the baby. I literally didn't want to leave. I think I was scared to come out after the trauma of Simone. She was fabulous but I was a totally incompetent mother.

This time around I felt very secure because I had a good business, I loved Rick and he loved me. Everything was in place in my life. I'd recommend that, rather than being unsupported, unprepared and, as a result, terrified. I'd arranged to have a maternity nurse for when I got home and I wasn't breastfeeding, so that made it easier. Whilst I was in hospital I'd discovered these Cow & Gate tiny little feed bottles with throwaway teats. Sissy was started on that and as we were leaving I said, 'How do I get some of that?' You didn't have to mix it or anything. You just took off the foil, attached the disposable teats and hey presto! No messing around. Rick and I had to go and buy crates of the stuff from the hospital chemist and they were quite expensive but I was in love! They were just so convenient.

I'd tried breastfeeding with Simone and just thought it was horrible so I was given pills to stop the milk coming. It's bloody painful; I don't know why anyone elects to do it voluntarily. I know it's not very PC to say that but I'm just not into it and I don't think it did Sissy and Jack any harm not being breastfed. Plus I couldn't go back to work with big milky boobs, could I? I'd feel like a cow, quite honestly – it would make me feel like I was ill. So we staggered home with crates of this wonder milk.

Because I was running my own business I had to be

super-organised at home so I employed a really good maternity nurse called Anne who slept in Sissy's room at night so that I didn't get disturbed except at weekends. I went straight back to work after a week. It was a streamlined pregnancy and birth, very regimented and planned. It worked for us this way because I know I'm not capable of being a stay-at-home mum. It wasn't an option either, running such a busy agency. That said, we had the most amazing time with Sissy. Rick fell in love with her. She was his first child so he doted on her and took zillions of pictures. She was lovely, just gorgeous and we were besotted with her.

We'd not been back at home that long when I decided we needed a bigger place so we moved from the flat in Castellain Road to a three-bedroom maisonette in Elgin Avenue, where I still live now. I sold the flat to Susie Bick. The poor thing moved in and she got all these bites so she went to see my doctor who told her she had chicken pox but in actual fact she had fleas – she'd caught fleas from our British Blues!

So we moved into Elgin Avenue. I loved it, and still love it now. It's got high ceilings, and the kitchen and living room are at the back and lead into a gorgeous garden that isn't overlooked. The rooms sort of wind into each other and it's filled with character. It's quirky and homely. It's our home.

Anne, the nanny, moved with us and had a room upstairs, then Rick and I were in another room and Sissy was in the third bedroom. One day we had guests at the house so they were staying on the sofa bed in the lounge.

It was one of those big proper bed-type sofa beds, not a flimsy thing, which is kind of crucial for what comes next. Blue, our girl cat, disappeared. We were looking all over the place for her but thought, well, she's so stupid she's probably walked up to somebody else's house. A few days later, Rick's sitting down in the living room with the nanny and there's this funny smell so he says to her, 'Have you farted?' She says, 'no no!', absolutely horrified. I get back that evening after I've been to a party with another booker and we stumble back home all merry to find Rick, ashen, in the living-room doorway. He says to me, 'You won't believe it, I found Blue.' So I say, 'Great, where is she?' Blue had gone to sleep under the sofa bed and the guest had collapsed the sofa bed right on top of her. Rick found her and she was like one of those cartoon cats: totally flat. So Blue had to be scraped off the carpet. Because the bed was so heavy we like to think it would have been very swift. Poor Blue.

At this point Rick was doing a bit of photography but he was also working at Premier with us, helping out with accounts. He started to ring around all the people who owed us money and managed to make us more of a priority on their people-to-pay lists. He basically just chatted them up. We had a very organised life – working every day, then the nanny would go away at the weekends so we'd hang out with Sissy. I felt guilty, especially because Sissy got so attached to the nanny, but I couldn't give up work. For me at this time it was all about efficiency and routine. I'd get up in the morning, go and get Sissy, have breakfast, the nanny would come down then we'd shoot off to work, come back, Sissy would have been bathed and we'd say goodnight. We really didn't see her in the week much at all, but weekends were family time. We'd go to the park and the Clifton nurseries, or we might go and see Chris and his daughter Olivia who was born one month before Sissy – they lived in Maida Vale, too. Chris had married Huggy, an Icelandic model he had scouted in Madrid, who went on to become a brilliant photographer.

In 1989, changes were afoot at Premier. We were really rocking. We had Susie who was working all the time, and John and the boys were the hottest men around. It was also the start of what would be the biggest movement in our industry – the rise of the 'supermodel'. There were a select number of girls, all dotted around different agencies, who were storming the industry. Their names kept coming up and they were working all the time. One of these girls was a beautiful blonde German model called Claudia Schiffer. She was on covers everywhere and everyone was talking about her. We knew we needed to be her agent in London and Chris was very friendly with her agent in Paris at the time, so we just kept asking until eventually we wore them down and they agreed to place her with us in London. It was the same with another model called Christy Turlington, who was American and one of Eileen Ford's protégées. We just kept banging on the door of Ford in New York saying we really wanted her and we managed to get her. Of course it was very controlled by Christy's New York agent and Claudia's Paris agent in terms of what we could do, but we were getting big buck clients. This kind of persistence and tenacity was definitely one of our strengths because relatively speaking we were still a small, family-run firm. We weren't giants like some of the other agencies.

Speaking of giants, the Elite network was like McDonald's – they were everywhere! John Casablancas, who was the founder of the Elite network, approached us to become Elite in London. It was quite a big deal because they were already the biggest agency in the world, with offices in about ten cities. Gérald Marie had gone from Paris Planning to head up Elite in Europe, from the Paris office. We turned them down because we didn't want to work for Elite; we had our own business, our own name and it was too much to lose. In the end they opened Elite London with Beth Boldt, founder of an agency called Synchro. Beth had recently discovered the young Naomi Campbell in Covent Garden. She had a very good eye – she was a great scout – but she didn't know much about being an agent. Elite had high hopes for Naomi and within the network they also now had Linda Evangelista because politically she had to be with Elite as she was Gérald's wife. They were a superpower.

Then, something happened that was going to change everything. I got a call from George Michael. He wanted some models for a music video . . .

12

THAT MUSIC VIDEO AND THE START OF A PHENOMENON

Was I partly responsible for George Michael's 'Freedom' video? Yes, I suppose I was! One of our bookers, Becky Peach, was dating a guy called David Austin, a musician who co-wrote one of George Michael's tracks. They were also big friends. Becky mentioned that George wanted to feature a particular group of models in his latest video and perhaps I could help? The models in question had recently graced the January 1990 issue of British *Vogue* in a now-iconic cover shot by Peter Lindbergh. They were Naomi Campbell, Cindy Crawford, Christy Turlington, Linda Evangelista and Tatjana Patitz. It was the first time a group of models had been put together like this, something that Peter notes in David Bailey's documentary *Models Close Up*, and it was to be the beginning of the 'supermodel' phenomenon. Others soon joined that famous group.

Becky invited Chris to meet George at her apartment in Regent's Park for dinner to discuss the idea further. With my connections and the fact we had a direct line to George through Becky I hatched a plan to take on all the bookings myself. Now how this usually works is that bookings of this nature would be made direct through the girl's main agent – what's known as the 'mother agent'. I booked Christy for her London jobs and Claudia too sometimes but they weren't my girls. And the others certainly weren't my girls. But I had George on my side so I thought I'd give it a try and see what happened.

I called up Annie Veltry, who was the lead booker at Elite New York, and explained the job to her. I told her how amazing it was going to be and said how it would make the girls world-renowned. I just went on and on and on and wore her down until she said OK and let me book them.

In a way it sort of made sense to have all the bookings done from one place because big production jobs like that are akin to herding cats, in other words, a bloody nightmare, but I was surprised the bookers relinquished control so readily. We put it to them that this was an absolutely unique experience and they had to do it.

We got Christy from Ford because we said she'd be missing out if she didn't do it – *all the other girls were doing it*. So now, these girls (and boys, including our very own John Pearson) who so far had only been seen in 2D were suddenly brought to life in this amazing video – *en masse*. They were powerful on their own but as a group they were mesmerising. The director was David Fincher who went on to direct huge Hollywood movies such as *Seven* and *The Social Network*. 'Freedom' was a massive hit and a breakthrough for the cult of the supermodel.

The only girl we couldn't get to take part was Claudia Schiffer, because her agent was immovable about her doing a pop video! Chris argued for days with her and couldn't convince her, even with a fee of $100k at stake. I think she was hoping the record company would call her direct, either that or she just didn't get it! Claudia was furious and called Chris for an explanation. He was diplomatic and left Claudia to draw her own conclusion as to who was responsible.

After the 'Freedom' video, we were re-approached by John and Gérald from Elite, saying the London office wasn't doing what they needed it to do. We ended up negotiating an offer where we did not become Elite, instead we merged our two companies together – we were 50/50 partners with no casting vote and Premier was incorporated into the title. We became Elite Premier in 1991. It would have been Premier Elite had Chris not lost the coin toss to Gérald. C'est la vie! Actually this was a good deal for us. We were the operating partners and therefore able to run Elite Premier pretty much as we had run Premier previously and we were able to prevent ourselves from being sucked into the empire, like so many other agencies in the lesser markets.

Despite us having the beautiful New Bond Street

premises, Gérald wanted us to relocate to a building on Parker Street in Covent Garden, which he had recently bought. Very reluctantly, we agreed to move. The rent in Bond Street was astronomical anyway at this time and, as the recession took hold, Bond Street became like the Blitz: shops were going bust, people weren't renewing their leases because the rents were going up, and landlords were getting more greedy and the rates were also being reassessed by the council. We're still in Parker Street now and I really like the premises; everyone knows where we are and it is so central. I just wish I'd bought them when Gérald sold up, but I'm not quite that astute.

We had a choice between the downstairs or the roof and we decided the ground floor was a better place. We joined forces and moved in with the Elite team and it was ridiculous – there were so many staff. We had double bookers and we were all sharing chairs. I was the 'conductor' and it was absolutely bonkers. They had a men's section, we had a men's section – it was double everything. Gradually over the months people started to leave, which is what tends to happen when two companies merge. There's always a natural wastage but it was mainly the Elite people who left. Some of the bookers stayed but it all sorted itself out eventually.

By 1991, the recession was really bad in the UK but because suddenly we had so many supermodels, we were able to buck the trend and go from strength to strength. We had Claudia Schiffer and Christy Turlington who weren't in the Elite Group and then we inherited Naomi

Campbell, Linda Evangelista, Tatjana Patitz and Cindy Crawford from Elite. Unfortunately we didn't have Kate Moss – she was only just breaking through. In a recession people tend to play safe and book models they know will sell. Boy, could those girls sell: they were million-dollar babies. During a recession, it's not a time to experiment so these girls were getting booked at exuberantly high rates, much higher than you get nowadays or probably ever will again. Plus, the industry was still quite small at that time in terms of the number of models. There were no Russian and Eastern European girls flooding the market at cheaper prices. That came later.

At Elite Premier, because of the supermodels on our books, we were thriving whilst many others were struggling. I could feel this sea change happen. After about a year I remember thinking, my God it's so safe, which isn't actually a great thing in a business because you get a bit complacent. You get complacent because you're not panicking. I can remember feeling exceedingly safe. And smug really. The money was insane. You could just hold your nose and come up with a figure. Everyone wanted these girls so much, they just paid it.

Who made the supermodels?

This is a question I am often asked and the short answer is 'no one person' but there were definitely a number of key players, significant happenings and mitigating circumstances. I'm fond of the editor Liz Tilberis's thoughts on the matter when in Bailey's *Models Close Up* documentary she quips: 'We grew them. They became our hothouse flowers.' Tilberis was definitely one of the puppet masters. She was at the helm of British *Vogue* in January 1990 for that iconic Peter Lindbergh cover featuring all the girls together for the first time. Of that particular shot, Lindbergh himself said: 'I had a tendency to put them in groups and they became the supermodels.'

The designers rising to fame at that time were also key drivers thanks to their insatiable hunger for these girls. After what had been a more experimental time in the Eighties with the Japanese invasion and a fondness for androgyny on the catwalk, designers like Azzedine Alaïa and Gianni Versace brought sexy back with a massive bang. Their bodycon dresses put glamour and sex at the fore. They were both obsessed with the flawless female body, rejecting all but the most perfect specimens, thus helping to create a 'master-race' of models. Versace in particular made sure to use only the top, top girls with the hot, hot bodies in his shows. The combined star power of having all those girls in one giant, glittery, over-the-top show was overpowering.

Traditionally, you had two types of models. You had the show girls who did the twice-yearly circuit around the world, and the photographic girls who did the advertising and magazines. They were separate. Then, in the Nineties, Gianni Versace was the one who realised: I've got these girls in my campaign, why can't I have them in my show too? The girls themselves have all acknowledged the key role Versace played, and they were certainly grateful to him.

The supermodels became part of Versace's über-glamorous DNA. Some might say the models were more important than the clothes they were wearing: get the models and be guaranteed the attention. He helped to make them superstars by worshipping them like queens on and off the runway. The fascination with the super-models was that they were really young, gorgeous and, crucially, they were friends. This meant they were out together a lot. Versace realised that if he dressed them, gave them free clothes, they'd wear them out and then suddenly the press would capture them looking fab, young and glamorous, going into restaurants and clubs or out with their latest beau.

When we started with them around 1988, everyone knew Claudia – she already was a name. She was on every single cover and her look – insanely pretty, blonde, blue eyes – it sells, particularly in bad times. It was the iconic 'Guess' campaign using the sexy Bardot-like image of her by Ellen von Unwerth that launched her. Christy wasn't as well known apart from in the States but she was coming through. Christy is probably one of the most beautiful women ever. She's elegant, flawless and timeless. They all were, quite honestly, but she was the most classically beautiful girl. And so refined as a person as well. That said, certainly in the beginning, Claudia was an easier sell than Christy.

Cindy was drop-dead gorgeous in a very American-looking way and became pretty unreachable, as she was married to Richard Gere, which had placed her auto-matically in the Hollywood elite. She was the wholesome, pretty girl next door with a fab body. I didn't know Cindy very well, we were never that close. These girls would walk into a room and everyone would just stop dead.

Also, at the time, actresses didn't ever condescend to do an ad campaign, ever. They didn't touch it. So you had the supermodels that were doing the big ad campaigns and becoming highly exposed in the process. Paparazzi were suddenly interested and wanted to know what they were doing in their lives. They were out all the time with fabulous boyfriends; they had big personalities. And of course, models are fascinating to the public because they don't talk. They were like silent movie stars who just looked amazing. Everyone wanted to know – where did they go to eat? What did they wear? The public was really intrigued by them. Coco Chanel's quote about models – 'I pay them to make women envious' – had never seemed more relevant. More than inducing envy, I think models reflect or predict a new era or mood. Supermodels evolved because their image reflected the times, or the fantasy of the times. It was all about larger-than-life glamour and excess.

People started to know their names, they suddenly started appearing on chat shows and they were becoming celebrities in their own right. The public knew who they were so they were tremendously powerful as a sales tool. They just took off like rockets. It was quite phenomenal how these girls were everywhere. Whatever they did was instant news.

Then they got so big, the press kept asking for interviews, which was a new thing for models, and I got fed up with it. So I started to say, 'It will cost you £5k,' and to my surprise they said OK. So they were loving it because they got the girl and I set a precedent around the world at the time. It became the norm. For a period of time, any interview was paid for.

The funny thing was, I invented it as a way to get rid of the journalists – I didn't necessarily expect it would take hold but it did. This was the start of models becoming personalities. Before then, nobody cared. I think it was a good idea, by me(!), but also the girls didn't have a lot of time. They were working back to back so squeezing in an interview simply wasn't a priority. Of course it isn't just sit down and have a chat. It involves hair and make-up and what they're going to wear. A photographer has to be arranged. It's a performance, really. And then they've got to divulge their personal lives without divulging anything at all!

Another precedent was set when we booked the Corsa Cars ad campaign in 1992, a massive production that comprised a really rather brilliant TV advertisement and a billboard ad campaign. In terms of fees, it was a landmark event. Each girl – Linda, Christy, Tatjana, Naomi, Kate – was paid a record-breaking amount. For a day's shooting. The car was (aptly/shamelessly?) called 'the Supermodel' and there was a lot of fuss leading up to the final event. Claudia was in the initial line-up, she was such a huge star and very much on the client's wish list. But there was a problem: Claudia's agent wanted almost twice as much again for her. We tried so hard to get it for her but of course if she were to get it then the other girls would have to get that too. The huge fees for this campaign were on a favoured nations agreement, in other words, all the girls would be paid the same fee.

Plus, it was already a humungous deal. In the end we had to swap her for Tatjana Patitz. She was well known at the time but nowhere near as famous as Claudia so she lucked out. And then Kate Moss came in as well – bear in mind that Kate had only just started rising through the ranks at this stage. She was a newbie.

The day after the contracts were signed, Claudia rang and said she would accept the original offer. It was too late. Aghhh. So, just like with the 'Freedom' video, she missed out on a big thing. It was the first time these girls had all come together for an advertising campaign. Corsas are pretty basic cars and models are quite picky about what products they do so Vauxhall (or the advertising agency they used) pulled off a real coup with that ad. And it was a really cool short film. Suddenly these silent movie stars had come to life. They spoke! And they took the piss out of themselves – double win! The whole premise was that each girl saw this new 'Supermodel' as a threat. They were all vying to be number one – talk about art imitating life! The director, Tarsem Singh, was one of the biggest names in the business for both TV ads and music videos. He was definitely part of the pull for the girls too because he was so respected. He'd done iconic commercials for Nike, Levi's and Pepsi and music videos for REM, En Vogue and Vanessa Paradis. In those days film and commercial directors had quite a lot of pull and power, which they don't seem to have nowadays. So yeah, there was that and the fact that the money was *insane*!

Chris was involved with a lot of the negotiations for

this job. You can only imagine the number of phone calls and meetings it took to arrange. Another key player in this deal was Alan Cluer, the Mr Fix-It for the London and New York ad agencies – a real 'Mad Man'. Alan was a no-nonsense producer – charming, sharp, articulate but utterly ruthless. He did not suffer fools lightly and we had to be fully prepared for him. Once we had delivered the girls he was hugely complimentary, as we had helped make him and his already awesome reputation look very good indeed.

So our first year as Elite Premier got off to a flying start. Our first day open we took a US$1 million booking for Heather Stewart Whyte, Yannick Noah's wife, to headline the Shiseido worldwide cosmetic campaign via our good old friend Masa in Tokyo. We had a huge fight with Gérald, who was her mother agent, and John Casablancas had to referee on a four-way conference call, but we would not back down, so the billing went through Elite Premier. A fantastic start for us. It was the start of a new decade, a crazy era for modelling.

13

THE SUPERMODEL COMMANDMENTS

After Beth Boldt discovered Naomi in Covent Garden when she was sixteen, she took her from Synchro to Elite London when John and Gérald approached her to open the London office. I met her in 1991 when Elite London became Elite Premier. I thought she was lovely. She was twenty-one and this bright young thing. She sashayed into the offices in Covent Garden wearing a short black mini dress and her body was just incredible. She was so pretty too with those high-planed cheekbones and now-famous lips that turned into an amazing smile. She was really confident and bubbly and we just sort of hit it off.

She'd been on the cover of *Elle* at just sixteen, she was the first-ever black model to go on the cover of French *Vogue*, which she did in 1988, followed by a

US *Vogue* cover in '89. It was March '91 that she'd strutted down Gianni Versace's runway link-armed with Cindy, Christy and Linda, the four of them mouthing the lyrics to George Michael's 'Freedom'. Let's just say, she was a pretty hot property.

Straight away I started to look at how I could book her. The press were going nuts – it was Naomi they wanted to get access to the most – but I realised that she'd hardly worked in London, which was weird. She was this huge model and never worked here. That was my challenge. I started off in the UK by getting her press: paid press. Then suddenly all the work flooded in – advertising and editorial. I'd ring up the key editors and photographers and ask, 'Why haven't you used Naomi?'

Around the same time, Monique Pillard, John Casablancas' long-term right hand in New York and head of Elite Celebrities, suggested Naomi be repped by me in London. I said I'd be her agent but only if we were made mother agent.

So, Monique and I made the agreement and I set to work. She obviously felt I was up to the job and there was a mutual respect thing going on too; I liked Monique. She was a powerful character – hugely respected, funny, utterly charming and a brilliant agent. She knew everyone and kicked off many iconic campaigns for most of the top models/celebrities of the time. To name a few: Cindy Crawford, Christie Brinkley, Beverly Johnson, Uma Thurman, Kelly Emberg, Patti Hansen, Kelly le Brock, Isabella Rossellini, Monica Bellucci, Janice Dickinson, Iman, Stephanie Seymour, Lauren Hutton, Nastassja

Kinski, Elaine Irwin and Brooke Shields. We were officially in the big league now.

Naomi was such a special model, and her walk was extraordinary, 'like a cat, with no self-consciousness at all' is how fashion documentarian Douglas Keeve described it to the *New York Times* and I couldn't put it better myself. She was beautiful to watch. One of Naomi's gifts was that she knew instinctively what was right for her, from the pose to the clothes to the hair and make-up. Very quickly she assembled her talented dream team of Sam McKnight and Mary Greenwell who did her hair and make-up, respectively.

Stylists had a lot of respect for those models who had an instinctive style of their own, like Naomi, Linda and Kate. Fashion editors loved to work with them because they always knew what was the next thing. Designers were interested in what they were wearing because they'd pick up things in countries they'd travel to. They had an inbuilt sense of style . . . model style. And sometimes my girls would find an item of clothing in one part of the world, and just by wearing it, would make it the must-have item in another part of the world.

The first striking thing about looking after supermodels is how much time they take up. I used to have two phones in my house – this is before email – so I had a line just for work. Then I got a fax machine, though I could never work it properly so Rick always had to do it. When finally I got a mobile, that's when the fun really started because I could be contacted any time, anywhere, by anyone. The thing is, as much as people are often shocked to hear about being on call to somebody in that way, it was my job. I took it on and I wanted to do it. I wanted to be there for them. But I did soon wise up to not taking my mobile up to bed with me, after too many silly o'clock calls. I left it charging downstairs.

When you consider the life they were leading, jetting all over the world, never quite sure who their real friends were amongst all the wannabes, co-dependents and hangers-on basking in the reflected glory, you can understand where their brittle outer shells might have come from. I saw it as a vulnerability and felt the need to protect them. I'm fairly tolerant but I have a level I can go to and then – boom! – it'll be my turn to start swearing. Those of you who watched *The Model Agency* will know that about me.

Those top girls could be difficult because of the amount they were travelling. Some of them had no concept of time at all. They were constantly in different time zones and often exhausted. Sometimes it made them tetchy. They liked to test people to see if they could magic up whatever crazy request they might have that day/hour/ second. Whereas some people might wilt at that thought or even find it demeaning, I saw it as a challenge. In that way I was well suited to the job because I never refuse a bet. I'd do it just to spite them sometimes. Let me try and give you an insight into the world that we shared, that hedonistic, all-powerful supermodel era of the Nineties.

I have never learned as much or as quickly as when I was with the girls. They were fascinating to work with for that reason. It's true of those 'big' girls in general, they were so busy, so successful, so adored, so pampered, so stunningly beautiful, so . . . super, that occasionally being ungracious and entitled was part of the mantle of success and no one thought about the raison d'être behind it. It was an unstoppable avalanche that swept us all along. There was a lot to learn. It was so new, this crazy supermodel phenomenon; we were basically all treading new ground together.

So what *did* I learn? I thought it would be fun to do this as a sort of 'Model Commandments': a handy (tongue-firmly-in-cheek) manual to be passed down through generations of stressed-out bookers, should the likes of those creatures ever walk this earth again . . .

The Model Commandments: An Agent's Guide

1. *Thou shalt have no other gods before me.*

OK, that one speaks for itself.

2. *Thou shalt never get anything wrong. Ever.*

So does that one.

3. *Remember the mornings are for rousing the goddesses from their beds. Persist, even if they at first resist.*

The wake-up calls. If Susie Bick was my training pants, some of the other girls were my potty training: the messy bit, filled with tantrums, that you think will never end. Getting certain people up and out to a job was an absolute nightmare with a specific routine that replayed and replayed like some kind of horror montage. My first trick was to say the call time for the job was two hours before it actually was – plenty of time, right? No. Eventually they cottoned on to that so you'd have to make it three hours.

I'd always have a key to the hotel room, let myself in, wake whichever beast I was chaperoning that day and swiftly be told, 'Fuck off, go away!' I'd adjourn to the lobby or wherever, have a cup of tea and then go back in and give it another go. Then, Madam may continue with the obscenities or, to keep things inter-esting, turn coy and say in her most charming voice, 'I'm getting up, I'm getting up.' But she'd be lying.

I'd go back in, like a boxer getting back off the ropes, and she'd still be in bed, texting or talking to somebody. She's now two hours late so you're shitting yourself. You are waiting outside the suite pacing up and down furiously, swearing. She's being paid a fortune, the client's ringing, the (really famous) photographer's ringing; hell is slowly revealing itself to you from beneath the door of the five-star hotel suite.

Eventually she stirs, shifts those million-dollar limbs to the left, shrugs off the gazillion-thread sheets and shimmies off the royal bed. On a good day, the royal ablutions will start; on a bad day, illness strikes. 'There there,' you soothe. 'You're all right. It will be OK' – simultaneously checking your watch, aware that she is now fully taking the piss. 'You don't care about me!'

comes the childlike shout: 'I'm ill, I'm ill!' You are living in a nightmare. Another hour goes by and somehow you find a cure for the mystery illness, order room service breakfast – which is barely touched due to lack of appetite and shaky hands – clear away the assorted evidence of last night's party and haul ass to the car that has been waiting for the best part of half a day. You will already have told the photographer/creative director/client/ whoever happens to be swearing down the phone to you 'where the fuck is she?' and other unrepeatable but classic 'sound bites' that you had actually got in the car hours ago.

Easy.

Of course, there are exceptions to every rule and some of them were like Swiss Watches: always on time.

4. Thou shalt always be late.

See Commandment 3 for the origins of this decree. You have done the waking ritual and now you are in a car and you are late. You are in a house and you are late. You are waiting outside their lover's house and you are late. You are holding a flight on the runway – you are late. You are trying to locate a missing belt/bracelet/foodstuff – you are late. You are late. You are late. You are always late. You learn how to manage said lateness with a series of updates (lies) to those concerned (no wonder talent agents have such terrible reputations). 'We are just leaving the hotel!' (still in sleep coma; one hour late); 'We're in the car!' (just out of bed; two hours late); 'We're in a traffic jam!' (just got in the car; three hours late); 'We broke down!' (almost there; really pushing our luck).

The thing is, like the lark sings in the morning, like the bear shits in the woods, the supermodel is always late. Everyone knows that, don't they? There will be fire breathed and expletives expelled – usually down the phone to the beleaguered agent – but then the bright light appears, the saviour, the supermodel cometh, and it's 'Hi, darling! So great to see you!' Then the fussing and pampering begins. No one will ever tell her off, all they care about is getting her perfect bottom in that make-up seat and ready to work the magic they – and she – know she can do. She smiles, she knows; she wins.

5. Thou shalt deliver unto me candles and a shade of lipstick that doesn't yet exist.

Diptyque Tubercuse has a lot to answer for. Candles, candles everywhere! When you're a model of a certain stature, you need to be in the presence of a £50 scented flame at all times. Your skin can be touched only by the finest lotions, your lips kissed by the latest tincture. A bevy of servants (assistants, or me) lie in wait, twitching, knowing it will come: the impossible request. Inevitably, we'd go, 'What the fuck is she talking about?', write down the latest fad and try to decipher it *en masse*. It would turn out to be a new skincare range that we'd never heard of, that only Harrods stock and that only came into the UK that day, which would be fine apart from the fact we're in Germany. Every day, a new puzzle to solve; a growing team of disciples constantly trying to decipher the latest whim. An assistant returns triumphant, arms aloft like a marathon runner severing that finishing line ribbon, only to be told 'It's the wrong colour!' and have to go back.

Then there's the far-flung request. I remember once having to find these special green candles from Tibet that were something to do with a witch doctor that had special energy or something. I mean, fucking ridiculous. There's me, a grown woman, trying to find these absurd things. So I'm ringing my PA saying, 'Find these fucking candles.' We're all losing our minds to find these damned candles that were just the most inane things but 'life and death' important to these models. I think now, for fuck's sake, what was wrong with me? I needed a lobotomy. But it's what I did at that time.

6. *Thou shalt assist me in my pursuit of love.*

The presidential suite at the Lanesborough? Champagne on ice? Rose petals on the bed? Sex toys located and delivered? No problem! Have a suit hand-tailored, purchased and couriered to LA? Sure thing! Oh, and could you take me to that famous actor's apartment in Little Venice? But whatever you do, don't tell my boyfriend!

7. *Nourish my body with foods untold.*

The supermodel will fuck you up with food. 'Bring me Chinese but only if it comes from Mr Chow.' 'I crave

Premier's giant 1995 poster.

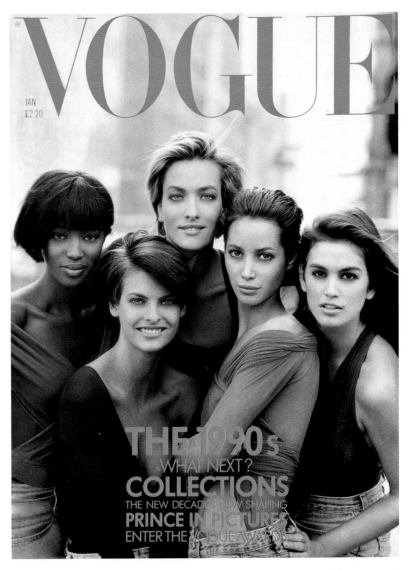

Peter Lindbergh/*Vogue* © The Condé Nast Publications Ltd.

Opposite, clockwise from top left: Christy and Olivia at the Fashion Café, New Orleans; Chris and Linda backstage; Olivia and Sissy autograph hunting; drinks with Gerald and Peter; travelling with a grumpy Sissy; Corinne and Susie during model party days.

Clockwise from top: Nelson Mandela meeting the supermodels
at the Versace Children of Soweto charity show; Linda and Olivia;
Chris with Olivia on the road; Chris, Naomi and Dr Guertler in Köln
at a Wella publicity photo call.

Left: Nelson Mandela book-signing on the Blue Train trip.

Above: Sissy and Olivia.

Below: Claudia judging Miss Iceland with Huggy, Eyglo and Olivia at Perlan.

Clockwise from top left: Claudia in Monte Carlo; Naomi Campbell for Agent Provocateur; Karen Mulder cover for *Marie Claire*; Linda on tour with *Elle* magazine; Huggy Ragnarsson/Singapore *Vogue* © Condé Nast Australia; Susie Bick by Rick Best.

Clockwise from top left: Cindy's model card; Karen Mulder for Vivienne Westwood by Huggy Ragnarsson; me on Flavio Briatore's yacht; Linda's *Marie Claire* cover shot; Naomi's famous fall at the Vivienne Westwood show, 1993.

Clockwise from top left: Rick with Sissy and Jack at home; Simone ready to go out; Rick at his desk; young Jack and Sissy; Jack and me; Chris in the South of France.

Penne Arrabbiata, but it must be made by Lorenzo.' 'I *need* a giant Cadbury's Fruit and Nut bar and I need it now!' That thing about supermodels not eating? Bullshit. They eat loads. And they eat specific. The caviar must be black, and Russian. Water – Fiji (or, in certain cases, replaced with Stolichnaya). The main thing to remember is that, whatever continent you happen to be in at the time, she will want a food indigenous to the continent that is furthest away. She will *need* the food that the little country you are in has never heard of; it has never passed their naïve lips – but you will find it. You will grow it, harvest it, pluck it, prepare it and cook it yourself if you have to. Can I tell you what the Special is today, madam? Llama curry. Or Llama Fucking Curry as it became affectionately known at Premier HQ. The first time we were asked for llama curry, we flew into a mad panic – a whole team desperately trying to find a restaurant that does this South American speciality. Then – hooray! – we find one and she says, 'Oh that was awful,' or, hopefully, 'That was brilliant,' and you have to remember where the good ones came from. The model is boarding a private jet and asked what food she'd like. She's in Milan – land of pasta, delicious cured meats, antipasti and pizza. What would she like to eat? Llama Fucking Curry.

8. Thou shalt covet thy agent's holidays.

I enjoy this story that concerns my brother Chris and one of our models. He gets a call from said model screaming and crying that she is in terrible danger. She is in danger from her boyfriend who has violently attacked her – he must come and get her immediately. In Mauritius. He knows it's probably not true, having been privy to exaggerated circumstances countless times before, so he firmly says 'no' but she keeps on calling. Even his wife Huggy says, 'You've got to go' and books his flight for him, so that's him, British Airways first class to Mauritius. *On Good Friday.* Chris was really pissed off missing out on a nice family Easter weekend but it was yet another crazy adventure. On arrival, the boyfriend is nowhere to be seen and said model (who at least had the grace to meet him off the flight, proffering a very welcome ice-cold beer) has not a scratch on her, is remarkably chipper and informs him to get a move on, there's a boat party they must attend!

What follows is a very bizarre sequence of events akin to a plot in *The Hangover* and involving, in no particular order, a yacht owned by a majorly odious mogul rumoured to have syphilis and a raging coke habit; a tough-guy actor, topless, playing the bongos; liquid ecstasy; a private plane to Zanzibar; and a very near miss for our model with a proficient martial arts expert who was the favourite daughter of one of the most powerful men in Hong Kong and who hasn't taken kindly to her attitude and abuse. 'I could kill you with one blow, bitch!' was the threat. It worked. She shut up after that.

9. *In sickness and in fake sickness, thou shalt be by my side.*

When a model is sick, she is really sick. Like, 'call the doctor before I die' sick. It is important when the need arises to have a plethora of 24/7-accessible, unshockable, sympathetic doctors to magic out of thin air. Now we're not pulling them from the ranks of those doctors who get called to sew up the bullet wound of an injured Mafioso, nothing that dodgy, but these A-list doctors have a special set of skills/disposition and, let's face it, tend to be a bit more generous with the good drugs and a verified medical note should the need arise.

There was a particularly nasty case of self-diagnosed appendicitis one morning that came on strong and sudden in the suite of a Paris hotel after a pretty heavy night the evening before. We phoned a dial-a-doctor and this guy really thought our model was the dogs' bollocks. He was great because if a model ever missed a shoot, we just called him. In this instance he put the model in the private clinic saying she had appendicitis, just as she had told him, whilst dramatically hugging the wrong side of her body and sobbing like a toddler. The downside for me was I was forced to sleep on this little truckle bed next to her and she was farting all night. You know, because she had wind. Wind.

10. Thou shalt respect my religious beliefs, whatever they happen to be this week.

It's good to get in touch with your spiritual side(s) from time to time, especially if, say, your current squeeze is Buddhist and doesn't drink (or reckons he doesn't drink).

Adjustments must be made, meaning a new regime is upon us and, as is only proper, we make sure all alcohol is removed from the minibar in your room and that it is stocked with only Volvic water, this time.

> 11. *Avail yourself to the task of gift buying for a seem-ingly endless list of 'friends'.*

Tiffany made a silver straw for a while in the Nineties. I know, a curious invention. They became very popular gifts until the jeweller cottoned on to what they were probably being used for and promptly wrapped up production.

14

PLANES, HELICOPTERS AND AUTOMOBILES

Concorde gave the supermodels supersonic power. It became a matter of course that if you booked one of those girls they flew in on Concorde. And often it would be two tickets: one for them, one for their assistant/boyfriend/ long-lost cousin. The fare cost about £6k and it meant they could leave London in the morning at 9.30 a.m. and be in New York by 9.30 a.m. ready to work – on time! The service ran between the key cities – London, Paris and New York – so it enabled them to work back to back. I loved Concorde, it was amazing. I've been on it about four times. From an agent's point of view it made things possible that simply aren't possible now. You have to allow a day between jobs in New York and London whereas then you didn't. It was a miracle. Why we've never replaced that wonderful technology is a mystery to me.

Literally every big shot and high-profile name wanted these girls so you'd choose the job and it was about money or prestige in terms of what was the right job for them, but underneath that there'd be probably five or six clients waiting to see if they could get them on the same day and you'd choose which one you were going to take. It had lots to do with the calibre of the photographer and the prestige of the campaign or editorial. Then, I'd think, how can I get them back to New York to do the job the next day? Concorde.

They were hopping on and off planes like rock stars on tour, the difference being rock stars always had a break and it wasn't as imperative for them not to look like shit in the morning. This time-zone surfing and the back-to-back jobs were, I believe, one of the reasons they got a reputation for being diva-ish. They had no time to themselves. A lot of the girls always said their favourite time was on the plane because nobody could get to them. As an agent, you would try and give them a day off but then a job would turn up that you simply couldn't turn down. You'd think, *oh God, I've promised her a day off but this job is really good*. Then you'd have to ring them and say Richard Avedon wants to use you for blah blah and feel awful telling them because they thought they had this fab day off.

It was quite an extraordinary thing – people were practically fighting to use them to the point that it became like an auction. We'd play clients off against each other and then have to pretend the girls were sick or something. Their schedules were just incredible. It was all massively high-calibre stuff and the rates were incredible, not like now. We just used to name our price. You could get £300k a day for doing a campaign and for a catwalk show, £25k. With all these girls they had so much power so the clients always knew they were in a queue. If it didn't come down to the prestige of job or photographer then it came down to money. On top of that there was a range of things we had to demand for them. I guess it would be the same if you were booking a huge music star like Madonna or Mariah Carey. So it would be a fee of £300,000 *and* a private jet *and* a limousine *and* body-guard, a suite not a room, food from Mr Chow, *and and and* . . . Once they'd committed to the money, then they'd gulp – an additional £30k just like that!

It was a steep learning curve at this time and there were a lot of firsts for me, like the first time I booked a private jet – another preferred mode of transport for your not-so-average supermodel. There was a big job in Denmark, and for one reason or another we had missed the flight. The job is worth a ton of money and I'm scratching my head thinking, how on earth are we going to get there? One of my bookers piped up, 'Private jet,' which begs the question – how the fuck do you book a private jet? 'I've got an uncle who knows somebody,' she says, and gives me the name of a company called Chapman Freeborn. The clock's ticking so I ring them up straight away and I'm actually quite scared, thinking they might be a bit snotty, but they weren't at all, they were brilliant. Straight away it was, 'Yes, we can get you there, where would you like to fly from?' And there were two choices – Farnborough or Northolt airport. I'd never done this before so I literally had no clue if just anyone could book a private jet or what it would cost. It turned out to be £8k which, when you're talking about a £170k job, is positively reasonable! Who would've thought it could be so easy and so quick?

Once I had done it once, of course, it quickly became the norm, as my girls became addicted to private jets. It quickly became another norm on an ever-growing list of demands. The trick was to get the client to pay for it. So, now that I'd learned how to book a private jet I did it all the time – as easy as making a doctor's appointment (just a bit more costly). I got quite a buzz from solving the various different puzzles that would come up all the time. It certainly kept things interesting.

I soon learned that it was a very delicate process, the business of luxury logistics, with no room for error. Often the girls would specify a particular seat on their luxury flight (1C on Concorde, 1A on a BA flight) or, when going private, there would be a preferable private jet company, favoured airport and even type of jet – Lear versus Citation. Then there was the car to consider. You couldn't just call a local cab firm and say can you go pick them up? They wouldn't just take any old heap. So it would be a Mercedes S-Class with a specified driver.

There would always be a favourite driver and possibly a bodyguard, too. These poor drivers didn't know what had hit them (no pun intended), especially when their role suddenly shifted and they became an overnight guest as was the case with one couldn't-believe-his-luck guy. He had a good run of it with one of our models until it came to the point where she was done with him and he took on the new role of jilted lover. They had to be built of stern stuff, those drivers. I was particularly fond of one bodyguard-cum-driver who was reminiscent of an East End gangster type. He was great because you knew he'd get your model to the airport in record time. He'd break the law and get you to Heathrow in ten minutes. Sometimes ten minutes was all we had.

We developed a close relationship with British Airways' special services at this time and often they'd hold the plane for us. We'd send a car in advance with all the luggage, which would never happen now. That all stopped after 9/11. The assistant would check everything in then wait for the model along with special services who, when she arrived, would rush them through on little buggies. We'd go sailing past everybody – it was really good fun actually. We'd ring and say she's ten minutes away but of course she wasn't. It always made you sweat but a couple of them, for example, never even perspired, which is quite a good trick for a model. I, on the other hand, would be stressed-out, sweating and boiling.

Once the transport had been arranged, then there was the hotel to consider. No Holiday Inns for these girls – this was a glittering portfolio of the world's top 'fashion' hotels. Fashion being as it is, hotels would fall from grace and the agent must bloomin' well know it. London in particular went in fads. It was Claridge's at one point – *everyone* had to stay at Claridge's. A big show would happen and you had to produce these rooms, which often, if it was last minute, was bloody hard. And if you couldn't get all your girls in the same hotel they felt like you'd failed them. So you had to. And then of course because they were all in Claridge's that's where all the fashion editors wanted to stay, too. After a while the Berkeley in Knightsbridge became the serious place to stay. Then the Dorchester. Then the Metropolitan – especially because the Met Bar was such a celeb hotspot (and den of iniquity). It was difficult to get into. When the Berkeley Hotel became popular it was all about the Blue Bar.

In Paris you had to stay at the Bristol. You could walk into the lounge bar and see Claudia Schiffer, Naomi Campbell, Stephanie Seymour, Cindy Crawford, Alexander McQueen . . . *everyone* stayed at the Bristol. And because they stayed there all the agents had to stay there. I would have to get my PA to book the Bristol for me every season a year in advance. The Bristol's beautiful, everything's white, it's classic but airy with lots of light. I still love it, but it's so expensive it makes you faint – 32 euros for a bowl of soup; 22 euros for a vodka and orange.

Suddenly, one year the lovely Bristol fell out of favour. Nobody knows why this happens and there is certainly no memo to say it's so, but you'd better be sure you act appropriately. Imagine booking into the wrong hotel? Disaster! So the fashion pack dispersed and migrated to the Ritz and Hôtel Costes. There wasn't that same community feel as there had been at the Bristol, though. I'm not keen on Hôtel Costes. It's like staying in Dracula's Parlour – we'd all be stumbling around in blackness. The best thing about the hotel is it has a nice outdoor area to eat and smoke. Even now it's still full of fashion people but I only suffered it once (during the trendy period).

In Milan it was the Principe di Savoia that you had to get into, and Soho Grand, Morgans and the St Regis had the hottest fashion rooms in New York. Of course, the trendier these hotels became, the more the room rate soared. There was no sense of keeping costs down, you just had to book it and become part of the entourage. Sometimes the client would foot the bill and occasionally the agency or model herself. The agency had to stump up quite a bit but it was like having a magic key – you could get into anything. It was a time when queues didn't exist. You just followed Christy, Claudia, Linda or Naomi and you were in.

Some of the girls could be very demanding. And of course they were in competition with each other over who had the most. They'd be like, 'I got this from my agent.' Waah! Suddenly the stakes just got ridiculous and became their currency. It would be, 'I got my client to hire a private jet,' and then you were under pressure to get it the next time. They were friends but they were rivals, too. They'd gossip amongst themselves and some of them were dead bright when it came to this. If they got wind of somebody being up for a job and they weren't, or a fab perk, they'd want to know why and I'd have to go and sort it out.

We'd each travel with different models. Chris would sometimes go over Christmas and take Huggy and Olivia to basically protect our investment. You couldn't send them off to do a £300k job on their own because as soon as anything went wrong – and something often did – it was your fault. You'd say to the client, she has to have this kind of vodka, Hermès soap, Diptyque candles, etc. Often the client would think it was trivial so they wouldn't do it and we'd say, 'we asked for this'. Some of them would blow up. Christy was never like that, and Claudia wasn't too bad, but sometimes some of them would really freak out. They were so powerful and they knew that the client had invested so much money in them that they could just misbehave. It would be 'I'm leaving the agency' all the time.

Being cooped up in a cabin for several hours often made for uncomfortable encounters. Chris recalls 'Boiled Egg-gate' (as we like to call it) – the time when a model had a major fit over a four-minute egg request that arrived a little on the well-done side. What do you do if your egg is not to your liking in BA First Class? You stand up and throw a fit, abuse the stewardess then demand to speak to the captain just as he is trying to land a jumbo jet with 300 people on board! Since when did the pilot have anything to do with breakfast? Luckily, the model realised the error of her ways afterwards and saw the funny side once Chris had told her she was being an idiot. She even posed for a picture doing an impression of a diva.

Even though there was some rivalry, the girls were

big friends. They'd ring each other up and say, 'Hi, it's Wagon.' God knows why they called each other that, but they did. Because they were all doing the same thing and living the same crazy life, it brought them together and some of them became close. Other girls of their age couldn't possibly envisage their lifestyle, it was mad. Kate, Christy and Linda were all really good friends, they'd all hang out together. They were really tight. They used to go to Dublin a lot because Christy was close to Bono and his wife.

The supermodel lifestyle meant I found myself on private jets, helicopters and yachts quite a bit, as well as at some legendary parties with all the big fashion people – models like Amber Valletta, Kirsty Hume, Shalom and Eva, a lot of socialites like Annabelle Neilson who'd bring along about a thousand people, Alexander McQueen, John Galliano, Peter Lindbergh. It was very exciting – I loved the parties on the yachts.

You'd go on there and stuff yourself with caviar and sit next to politicians or famous people. I remember being on a deck having a dinner with a load of Italian politicians one time and I had my daughter Sissy with me. She went to the loo and came back and said, 'Mummy, mummy, there's money in the loo.' I went to have a look and there was a $100 bill rolled up. I said, 'Oh, that's nice, darling,' and put it in her pocket!

I remember chatting to P. Diddy one year on a boat. He was good fun. I knew who he was at least, but more often than not I didn't have a clue who these people were. The funniest example of this was back in London when I was rushed out to lunch and sat for a good two hours at a table with a charming man who seemed very familiar to me but I couldn't quite place him. It was Kevin Spacey!

15.

WAIF V WOMAN

Fashion is full of surprises. The waif and the cultural revolution she spawned (or which spawned her?) in the early Nineties was one of those surprises. It was a unique era because it was a time when one movement – the goddess-like supermodel – was at its height but in the background something altogether more grungy was happening. An alternative scene, vibrating on its own low-key frequency, was slowly building momentum and then, when it properly hit, nobody really knew what to do.

What was this strange new look? This rebellious mood? For those of us who were at the epicentre of the supermodel phenomenon, helping to create it and move it along, it seemed like the riches would never end. These unbelievably beautiful women had a near-monopoly on the industry. OK, so they were the biggest pain in the ass (to quote Isaac Mizrahi), but their beauty allowed and facilitated their divadom. They were goddesses to be adored and pampered and placed on high. They ruled the fashion kingdom . . . but like any empire, it toppled eventually.

A cultural snapshot of 1990: the supermodel era begins with George Michael's 'Freedom' video; Paul Gascoigne cries when England lose out to Germany in the semi-final of the World Cup in Italy; and Kate Moss appears, toothy, freckled and aged just sixteen, on the cover of *The Face* magazine, photographed by Corinne Day.

The issue was called the 'Third Summer of Love' and the cover lines promised 'Stone Roses on Spike Island, an A–Z of the new bands, Daisy Age fashion, Hendrix and psychedelia'. Who better to convey this than a fresh-faced, smiling teenager in a feather head-dress? This was British youth culture at its most carefree. It was 'real' and the proverbial chalk to the supermodels' rich and indulgent cheese.

The slightly confusing part in all this though was Kate, because even though she was the poster girl for the new counter-culture, she was embraced by the establishment, too: she could straddle both worlds. The powers-that-be wanted some of her magic dust for themselves. John Galliano kicked off what would be a lifelong collaboration with Kate when he featured her in his first Paris show in 1990, and then, in '92, she landed a huge Calvin Klein contract, dressed as a waif – dressed as herself. The new mood had officially crossed over and Kate was the conduit. About the casting, publicist Nian Fish of

KCD told *Vogue*: 'The big girls were there – Cindy [Crawford], Nadja [Auermann]. And then Kate Moss walked in. She put on this beige chiffon slip dress, and it just fell on her body. We put her in flat shoes, and when she walked, the fabric was like liquid flowing around her body. I got goose bumps. We all knew we were witnessing one of those fashion moments.'

It was clear that Kate was treading a new path in both worlds when, also in '92, she appeared in Marc Jacobs' notorious grunge show for Perry Ellis. It was clear where Jacobs had got his inspiration when he told *WWD* soon after: 'The images of Kate Moss by Corinne Day and Juergen Teller really changed fashion. That was a moment when we looked at beauty and glamour in a different way.'

Also in 1992, Kate was officially crowned 'supermodel' along with her more established super-sisters in the Corsa car TV commercial that we pulled together. In a way, that ad said it all because Kate comes in right at the end, with the little red car, as the slogan booms out 'the New Supermodel'. Fair enough, she's booted off the stage to make more room for the car but her look is cute and girly versus the more statuesque, Old Hollywood glamour of Christy, Linda *et al*. The waif had officially arrived – but how would the goddesses respond?

This was the challenge I was faced with. Because these supermodels were so, so beautiful you couldn't really waif them up. They were simply too beautiful to be in that category – it was so different. The waif thing wrong-footed many of the fashion fraternity because before we were looking for beauty – admittedly in many different forms – which is enduring and very symmetrical; it's what beauty as we all understand it is and to a degree that will never date. But this new waif stuff? It was about something completely different. Many of us thought it would be over in five seconds. It wasn't, it defined a whole generation.

Photographers like Corinne and Juergen ushered in a new era which was about deconstructing beauty, and in the end it made being glamorous almost naff. All that make-up, all the glitzy Versace stuff, suddenly started looking dated. It was a massive shock for fashion in general. Nobody quite understood it. First of all, we thought it was quite ugly but then, as I'd experienced before with Gillian at Bobtons, your eye adjusts, starts to accept it and you get it.

The new photography style made the pictures look almost like amateur snapshots. The production values were low and the environments completely naturalised – skinhead guy crossing a street wearing Nike Air Max; gangly girl stood in a puddle in a simple black ensemble and bare feet. It was that street-style look that's become so common – and diluted – now. The buzzwords were truth and realism, almost like taking a documentary style of photography and applying it to fashion. It was contrived photography but basic in that it had everyday props rather than, say, a tiger, or something equally OTT. This realness is something I know Corinne was so passionate about. I read a piece in the *Evening Standard* soon after she died and this quote from her has really stayed with me: 'Fashion magazines – it's all fantasy, isn't it? I've always liked to go in the opposite direction.'

Of course the change needed to happen. It's like anything – there has to be a shift. In a way, what Corinne and her contemporaries did was offer a palette cleanser to the really rich courses that we'd been gorging on. When Corinne first started it was really raw and uncompromising. But then she toned it down, when the likes of *Vogue* wanted in, and it became softer. Magazines like *i-D* and *The Face* could take it in its purest form. I know Corinne would struggle with the thought that she'd sold out. But I guess she had to eat! Even if it was unconscious and she didn't know she was doing it, she did refine it. Then Juergen would go from his gritty pictures, into advertising, where it also becomes more refined. If you look at Juergen's book it's like snapshots really, then you look at his advertising and it still has that gritty quality but it's become much more sophisticated. This is bound to happen – things adapt almost by osmosis.

Everything that goes into *Vogue* is adapted for *Vogue*. It's not based on truth – it's a dream. How can you have dirty sheets, Tampax on the floor and fag ash everywhere, in *Vogue*? I mean, really. The Corinne look is really hard to style, but *Vogue* is *Vogue* and they have to acknowledge what is going on, albeit in a slightly more sophisticated way. So it becomes not true. By *Vogue's* standards, though, Corinne's 1993 shoot – showing Kate in mismatched underwear and in a very ordinary-looking bedroom – was pretty damned gritty. In some circles it provoked outrage, which I'm sure Corinne would have been more than happy with. It shook things up in a big way. It's one thing featuring a waif-like Kate, skinny and half-dressed in magazines like *i-D* and *The Face* – they're in the niche box over there – but *Vogue*? Suddenly everyone, including (somewhat randomly) Bill Clinton, had something to say! There were some really heavy accusations made after that 1993 *Vogue* shoot, referencing paedophilia, anorexia and 'heroin chic'. It got pretty nasty, to say the least.

And while the bitches were bitching, the adapters were adapting, or trying to. I think Christy being signed up to an exclusive contract by Calvin Klein was a good example of this. Hers was a less gritty vision of beauty than Kate's in the Obsession campaign but it was certainly very natural. It was quietly glamorous, which was the compromise from the distinctly unquiet glamour of the late Eighties and early Nineties that preceded it. Kate certainly caused a stir in that ad campaign but I wouldn't be surprised if it wasn't rather less successful in Middle America where all the money is. Christy is a good alternative and I would say she probably appealed more to the American market. She rounds off the edges a bit.

Cindy Crawford was the all-American girl but her relevance was very much bound in the true super era. She was hit very hard by the waif. It hurt those girls in a way because then you had your second wave of models coming through, like Shalom Harlow and Amber Valletta, and they could do this new look (or versions thereof) and, of course, Kate was riding high. She was enjoying a different success because she was doing all the premium editorial as well as some of the really big campaigns. The other girls were still hugely successful – they would do money jobs – but they wouldn't do as much editorial, which is so necessary to keep you in the cool groove. Compared to Kate they were waning a little. I remember really hunting for editorial for the supers at this time. Their look wasn't right for those magazines like *The Face* and *i-D*.

Kate Moss is such a unique model thanks to her chameleon qualities. Peter Lindbergh's work with her for *Harper's Bazaar* in the mid-Nineties is a brilliant example of this. He managed to capture Kate in a way that moved everything along and created a more naturalistic form of glamour. Peter had, and still has, a gift for capturing those girls in a really candid way. His special brand of glamour wasn't as glossy. When Kate started out it was all very young and crisp and real, then it evolved and it's in this evolution that her success lies. I think people like to see a girl that's quite raw like that and then suddenly she turns into this sexy person from that almost pre-pubescent girl look. Everyone's like, wow she's actually really beautiful and sexy and grown-up. It's like we grew up with her.

Kate was somebody who was beautiful but obtainable. The supers weren't obtainable – they were looked up to and dreamed about. She's so relevant, Kate, it's really peculiar. Everyone could relate to her. She wasn't *oh my God, you are so beautiful* straight away. She grew into it. She was the of-the-minute girl who remained of-the-minute for more than a decade. I know from experience how rare this is in a model. The classical beauties that had been celebrated in the past gave way to more varied and alternative forms of beauty. Models became muses for an entire generation, with Moss as head muse. Kate Moss did for the Nineties what Twiggy did for the Sixties – she said to women, here's the face to this revolution. In the documentary *Kate Moss: Creating an Icon*, Peter Lindbergh says about her: 'Kate has something you can't describe, something inimitable, something extra. Kate is cool.'

Cool is the word. Kate was the poster girl but other models, such as Annie Morton, Rosemary Ferguson and Karen Elson, followed in her wake. They were fresh, perhaps a bit gawky, certainly skinny and – crucially – very British. They were photographed by the up-and-comers such as Wolfgang Tillmans and David Sims who, like Corinne and Juergen before them, were much more interested in a candid setting and a gritty finish. Humour had even started to creep in. It was a very cool time for British culture in general. It was the beginnings of 'Cool Britannia', another media construct that bled through the consciousness of the time.

It got to 1994 and Kate was firmly established as one of the supermodels and they were all friends but she did start taking the cream of the work. I wouldn't say there were squabbles but they would find out what she was doing and ask, 'Why aren't I doing that?' I'm sure there were some tensions but they were genuine friends so it never became a huge problem. It's quite a difficult thing because there were these top girls who'd always get in everything and then suddenly this new little girl comes along. It's quite hard to say to a model, 'Well, your look isn't actually that current.' You had to say, 'All right, I'll get on to Juergen' or whoever, and very often you'd get 'oh, she's not right.'

At this time Kate just had a more varied appeal, and that all-important cool factor. The supers were still powerful as a group too and the British factor was so important. It's when designers like Vivienne Westwood and Alexander McQueen were riding high, promoting the creative eccentricity of our small island and using British girls to do so. When you see what comes out of this small country it's quite incredible. The invention is here. Vivienne recognised the power of these girls. She used Kate, yes, but she also used Naomi and other girls. She knew the power of the personality and the muse. It was '94 when probably one of the most iconic images of Naomi appeared, when she toppled on those giant platforms on Vivienne's catwalk. I didn't see it because I was backstage. But she handled it so well. She laughed and you don't expect to see that from a goddess.

I remember this period of time as being really interesting because on the one hand, the waif had usurped the woman, but then the waif grew up to be a woman herself. There was still a lot of buzz around that group of girls, though, in no small part I think because they were such good friends and they supported each other and the designers that they revered. In a way, it was no different to those girls appearing on the Versace runway together, they had massive power *en masse*. It's just the clothes, the aesthetic and the designers that changed. Stella McCartney is a perfect example of this. I was at her Central Saint Martin's graduate show – another iconic fashion moment involving some of those girls. You couldn't ignore the buzz and the rebellious spirit that ran through the show. Oh, and the fact that a student (albeit a McCartney) had managed to pull really awesome models like Kate Moss, Naomi Campbell and Yasmin le Bon to strut the runway in little dresses, tiny bowler hats and, in Kate's case, with her signature fag in hand. Stella was smart enough to harness Kate and Naomi's celebrity power for that show. Vivienne Westwood also understood this, though I think Vivienne loved Naomi's aesthetic, too. She was partial to a goddess! But it wasn't so easy with some of the other big designers that were coming through – and had the all-important cool factor – at this time.

16

MODEL-TURNED-ACTRESS-TURNED-SINGER-TURNED-AUTHOR-TURNED-DESIGNER-TURNED-RESTAURATEUR

The 'Model-Turned-Actress' adage is a bit of a joke but it actually makes a lot of sense. We always encourage our girls to diversify and have something else they can do once the modelling work becomes less frequent. Also, at this time, the supermodel boom was so superlative we weren't quite sure how long it would go on. It all felt a little bit too good to be true, so we took precautions.

The notion of models branching out and becoming brands just kept gaining momentum in the mid Nineties. In 1994, Chris became head of a joint venture created by us and Elite SA called 'Elite Special Projects', based out of London to develop the Elite brand and network and its licensing potential. Chris also looked after the Elite Look of the Year licensees in London, Asia and Africa. Then, an official partnership was forged and it was decided that Chris would head up the division in New York.

When Cindy Crawford left us for CAA, the hugely powerful entertainment agency in LA, John Casablancas realised that we needed to do something to fight back. Cindy was probably the first model who was taken by the agents and manufactured into a household name. But before she jumped ship to CAA, it was John Casablancas and Monique Pillard at Elite New York who secured her the lucrative Revlon deal that sealed her fate. Her fees skyrocketed after that, but as John pointed out on Bailey's *Models Close Up* film: 'We created our own monsters and became victims of our own creations.'

John realised that this was something that was happening and tried to forge alliances with William Morris and other entertainment agencies at the time, but he knew that unless he could do it in-house they would steal other girls, no question about it. There is no loyalty in agent world – it's daggers at dawn. This is how Chris came to be stationed in New York – he was the only person in the Elite network at the time who really understood branding. He and John realised that creating Elite's own branding/special projects division for these girls was the only chance we'd have to keep them. There was a tug of war for a while over where Chris should be located. Gérald wanted him in the European sector to do the same thing but John wanted him in New York because he could see the attack coming from LA. It was warfare! In the end, Gérald conceded that it made sense for Chris to go to New York because most of those girls lived or at least worked out of there.

It was stressful for Chris from the get-go. He told John that he wanted to be positioned on the main booking table at Elite New York; that way he could hear what was going on and be able to contribute and suggest deals. This is what Chris is brilliant at – spotting and seizing opportunities, the entrepreneurial stuff.

Unfortunately, the 'bitches and the witches' (as he liked to call them) who had control of Elite New York were all desperately protecting their own positions. And because John was always away travelling, he had to rely on them to hold the fort. Chris fought really hard to go on the table but they wouldn't let him, so he was given an office on the top floor out of the way. Now you'd think that the top floor would be the swish place to be, going by the law of the penthouse, but actually Chris's office had become a kind of cemetery: where Elite executives went to die. It's where John's brother Fernando was put to run the John Casablancas Schools and Monique Pillard ended up when they farmed her out to the celebrities division.

It was a shame because had Chris been given the opportunity by John to transform that booking table with all those top girls I think he would've done that. It was very tough for him without John's full support. He was on his own, apart from his assistant Lisa Smith, whom he'd brought with him from London. Unfortunately, as much as they tried to integrate with the team, 'the witches' felt threatened by them. Chris always says it was a typical New York welcome – blood pouring down your back from day one. I knew them anyway because of the work we were doing, but they were very difficult to deal with – they weren't willing to collaborate with Chris at all – it was a pretty classic case of turf wars. It was a massive missed opportunity for all of us. The booking team didn't create or develop brand-building projects, which is what Chris was doing – they pretty much serviced industry model bookings from an established client base. It was about strategic thinking, which model would complement and work with which brand or product and try to create something even bigger out of these opportunities than just a single job. Our vision was to build the top girls' own-brand identities and profiles with a view to the future.

Before this time, people tended to just use models as figureheads rather than as partners in a business. I think the first one to break new ground was John with Cindy Crawford and Revlon. That was the first big model attachment where the penny dropped, and all credit to John for that. She was identified as 'Cindy Crawford', not just a face, so she was a headlining model with a name and a personality, like a major actress would be now. That really was ground-breaking. John and Monique Pillard did that deal and Cindy must have been kissing their feet because it put her name on the map.

Managing own-brand and licensing opportunities for the girls was difficult without the full support of the

New York team. This lack of engagement – and some-times outright opposition – was very disappointing and damaging to a great initiative. Admittedly, it was a tight-rope for John – running an empire of twenty-six agencies is tough – but he just didn't seem to have the energy to back Chris against the old guard of Elite New York, which was unusual for him. In the end, Chris, John, Gérald, Alain and I decided to close down Elite Special Projects. Exhausted by the politics and the constant travel, Chris was very relieved to be able to walk away from it.

Rumbling along at the same time as all this was another 'model-turned . . .' enterprise: Fashion Café. Now this wasn't the brightest venture – and not one of ours, I hasten to add – pitched as a 'couture version' of Planet Hollywood, whatever that means. The idea came from Francesco and Tommaso Buti. Tommaso was married to Daniela Peštová, a Czech model, who was friendly with Claudia Schiffer. He approached Claudia with the idea first and she helped him recruit Christy, Naomi and Elle Macpherson.

Fashion Café first opened in New York's Rockefeller Center in 1995, then London in 1996. These were followed by six other outlets, including Barcelona and New Orleans. It encountered difficulties right from the beginning, especially around branding. I remember reading a hilarious quote a couple of years ago from Matt Haig, the author of *Brand Failures*, who said: 'The connection between models and food was not an obvious one, and "fashion" was not a theme that made people feel hungry.' Now I know that models do eat, contrary to popular perception, but it makes no sense having them as poster girls for substandard burgers and chips, that's for sure.

Despite its inherent problems, Fashion Café developed at a heady pace in a fog of private jet fumes and hedonism. Chris and I became quite involved with the management of the girls' time and appearances at the various outlets. Chris flew to Jakarta and then onto Manila on Tommaso's rented private jet (he never left home without it). We were both at the openings in New York, London, Barcelona and Jakarta. Chris took his daughter Olivia to the New Orleans opening. That was a funny story. She was treated like royalty by Claudia, sharing a limo and asking all sorts of awkward questions that only young girls can do, much to Chris's amusement. Christy was sweet and nice to this wide-eyed, eight-year-old: at her brief appearance at the after-party she kindly took her under her wing and Olivia is still a loyal lifelong fan.

I have fond memories of the Barcelona launch. We stayed in the Intercontinental Hotel and went to a gorgeous fish restaurant on the beach the night before the launch. The calm before the storm – as usual – because the launch was insane. It was packed – like being at Buckingham Palace for a royal wedding (not that I've ever been to one). I find it difficult to remember some of these big events because I was always so frantic. It was always stressful – but we just got on with it and joined the party later – and it was a great party!

Fashion Café was short-lived. London and New York both closed in 1998 and in December 2000 the Federal Government of the United States filed charges against the Buti brothers, accusing them of conspiracy, fraud and money laundering. Perhaps a case of too many private jets going to their heads!

A similarly ill-fated venture, presided over by opportunists, were the supermodel dolls. Remember them? Kind of like Barbie, but nowhere near as successful. The dolls were the brainchild of Karen Mulder's boyfriend, Jean-Yves Le-Fur, who was determined to up the exposure of Karen, who was something of an 'also-ran' in the supermodel league table. He mixed with Patrick Demarchelier and Peter Lindbergh, Gérald and John. He was a charming guy – very smart and wily. So he approached a guy at Hasbro about creating these dolls. Patrick did the shoot, which was a coup, but they didn't really gel and no one did any PR, so it was a complete flop. The dolls launched in Galeries Lafayette in Paris. Davina McCall, who'd just started presenting for MTV Europe's *Most Wanted* show (she used to be a booker at Models 1), interviewed Claudia and Karen about them.

17

MEETING NELSON MANDELA, THE BLUE TRAIN AND THE HAGUE

In the summer of 1994, I went to South Africa to do a shoot with Naomi and David Bailey. Naomi was doing a big ad campaign for a department store called Sales House. It was huge money and a huge production in Johannesburg. Our itinerary included a visit to some children who were living with HIV. This was the start of Naomi's charitable work with various organisations over there, usually related to children. So we visited this residential school in Soweto, the notorious township on the outskirts of Johannesburg, which was home to over a hundred kids who'd inherited HIV from their mums. It was so sad and we started to get emotional almost as soon as we arrived. We went from dormitory to dormitory, talking to the children. Bailey was there too and it was all being filmed. After a while, we were overcome by the awful plight of these small children. They didn't seem to know how sick they were, of course they didn't, they were only five or six. If anything, they seemed so happy, but maybe that's what made it so terribly sad. It was so upsetting, we were both in tears.

I remember Nelson Mandela sitting at a desk when I met him at the Soweto Children's Home, and I was totally in awe. I mean, what do you say to Nelson Mandela? He signed my copy of his autobiography *Long Walk to Freedom* and then we had some pictures taken with Bailey.

It was a culture shock going to South Africa, especially the first time. Johannesburg was really dangerous in those days, so when we were shooting the TV commercial and the film was ready to go to the lab, all these bodyguards with rifles would jump into this big car and speed off with the precious goods. We were constantly surrounded by a team of armed bodyguards. Bailey's great to have around in these situations because he's a very up person and extremely funny. I've seen him in the past when things weren't going to plan and one of the models would be playing up. He'd just walk into the studio and say, 'My God, you're so sexy when you're angry' and the model would collapse in laughter and just get on with it.

The second time I met Mr Mandela was on 25 September 1997 and little did I know that the events surrounding this meeting would go down in the history books and lead to me testifying at the International

Criminal Court in The Hague – one of the most terrifying experiences of my life. But let's start at the beginning. We had been invited on the inaugural trip of the Blue Train that used to run from Pretoria to Cape Town. The famous train had been restored to its former glory and Naomi was to be on board for the first journey, with a host of other – totally random – celebrities. I was really excited; it was like being invited to go on the Orient Express – you don't say no. I loved travelling with Naomi, but I told the organisers that we'd rather not share a compartment. Those cabins are tiny, even on a deluxe train, and I could just imagine the scenes of us trying to cram ourselves into one sleeper. It wouldn't even fit our clothes in!

Naomi and I fly to Johannesburg and for the first night we're staying in the guest house in Mr Mandela's compound – in Cecil Rhodes' house! It was a huge colonial building with giant Baronial doors with huge bolts on them and soldiers on guard outside wearing ceremonial red hats. It was quite daunting really – nobody was getting in or out of there in a hurry. Naomi and I had our own separate rooms so we got changed, went downstairs and suddenly all these guests started appearing. There was Mia Farrow and three of her children, Quincy Jones, Jemima and Imran Khan, and we were all staying in this house together. So bizarre. We gathered to have a drink in the main living area downstairs and then all headed to dinner at Mr Mandela's house. The controversial president of Liberia, Charles Taylor, was apparently coming to the dinner and Graça,

Mr Mandela's soon-to-be wife, was really annoyed that he'd been invited.

I'd heard of Charles Taylor and I knew he was the president of Liberia, but I didn't know that he was heavily involved in a civil war raging in neighbouring Sierra Leone. But Graça did, and she had very strong feelings about it and she didn't hold back in telling us about them. So here we were, rather an odd bunch: celebrities, politicians, a dictator and a very politically engaged Mia Farrow, who I'm sure must have been extremely uncomfortable at the presence of Charles Taylor.

The dinner was quite a formal affair – not exactly the occasion for getting pissed anyway, put it that way. This was the first event to promote the Blue Train so it was a big deal because a lot of money had been spent on renovating it. Charles Taylor was quite charismatic (as I imagine crazed dictators often are), but I wasn't aware of the truth about him. He'd obviously been well educated in the US as he had an American accent. I sat next to the Minister of Defence. I can't remember much of the conversation that evening. The defence minister and I didn't have much in common, funnily enough. It was also such a long time ago so of course my memory is quite hazy on the details. I do remember that the evening ended quite early, around 9.30 p.m., because Mr Mandela always went to bed early.

Everyone was in good spirits and we headed back to the house where more bizarre events unfolded regarding the now infamous 'blood diamonds', which I'm unable to discuss here. If you want to know more, then you can refer to what Mia Farrow and I said in The Hague, under oath, which is all available online in the court report.

The next morning, it's time for the Blue Train trip. Everyone's really excited at breakfast. Off we all trot from the compound ready to board the famous train. It's like something out of Agatha Christie, all these glamorous people with designer luggage gathered around an ornate train. There's a real fandango – a military brass band is playing and there are press everywhere, cameras flashing. It was all quite exciting.

Lunch is the same crowd from the night before but with the addition of a load of dignitaries who we have to meet. I'm introduced to Mr Mandela again and, shaking his hand slightly in a daze, I wouldn't let go! I was completely star-struck, which is rare for me.

The train was terribly posh – all mahogany and chandeliers and silver service. We were all sat on separate tables and I was, again randomly, sharing a table with Archbishop Desmond Tutu, who was a total hoot. We ate zebra, which was really good, a bit like venison.

I spent most of that trip in the toilet in our cabin – that became my office. God knows what I was doing but I was on the phone a lot. I was on my mobile constantly. We were speeding through this African countryside stopping off at African villages where we'd all pile out of the train and they'd get the brass band out. It was all quite happy but really rather surreal.

Dinner was black tie. We always seemed to be eating

or drinking on this trip, not that I'm complaining – I'm pretty good at both! There was a lot of drinking going on and I remember talking to Jeremy Ratcliffe a lot. Again, the court report has all the details of what we were talking about.

Late afternoon the next day we arrived in Cape Town and there was a big gala dinner at a beautiful hotel called Table Bay. We all decamped from the train and went off to our rooms to get ready for yet more food. There was a big auction in aid of the Nelson Mandela Children's Fund at the dinner and a dance afterwards. I didn't think much about this strange and exotic trip until thirteen years later when I received the oddest email that took me right back to South Africa.

Let's fast forward a bit . . .

My big day in court

On 28 January 2010 I received an email from Dan Bright, my lawyer in New York, asking if I knew anything about blood diamonds and Charles Taylor, the former president of Liberia, who was at that time coming to the end of a lengthy war crimes trial at the International Criminal Court in The Hague (Naomi and I had parted ways in 2008). Dan had seen a piece in the *New York Times* where Mia Farrow recalled the conversation she'd had with Naomi on the morning of the Blue Train trip, way back in September 1997. Mia stated that Naomi had told her she'd received 'a huge diamond' from Charles Taylor.

Until this moment I hadn't even known Charles Taylor was on trial. It had been going on for three years but had been pretty under the radar in terms of the press. Mia Farrow brought it to the world's attention by filing a statement with the court in Sierra Leone on 4 December 2009. Because, as the *New York Times* put it, 'it was suspected that diamonds mined in Sierra Leone were used to pay for arms and ammunition that fuelled Mr Taylor's proxy army,' Mia's evidence was crucial in linking Charles Taylor to the so-called blood diamonds, and therefore crucial to this case, which was floundering somewhat at this point.

She wasn't trying to implicate anybody – we hadn't done anything wrong, after all – but she had realised the information could be crucial to the trial. They couldn't pin the use of blood diamonds on Charles Taylor; he had sworn on oath that he had never had access to any and the prosecution couldn't prove otherwise, but effectively what he was doing was using these diamonds to buy arms. Apparently he was smuggling them in jars of mayonnaise. Mia stepped forward and told the prosecution what she had learnt at that breakfast in Nelson Mandela's home all that time before.

A little while later, in April 2010, Dan called me again and said, 'Do you know this is really serious?' The case had struck a chord with him because his grandparents were murdered in Auschwitz and so many innocent people had been killed and mutilated in this bloody civil war in Sierra Leone. During the trial several victims – women who had been raped, men whose limbs had been amputated with machetes – gave evidence. Dan said to me, 'This trial is not going well for the prosecution and you have to tell your story because it's very pertinent to their case. Would you mind if I contact them?'

I said no, so he rang the court in The Hague and asked to be put through to the prosecution. He told them that he had a witness who had seen men working for Charles Taylor hand over some blood diamonds. They told him that it was unfortunately too late, the trial had finished. It was really in its dying days. What they failed to tell him, however, was that he was actually speaking to the defence for Charles Taylor – he'd been put through to the wrong team! Dan thought about it over the weekend and realised that something wasn't right with the exchange, so he decided to call again on Monday and got the prosecution this time.

He relayed the story again and, within a couple of days, two members of the prosecution team were on a plane to London so that I could give my statement. Naïvely, I thought that was it, I never thought for a minute I would be asked to go to The Hague. A few more months went by – we were in the summer by now, and they got in touch again and said they would need me as a witness to support my statement, and I thought, OK, I just have to read my statement. Easy. Little did I know what lay in store for me.

Mia Farrow and I were going to be appearing in court in July, then it moved to August. The arrangements for this trial were extraordinary, and became increasingly ominous as we neared the day. First, the prosecution team asked if I would like to stay in a hotel with Mia

Farrow. Apparently, she really wanted to meet me again. Then they said it wouldn't be appropriate for two key witnesses to stay in the same hotel together. That makes sense, I thought. Then they asked if I would like to stay in a safe house. Now I was getting a little worried. Why would I need a safe house? They told me some of the witnesses had been intimidated.

'We can put you in a secret hotel location or you can have a safe house.'

'No no, I'll go in a hotel.'

My PR adviser at the time said, 'Carole, I think I ought to come with you,' to which I said, 'Don't be so silly' – all I was doing was reading my statement (or so I thought) – but then two days before I decided I would like somebody to be with me, after all, so I asked my daughter Simone to come along for moral support. We landed at Schiphol airport in Amsterdam and were met – they actually came on board the plane on the runway – by the chief of police of Amsterdam, and four armed bodyguards. Armed. Gulp. Then we were ushered into a bulletproof van. We had to go to the loo, which required bodyguards waiting outside for us, pretty heavy stuff.

We were then driven to the 'secret' hotel, which was by a beach. We got there, were shown to a suite and told we weren't allowed to leave – for a whole day and night. My response to this was: 'Don't be ridiculous.' They felt it wasn't safe for us to leave, but there was no way I was going to stay cooped up in a hotel suite for such a long time. I arrived a day before my appearance in court because the prosecution had to go over my statement. Eventually, they had a big pow-wow and agreed that Simone and I could go to the restaurant for lunch on the proviso we had the bodyguards with us. So we went to this beachside restaurant with two minders in tow and had a really nice meal. I'm pretty tough but I'll admit I was getting quite apprehensive by this point. Then a barrister for the prosecution came and went through my statement, which I elaborated on because the more you think about it the more detail you remember.

The next morning I have to be in court and the prosecution decide that I need to have my hair done by a hairdresser. Turns out, she couldn't do my hair – I could have done it better myself. With hindsight, the hair was the least of my worries, but I still didn't know what lay ahead at this point. We arrive at The Hague and Simone is allowed in the waiting room but not to be with me in the court. Then I have to go to the court and only then do I realise that the proceedings are being broadcast live around the world. My lawyer Dan was with me, attempting to calm my nerves with his chatty manner, but it was all feeling very real now. Special mention really does need to be given to Dan Bright. Without him, this wouldn't have happened and there might have been a very different outcome. He should be very proud of the role he played in bringing Taylor to justice.

So everyone had realised that my statement was pretty crucial. I'm on the stand in this incredibly formal courtroom, faced by four judges on the dais and about to be questioned by the eminent QC Courtenay Griffiths. I take a deep breath and just focus on the fact that all I'm here to do is pretty much give my statement, which is the truth as I remember it and the extremely important thing here is that hopefully my evidence will help to bring a brutal war criminal to justice.

Suddenly, very early on in the proceedings, a clerk hurries into the court clutching a load of papers that Simone said looked like printouts from Facebook. Courtenay Griffiths begins his questioning and immediately starts asking me about Facebook, which completely threw me. Number one, this has no relation to my statement, and number two, I know next to nothing about Facebook because I don't use it. I don't do it, I don't like it – I think it's an invasion of privacy. I literally didn't have a clue what he was going on about. He asks me, referring to the printout: 'Did you have a blood diamond party?'

'No, I don't know what you're talking about.'

'On August the 5th/6th you had a blood diamond party.'

'No, I didn't. I went to a party for my brother's birthday in a pub.'

'No no, you went to a blood diamond party.'

The day after my brother's birthday Premier had bought a house to accommodate girls during the shows, which was really nice, and I took all my bookers around to see it so they knew where they were putting models, and we had pizza and wine and stuff. Turns out, one of my bookers, Annie, was taking pictures and then uploaded them onto Facebook with the strapline, 'Blood

Diamond Party'! It was all in jest but still, not ideal while I'm sat in The Hague, being broadcast live around the world, and not knowing what the fuck this attack lawyer is talking about.

Back in London, of course, the entire Premier office, including Annie and my brother Chris, are all watching the live feed and no doubt feeling sick on my behalf. Especially Annie. Imagine how surreal that is? Her name, and the names of my other staff members who were in the model house that evening, were read out by this QC. In a war crimes trial! I mean, WTF?

It looked so bad and I had no knowledge of it so I was immediately on the back foot. It's quite hard to explain that one of your idiotic bookers had done it for a laugh. But this was only the first in what turned out to be an onslaught of allegations made against me. Annie thought I was going to fire her. In the *Evening Standard* she won the worst employee of the year award! Poor Annie, but that was quite funny. I had no intention of firing her, it was just a silly mistake and anyway she'd been punished enough.

What followed was a full-on interrogation. Courtenay Griffiths was so horrible to me. At several points he actually said I was a liar, which was hard to take, and when I tried to tell my side of the story, he just tried to shut me up.

Even though we witnesses couldn't agree on exactly how the diamonds came to be handed over (it's actually quite normal for witnesses to the same events to remember them differently), it was at least established that diamonds were delivered that night and the court felt that the evidence established beyond reasonable doubt that two men sent by Taylor delivered uncut diamonds on his behalf, which is what was crucial for the case.

Even though the whole experience was extremely daunting, I wasn't scared as such because I knew what I'd seen – all I was doing was telling the truth. I was trying to do the right thing because I knew how important it was that this man was brought to justice.

This all happened in August 2010 and it wasn't until April 2012, almost two years later, that Charles Taylor was actually found guilty and on 30 May he was sentenced to fifty years in prison.

This is how the *New York Times* reported the sentencing:

Mr Taylor was the first former head of state convicted by an international tribunal since the Nuremberg trials in Germany after World War II.

Mr Taylor was found guilty of 'aiding and abetting, as well as planning, some of the most heinous and brutal crimes recorded in human history,' said Richard Lussick, the judge who presided over the sentencing here in an international criminal court near The Hague. He said the lengthy prison term underscored Mr Taylor's position as a government's leader during the time the crimes were committed.

Diamonds, as well as atrocities, also came up repeatedly in the 2,500-page judgment. The judges agreed with the prosecution that diamonds mined in Sierra Leone were used to pay for arms and ammunition for Mr Taylor's proxy army and that rough diamonds were delivered to Mr Taylor's house in Monrovia, the Liberian capital.

One diamond story that received a lot of attention during the trial involved the court appearance of the model Naomi Campbell. Prosecutors said Ms Campbell had been sent uncut diamonds as a gift from Mr Taylor after they attended a charity dinner hosted by Nelson Mandela when he was the president of South Africa.

Two of Ms Campbell's companions who recounted the episode in court – her agent, Carole White, and the actress Mia Farrow – were repeatedly called 'liars' during cross-examination by the defense. But the judges wrote that the two women were 'frank and truthful witnesses'.

It felt good to be vindicated by the court and in the press as being truthful after all the accusations of lying when the trial was taking place. Recognising the ordeal I went through, prosecutor Brenda Hollis sent me a lovely email thanking me for having the 'courage and integrity' to testify before the Trial Chamber. In the end the truth was recognised, where it really mattered, in court.

Fast forward to now, in 2014, with even more water under the bridge, what else is there to say about this? Obviously writing this book I've had to think about it again and it's stirred up those memories and feelings. One of the things that will stay with me is how awful I felt immediately after appearing in The Hague. I'm usually a very strong and resilient person but it really hit me hard.

So there we have it – what a story! I'm sure there's so much more to say, so much that can't be said (unfortunately), but the Blue Train, Nelson Mandela, Charles Taylor, 'blood diamonds' and The Hague are memories I'm not likely to forget any time soon. What a ride.

18

WHAT GOES UP
MUST COME DOWN…

It was 1997 and 'Cool Britannia' was in full swing. Tony Blair had won a landslide victory in the election and threw a party at Downing Street for all the faces making waves in music, art and fashion – people like Noel Gallagher and Vivienne Westwood were there, sipping champagne and 'exchanging pleasantries' with the prime minister. I wouldn't say the atmosphere was as exciting as what I'd experienced in the Sixties but there were certainly some parallels. Brit designers had never been so cool, the so-called Britpop bands were riding high and artists like Damien Hirst, Tracey Emin and the Chapman Brothers were making an indelible mark as the new *enfants terribles* of the art world.

In March 1997, *Vanity Fair* published a now-iconic special edition on the capital with the then 'it' couple

Liam Gallagher and Patsy Kensit on the cover, featuring the title 'London Swings Again!', and British *Elle* followed it in June with a Naomi cover shot by David Bailey. It was all very happening, and Naomi and Kate, along with other Brit girls like Rosemary Ferguson, Kirsty Hume and Erin O'Connor, were all on the scene. It's when the Primrose Hill set was getting up to all sorts of shenanigans too: Sadie Frost, Jude Law, Pearl Lowe and all that crowd.

The hangouts of the time were places like the Atlantic Bar where I remember going to an *Ab Fab* party after the girls had appeared in the show, or the Met Bar at the Metropolitan Hotel where they used to hold all the Brit Awards after-parties. Oh, and there was always somebody stumbling out of Brown's in the early hours. It was a very hedonistic time and this overspilled into the mood in the office, too. A sort of sense of people being invincible, which is extremely dangerous. The other thing about a high period is that there will always be somebody waiting in the wings to bring you down, which is what happened in spectacular fashion. First up, *People* magazine ran a cover story in 1998 with the sensationalist but undeniably catchy headline 'Supermodel Meltdown!', featuring supermodels in their various alleged states of falling from grace. Second, and much more damaging, was the exposé of the seedier side of the modelling business produced for the BBC by the investigative journalist Donal MacIntyre.

Let's start with Supermodel Meltdown. Kate, Naomi, Linda and Cindy shared the cover with a special angle

Top: The Versace Supermodels © Maria Valentino.

Above: Linda for The Supermodel Club Japan press shot.

Left: David Bailey's *Models Close-Up* documentary for Channel 4.

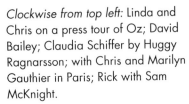

Clockwise from top left: Linda and Chris on a press tour of Oz; David Bailey; Claudia Schiffer by Huggy Ragnarsson; with Chris and Marilyn Gauthier in Paris; Rick with Sam McKnight.

Opposite top: 'Model Secrets' with Sarah Doukas by Huggy Ragnarsson.

Opposite bottom: Simone and Steve's wedding.

Polaroids over the years (clockwise from top left): Ranya; Alice Gibbs;
Suvi; Lara Mullen; Bambi; Jeneil.

Clockwise from top left: Katrin Thormann; Tao; Malaika Firth; Hannah Holman; Julia Nobis; Meghan Collison.

Clockwise from top left:
Bookers out having fun;
Harvey Goldsmith and me;
Graduate Fashion Week prize-
giving; with Jacqui on a train;
Annie and me sitting outside
Versace's house in Miami.

*Opposite, clockwise from top
left:* Model dinner in New
York; Doug; Phillipa in Paris;
Lara and me out for dinner;
John Pearson; Malaika's
model card.

DOUG
premier DIVISION

JOHN PEARSON
premier

LARA MULLEN

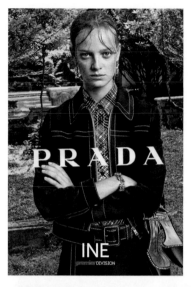

PRADA

INE

PLAYFUL

#hailey #luma #cinematic #beautiful
#games #intimate #chic #sexy #vsmag

ESCLUSIVO! IL CALENDARIO MITO

Clockwise from top left: Lara's
Dazed cover; Ine; model dinner in
Paris; Ty Ogunkoya model card;
Sasha Luss *Vanity Fair* cover;
Hailey Clauson and Luma Grothe
VS cover.

on each of them spelling out 'their own personal crises'. For Kate it was 'too much partying', with the suggestion she'd checked into rehab. Linda meanwhile 'loses her footing', referencing her falling off the catwalk, allegedly drunk. For Cindy Crawford, it was 'her TV show tanks'. Now none of these girls were strangers to headlines, or scandal for that matter, but for some reason this cover really hit home and had a devastating effect. It definitely had that air of 'they had it coming' after all those years of excess and entitlement. The biggest impact for us was that Linda Evangelista's fragrance deal fell through right at the last hurdle – literally on the day that Chris was due to sign the contract in New York – because Procter & Gamble were worried about allegations in the press that she was drinking and a general weariness of the public towards the apparent overindulgences of the supermodels.

Our first forays into fragrance began in the Nineties. Linda took a lot of convincing to do a fragrance deal – she was rightly very image conscious, but she also listened to the many 'advisors' and 'managers' in the entourage that surrounded her, many of whom claimed she could get a better deal somewhere else with someone else (although nothing better ever materialised). Linda would simply not commit to signing up to the project. Eventually, she signed the deal after months of prevarication and negotiation. Linda's team's counterproposals were sometimes quite simply outrageous. Unfortunately all this dithering was to be her undoing – and ours. Why? 'Supermodel Meltdown'!

That *People* cover and the feature article that went with it unquestionably screwed Linda's fragrance deal with P&G. So that was that: all those months of hard work out of the window – for the Linda deal anyway. But we did do some huge deals: these were kind of pioneering days because the previous models/celebrities who did an own-brand fragrance campaign were Cheryl Tiegs and Cher and neither were that successful. The exception, of course, was Elizabeth Taylor's, which was huge. Look at this area now – everyone and their mother has a fragrance deal!

So these were exciting times for the supermodels and our industry in general. Looking back, it felt like everything was heating up in a pressure cooker and it was just a matter of time before it blew.

Back in London, relations were beginning to sour between us and Elite. When we went into business with them it was a ten-year partnership but we discovered we were paying three times the rent as anyone else in the building and the rent was huge. Their argument was: 'Well, you've got all those supermodels so you make three times the turnover,' but that wasn't the case really because we could never overcome this massive rent and the manufactured 'service charges'. We were horrified that our partners would do that. Every year we battled to get the rent down but the issue was never resolved, so after Chris's New York experience the writing was on the wall and we decided, 'let's get out'. Then came MacIntyre – the beginning of the end. Or maybe the end of the end.

It all started with a girl called Lisa who began working as an intern with us. She was a bit older than the usual candidates, at twenty-six, but she told us she was a student, gave us good references (obviously invented) and was keen to gain experience to help with her thesis. So she came in and started doing all the usual horrible things that interns have to do like organise the models' cards. But then she kept asking for more work so we were like, great, we've got this slave, she'll do anything! It was quite wacky here at the time; the team I had were, in hindsight, not as focused as they should have been. There were too many crazies, and they partied too much – a lot of personalities, shall we say.

One day, Angus Monroe, who's a big casting agent now but who was working for me on New Faces at the time, came up to me and said: 'Carole, that girl Lisa is acting weird and we think she's filming us.' We thought she was doing her thesis, which was why she was interviewing the bookers, but Angus and some of the other bookers were suspicious. 'She's got this handbag,' they said, 'and she keeps putting it on the desk. We think it's a camera. Can you steal her bag?!' Everyone was in a big flap about it but I said, 'No, of course I can't steal her handbag.' They wouldn't let it go though so in the end I said: 'Oh, for fuck's sake, why don't we just ask her?'

Of course no one dared to ask her so it was down to me. At that time we didn't have the one big booking table, we had two – one for the main board and one for New Faces where Angus and this girl sat. He was now pretty certain she was filming him but he carried on with the interview she was conducting when I sidled over to investigate.

'Lisa, could you open up your handbag?' I asked.

She grabbed it defensively: 'Why?'

'We think you're filming us and I'd like to look inside your bag.'

We didn't know what to do past this point, so I got Rick and told him what had happened. Rick said: 'Call the police'.

'You've got to ring my professor on this number,' was her response, but then we rang the college and they'd never heard of her. Then we spoke to someone else who said, 'Yeah yeah, she works here,' but it was very dodgy.

The police came so we took them into the back room and they asked us to leave whilst they talked to her. When they emerged they said, 'Yeah, she's probably not who she says she is but this is a civil matter, it's not a police matter, there's nothing we can do.' Short of kidnapping her there was nothing we could do. At this stage we didn't know what it was for. We knew it was wrong but we thought it was *News of the World*. So then we let her go but we made our biker follow her. He lost her, of course. A little later, somehow, on the grapevine, we found out she was working for the BBC and that there was a big programme being done on the model business. Then it clicked. When I was in Milan for the shows Lisa had rung and asked if she could come and follow us and talk to the models and get the feel for it. Then I realised she was trying to get them involved, because of the extra publicity that their names would bring.

Once I found out about MacIntyre's involvement I rang up Elite Paris and said, 'Do you know Mac?' which was the name he was going by. Alex, the booker, said, 'Yeah yeah, he's part of this magazine called *Polka Dot* and Gérald loves him. He's a really good friend of ours.' I said, 'No he isn't. He's actually a journalist working for the BBC and he's been filming you secretly.' Donal MacIntyre had somehow managed, under the guise of being a fashion photographer for a frankly ridiculous-sounding magazine, to ingratiate himself with the upper echelons of Elite, including Gérald Marie, who was the big boss in Europe. And he'd managed to get a lot of incriminating footage of what some of the bookers and publicists based in Milan were getting up to with young models, how the girls were treated (not always respect-fully) and plenty of drug use. They all shat bricks and said, 'No no, you're wrong, Carole.'

I said, 'I'm not, he's been filming you for months.'

We didn't know Mac at all because he'd obviously been doing the bits in Paris and Milan.

'They're doing a big exposé.'

We didn't really know what Lisa had got in London but we knew her handbag had been left in all the rooms so, to put it mildly, we were also shitting ourselves. Our back office had witnessed some pretty 'strictly private and confidential' conversations with a variety of models, agents, clients and lawyers.

At this point, a number of bookers resigned – not all

at once but there was a quick succession of leavers, probably because of all the stress. So here I was in this crisis, losing all these bookers and wondering what would happen to the business. In actual fact it was the best thing that happened because as a result of this walk-out I got more dedicated people who were much more professional! It's funny, you get really close to people and think they're great but then you get new people in and realise that perhaps the last lot weren't so great after all. A lesson learned: no one is irreplaceable.

Our next step was to hire a big law firm to attack the BBC. We wrote to them, pointing out that their own filming proved that we weren't involved in anything untoward, and that we were actually in the process of splitting from Elite and we didn't want to be portrayed in this film at all, since – despite our innocence – we would be tainted by the connection to Elite. Could they guarantee that we would not feature in the film? I also rang John Casablancas and told him that it was a wide-ranging exposé, involving the whole Elite group. John was horrified. He was also in denial, so he was saying, 'No no, Carole, it's all about you.' Elite were riding so high at that time I think he probably thought they were invincible but MacIntyre had started their downfall.

Later I saw a trailer that confirmed my suspicions. It showed a clip of one of their bookers bragging about how they shag all the models who were very young girls. I rang up John and Gérald *again* to try and convince them to do something. The booker was identifiable as one of theirs because of his really distinctive tattoos.

'It's about Elite, not Elite Premier,' I said. I was trying to give them a heads-up. 'Guys, you need to prepare yourselves, we are preparing ourselves.'

They asked me to send them the clip. How did you get hold of a clip in those days? We were trying to video this clip and send it to them. It was such a ridiculous turn of events really because although we realised it was about them and it would be tricky for them, we knew it was also bad news for us. We were like rats leaving the sinking ship. They thought they were leaving our sinking ship but we knew we were leaving theirs.

When it aired in November 1999 we had just about made the move. The whole thing took about a year. I was in Australia doing a job and it was so frightening because even though we'd been told it wasn't about us you just never know. Everyone was watching it and London were calling me to tell me what was happening. I was so on edge about the whole thing. Anyway, it started airing and it was horrendous – but there was nothing about us. The BBC had been true to its word.

It was the beginning of the end for Elite. The BBC was trying to get it shown in America but Elite managed to block it. It was shown in Canada and the Elite office in Toronto started receiving hate mail and hate calls. Here, Premier didn't get so much flack, in fact we had more people ringing up and saying they wanted to be models than ever before because your name goes up all over the place and people just remember the name. We found that quite amusing actually, especially as the old Elite Premier web address was redirected to Premier's new website. We had to distance ourselves from them, though. At the end of the programme the BBC ran a full disclaimer that Premier were now separated from Elite so luckily no damage was done. It cost us a fortune in lawyers and crisis management – almost £100k – but this was essential at such a crucial time for us and allowed us to complete our split from Elite successfully.

I was appalled by some of the stuff I saw in the documentary, even though it seemed as if it had been salaciously edited for maximum impact. Most of the really bad footage was focused around the club scene in Milan, where so-called PRs were luring young models to nightclubs where older men lay in wait. It was so shocking. Thank God we only sent girls to Milan to do runway shows, which are back to back, leaving no time to go clubbing, so they didn't get into these dangerous situations.

The PRs worked for the clubs and worked on commission. They offered models free entry and food and drinks. Sometimes, the Milan agents would tell the girls that they had to go to dinner with 'potential clients'. The PRs were good-looking young men and they'd flirt with the models and then the dinners would happen and there were all these older guys. What's not entirely clear from the programme is the link between the PRs and the agents. The agents certainly didn't appear to discourage this behaviour. Seeing these men openly talking about 'fucking girls aged fourteen to fifteen' was pretty hard to stomach.

Drugs were a big part of the documentary, too. It

showed a Brit model called Carolyn Park being sold drugs by her Paris booking agent. At that point coke was just everywhere. It's just not around like that any more – thank God. Coke was the big thing and it was just considered normal. It was the downfall of a lot of people because they got so into it they didn't concentrate on what they were doing; they were all talk and no do. I've come across cokeheads – they think they're doing brilliantly and have all these ideas that they never do anything about. I was so shocked to see that booker selling drugs to her model. Bookers are in a position of trust and have a responsibility for the welfare of their models.

To be fair to Elite they appealed, took the BBC to court and won on how it was edited. Elite received substantial undisclosed damages. It was edited in such a way that anyone could be made to look like a pervert. Despite winning in court, Elite's reputation was severely damaged. John and Gérald, Claude Haddad, Jean Luc Brunel, Xavier Moreau and Dominic Galas were all branded by the documentary with varying degrees of sleaze and complicity.

Despite being very unfair in the way that it depicted some people, the MacIntyre programme was probably a catalyst for positive change in the industry: agencies have certainly become much more professional and now actively monitor the conduct of all their staff, particularly with respect to models. I'm happy to say that the era of the playboy-owned agencies is over. One of the things that bothered me the most about the documentary was how some of these guys talked about the models and what they got up to with them, sexually. It was very wrong and very misogynistic. Overnight, some of the icons of the business were exposed for what they really were: foul-mouthed, chauvinistic womanisers. They were all heterosexual men. I think it also opened the door for a lot of smart, hard-working gay men to become very powerful in the business.

Post MacIntyre, we became a lot more careful who we were giving models to. It was a wake-up call for us and took Premier into a new era. We came out of Elite and of course we had some huge mountains to climb because when you split you're arguing about who pays what. It was a dodgy period. That sort of stuff takes some time to recover from. We were owed a lot of big commissions from Elite, which of course we never got, and it seriously messed up our cash flow.

They came to us with a deal: 'Chris is out, Carole can stay, we'll give her 25 per cent and we'll take the rest and run the company. Or pay us a pound, we are out and you have the company.' What did we say to that? 'We will keep our company, thank you! Here's a pound.'

We took on all the liabilities and had to deal with it. It was really tough. We had no other choice but to call their bluff and fight for Premier. We nearly got another investor in Carlo Salvi, the owner of the Women Group, who Chris and I really liked and respected, but that initiative never materialised, mostly due to internal politics and a disgraceful attempt by Carlo's negotiator (unbeknown to Carlo) to insert himself into the deal, as a shareholder and CEO. It was so difficult and so frustrating. Another really great personal friend of Chris and Huggy's came to our rescue, providing us with much-needed cash – like manna from heaven. His help was invaluable at this really critical time. We were in sink or swim territory. You know who your friends are when the shit hits the fan. Barclays Bank were fantastic actually: in the days when they still lent small businesses money, they sent in a specialist rescue squad that stood by us and nurtured us through the immediate crisis. Elite had to shut down in London – they had had such bad press. Thankfully they couldn't open for ten years here and we kept a lot of the girls because we'd done a really great job for them.

It's a bit like what's going on now with all the BBC presenters and DJs. It happened in the Sixties, Seventies and Eighties when it was sort of accepted. Now everything was being reassessed and chaperoning, model houses and other safety measures came out of this. There was an ousting of the old guard.

We were now free and sailing on our own again . . .

19

PARENTHOOD AND THE PINK HOUSE

I need to catch you up on my family, which I appear to have neglected for the past few chapters. Some may say I'm work obsessed! Premier went through many changes in the Nineties, and the same is true for family life. In 1994, we welcomed a newborn son but we also said goodbye to my darling dad. Jack was born in the February and just two months later, Hack died, aged eighty-two. He just got sick one day, and it came as a massive shock for us all.

Looking back, I feel like life wasn't as happy for my parents after they'd sold the Old Rectory, because it was the family's hub and provided sanctuary for us all at different times in our lives. It was such a beautiful home and filled with happy memories. It's where Simone and Michael grew up and where I sought refuge after leaving

Don. That period of time really brought us all together as a family – everybody rallied to help me and to care for Simone, especially Mum and Dad. It helped us all understand the power of family relationships and how essential they are to your life.

When my parents decided that the Old Rectory was too much for them, Chris and I vaguely discussed the idea of keeping it on but we were both way too busy with work. Chris was travelling a lot and it wasn't an option for me to relocate there so the house was sold and we were pretty gutted. The reality for my parents though was that they were getting older and the house was too big for them to keep up – it had nine bedrooms and such a lot of land. It was also pretty remote and Dad wasn't able to drive as much any more so it could feel pretty isolating for them.

Generous as ever, they gave some of the profits from the sale of the house to us kids. I used the money to help buy our place in Elgin Avenue. Meanwhile they bought a new place in Canterbury, which I really didn't like. They went from this fantastic, huge, grand old house to a town house opposite a church with a zebra crossing so you couldn't even park outside. It was part of a terrace so had no privacy and it was so dark inside, which isn't good for the soul. Really, in hindsight, we should have put a housekeeper into the Old Rectory who could drive them around, and let them end their days there.

Whereas the Old Rectory had acted as our family's HQ and was like an open house at weekends with visitors coming and going, that was never really recreated with the new house due to lack of space. Our family get-togethers had become less frequent but I'd still speak to my dad on the phone every day. He was good with business so I'd tell him about any problems I was having at work plus I was always squabbling with my brothers so I'd talk to him about that too. It became obvious to me when we had these chats that he was deeply unhappy. We should never have let them move there; it's my biggest regret but we took our eye off the ball. I was pregnant at the time and Chris was away such a lot.

Dad had a lot to deal with because our mum Sheila's health had further deteriorated, which was a constant worry for him. She suffered with manic depression and it was a situation that got harder to deal with as the years progressed. Mum could be really difficult. Dad had always been very sociable in the past, but doing things like going to the local pub had become increasingly fraught because of Mum's unpredictable behaviour so I know he felt lonely. He was a real gentleman, my father, but didn't like to be embarrassed and she would show him up in public a lot, by swearing at the vicar and things like that. We'd go down to Canterbury and take him out when we could and our old friend Carol Macdonald-Bell would visit him at the house and go out for drinks with him. She was a huge support and that meant a lot to him.

We realised we had to find them somewhere to live in London so that they could be near to us and not feel so isolated. Chris and I found a flat in Sutherland Avenue in Maida Vale, just around the corner from us. It was beautiful and they were really excited about it. The flat was lovely and promised a new lease of life for them but we got gazumped at the last hurdle. They were heartbroken because they loved this place but we said, don't worry, we'll find another one. Then, suddenly, my dad got sick.

He had diverticulitis, which is a common digestive disease that occurs within the bowel wall. The operation should have been pretty straightforward but it didn't turn out that way. The surgeon found that he was missing a beat on his heart so he decided to do something about that, too. No one had noticed for eighty-two years but they decided to do both operations at the same time. We thought he'd be fine because it should have been a routine procedure, but he wasn't.

To make matters worse, after the operation they put him on the wrong pills. The staff who came onto the night shift misread the notes and put him on water retention pills, which really dehydrated him. One minute he looked fine and then suddenly he looked like a skeleton. We were shocked when we saw him and called for help. The doctors admitted the mistake and immediately put him on some fluids but it was too late by then, it was obvious he was dying. I really hated that hospital, the level of care was totally unacceptable. It showed me that sometimes it's not always better to go private. The guy was off playing golf every time we tried to speak to him. It made me feel quite bitter and I lost my lovely father who I absolutely adored. We were able to say goodbye but we weren't ready and neither was he. You think you're prepared for dealing with death but you're not – it's a very lonely thing and you can't understand it. He was my friend and confidant and even now I think of him every day.

After my father died my mother put on a stoical, unemotional front but behind it all she broke down in private. It was obviously a huge loss. Then she got ill. It started with colon cancer and eventually spread to her liver. We arranged a lot of her treatment at the London Clinic – after what had happened with our father we felt she'd receive a better level of care.

She was very brave because she had such a lot to deal with. She ended up with a colostomy. I can't handle things like that, I'm too squeamish, but Chris was amazing – he's more hands-on than me and would help her with it. Mum stayed with Chris and Huggy for a while and Huggy was fantastic with her, taking her out to visit churches and museums to keep her entertained. In the end though they couldn't look after her any more, she was in too much pain and needed round-the-clock care. It progressed to stage three liver cancer and then the doctor called to say she only had three months to live. She spent this time being cared for back home in Kent and again our friend Carol came to the rescue, visiting my mother every day. She spent her last few days in hospital. After she died we were given a bag of her jewellery and I noticed her wedding rings were missing so I called the hospital up, asking to know where they were. When they said they didn't know what I was talking about, I threatened to call the police. Ten minutes later I got a call back saying they'd found them in the Hoover. Give me a break! How disgusting was that?

I grieved for my mum, but her death didn't affect me as deeply as my dad's – I had never been as close to her as I was to my dad and I think I still had some lingering resentment towards her because of the way she had treated him over the past few years. I know it wasn't her fault but it took me a while to get my head around that and forgive her. Michael told me later that he felt exactly the same way – he knew that Mum was ill but it took him a long time to be able to forgive her. Chris, on the other hand, completely understood what she was going through – he never blamed her and showed her nothing but kindness and understanding. I was such a daddy's girl and I couldn't empathise with her behaviour at all, or comprehend how he could put up with it.

Sheila was an incredibly bright woman and in later life she took this theological degree and completed it in two years instead of five, which was an amazing achievement. She became a lay preacher at the church but then her manic depression hit and religion started to become a fetish. She did odd things like putting her jewellery on the altar at the church and you could sense people around the village not quite knowing what mood she'd be in or what to do about her, yet she'd been given this position in the church as a lay preacher so she'd do sermons and things. It was difficult for my dad because he was the most affable character. He'd be such fun and really sociable, but then suddenly his wife who used to host dinner parties and be central to their social circle was suddenly becoming this total nightmare. Dad would do anything for her but I know it used to make him really sad.

She had to take Lithium to control her mood swings but sometimes she'd just decide not to take it, which of course made her even worse. I think it impacted on my youngest brother Michael the most because he had to live with her, back when they were still at the Old Rectory, and could see first-hand her decline. When it all started with her he was twelve and really bright and going for a scholarship, but she was going nutty and trying to involve him in her religious fetish. They were close before all this happened and I think it disturbed him so much he didn't get his scholarship. He didn't reach his full potential in a way. He was so academic; he should've been a lawyer and gone to Oxford or Cambridge university. I think it really affected him. He must have seen things that we in our wildest dreams couldn't imagine and he will have seen our father in despair, too. Hack and Michael had a really strong bond and I know Hack had such high hopes for what his son was going to do. I would say Michael changed radically during that period. I found it hard to empathise with my mum. I just found it stupid what she did – there was no sense to it.

It's funny how when you get older and have more experiences, your attitude and relationship with your parents changes. When I'd had Sissy and Jack, I remember reflecting on mine and Chris's childhoods and couldn't get my head around a mother sending her four- and five-year-old on a plane to boarding schools in England and then not seeing them for months at a time. At Easter we'd spend the entire holiday at school. When you're a child you accept it because you think it's normal but it was really difficult – I know now that I was actually quite depressed, spending weekends alone in a big lonely school. We were on our own so we had a real lack of emotional support. It would have been preferable if my parents had had a base in England so that they could have been there in the holidays.

On the flip side, they were highly generous with Simone when I was a selfish brat. I got myself pregnant and had a child far too young and couldn't cope. Mum and Dad saw that and took the pressure away – they were utterly amazing. They were pretty incredible parents. I mean, you can get annoyed about some of their decisions but we all make bad decisions in life and it's always the benefit of hindsight or your children looking at you as if to say 'what the fuck did you do that for?' that makes you stop and think about things. Also, some of the decisions they made probably kick started what we wanted to do with our lives. Neither Chris nor I went to university but we were both highly ambitious and this probably comes from having inde- pendence and having to stand on our own two feet from such a young age. We didn't have that traditional home life. I think that made us individuals in a different way to people who had a very conventional upbringing. We were put into positions where we simply had to deal with it. We couldn't whine or call on Mum and Dad. It created a way of facing life that normal out-of-the-system kids don't have. Plus they always supported and believed in us. As Shakespeare once said, evermore thanks, Mum and Dad.

* * *

At the same time as my father was ill, I was a new mum to my boy Jack. It was sad because my father was only able to meet him once, though I am grateful for that – at least he was able to see him. Like my experience with Sissy, I adored being pregnant – men are lovely to you; you can eat what you want; it's really good. I didn't have any problems but I'm not so sure other people could stomach it. We were still with Elite then and John Casablancas was in the office one day and was horrified that I was pregnant at forty-four. Come to think about it, everyone was horrified that I was pregnant at forty-four!

I repeated my Wellington hospital experience again, almost to the letter. I had the same doctor, I watched a movie, had the boy I wanted by 12.30 p.m., ordered my lunch, ate it, followed it up with a candlelit dinner with Rick in the evening. I remember drinking champagne in my hospital bed. And, just like before, I didn't want to leave. Then I had to get organised with some help because business was so busy at that time. I had a maternity nurse and a variety of nannies for Jack. We weren't quite as successful with Jack as we had been with Sissy because he never got on with them. I remember him slamming the door behind one poor victim when she left and shouting, 'And don't come back!' He was only a toddler!

I didn't experience any problems with being an older pregnant person but it sure was tougher being an older parent. Jack was quite hard work because he was a very active child. Boys are physically more demanding, too. I remember being really tired all the time. On Saturdays we were nanny-less so we knew it was time to play but all we wanted to do was snore. He was getting more and more active and wanting to explore everything. Eventually I came up with this plan for a girl to come and play with him on a Saturday afternoon so I could sneak in a little sleep, which helped a lot actually. I work hard and I get tired. It's not a great advert for being an older parent, I guess, but I did enjoy my kids enormously all the same.

So, yes, it's tiring being a mum at forty-four. The one thing about being an older parent is the physicality of looking after a toddler, particularly a boy. I remember thinking that even at six months old he was so big. He's 6' 2" now so that gives you an idea! Physical exhaustion was definitely a problem because you felt really bad. You wanted to be there and charging up and down like younger parents. I tried not to go out in the evenings too much to conserve energy but obviously looking after such big models was really demanding and it was such a busy time for our business.

Being a busy working mum, you have to be really organised and your back-up has to be good. Our nannies did all our laundry and we had a cleaner who also did our ironing. I was privileged enough to be in that position where I could have all those things done for me. I didn't have anything to worry about like 'is my house clean?' and 'have I ironed his shirt?' – not that I'd be any good at that stuff anyway but it was all taken care of. The main issue was just trying to give the children enough time and of course you do feel guilty about that.

Sissy went to boarding school when she was eight. I couldn't have coped with both of them in the house, especially because she was so jealous of him. She'd had six years of us to herself so she was thoroughly spoilt. Jack went to the local private school up the road and then to an all-boys school in West Hampstead. He wasn't particularly academic – he has a way of getting into a subject and then getting bored with it. He joined the Cadets though and loved that. He was really good at shooting and at one point I thought he might go into the Army. I think it's amazing what they do in the Army but it wasn't meant to be. Like Sissy, he also went to boarding school in Canterbury at thirteen, which was actually quite a good thing for him.

We tended to do things at the weekend with the kids. When Sissy came back from school we'd go to Holland Park and feed the squirrels or head to the Science Museum. They both loved it there. And we'd go on holiday every year, often to Greece or Mallorca. It got really difficult with Rick because he's so particular when it comes to the standard of the food and the hotel. His tolerance levels weren't great. I started to take them away on my own or sometimes with Simone. We took Sissy to Marrakesh and Jack to Barcelona one year. It was easier to leave Rick behind. Now I go to Turkey every year for my holidays and I'd rather shoot myself than take him with me. I know he wouldn't like the food. Last year I took him to the Splendido hotel in Portofino, just the two of us, and the hotel and the food were both fantastic, but I'm a bit daunted now because I think he'll be hoping I'll take him somewhere like that every year.

After Mum had died and the house in Canterbury was sold, I said to Rick, 'I want to buy a house on the beach.' I became obsessed with the idea and wrote all these letters to the houses I liked in the little coastal villages, saying, 'Dear lovely home owner, we're a young family . . .' – we weren't really, we were an old family – 'we really want to live in your house on the beach. We're not an estate agent so there won't be any fees.' I stuck these letters in any house I liked along the coast. I liked Hythe in Kent so I did a lot of those houses, and went to Sandgate too. I probably leafleted about thirty houses. We heard back from the first one I'd leafleted, a town-house on the promenade. We were going to instruct the solicitors to buy it but the process was really slow and we ended up losing it. I was furious. We then found another house in Sandgate that was a beautiful villa but it wasn't right on the beach. We nearly bought that and sold our house in London because it was really expensive. It was a big decision – planning this new life where we'd commute every day. What were we thinking? It was bonkers.

We were nearly buying this house then one Saturday we were shopping on the Hythe high street and I realised that everyone was really old, on mobility scooters or with Zimmer frames. I said to Rick, 'We can't live here, people come here to die.' So we pulled out of the house. They were friends of ours too and they were furious with us but that's life, isn't it?

Then, a little later, I got a call from a doctor who said his sister had a house on the beach at Fisherman's Bay who'd got quite sick and decided she wanted to sell. I said, 'Which house is it?' And he said, 'It's the pink house.' I knew the house straight away, what with it being pink, and I loved it. I went to see it and she insisted on going through an estate agent. She said she wanted it all done properly. The estate agent valued it at £99k. I couldn't believe it. It was such a bargain. We didn't end up getting it that cheap in the end but it was still a great price.

The first summer we had the house it was really hot. We'd go there every weekend and take the kids. It was actually a big slog to get two kids and two adults down to Kent – wake up early, make sandwiches, get in the car, tell everyone to shut up arguing etc. Rick's vile in these situations – 'Don't talk in the car, I'm driving!' – but then you get there and it's great because you feel more energy than if you were just slobbing around in London. It worked really well for us and it was our big thing to go away every weekend, then I took the whole of August off that year. We were on the beach every day, I was brown as a berry; we couldn't believe our luck. There was this fishmongers just down the beach from us so we'd go there and every morning get the catch of the day – crab or oysters. Yum yum! We'd invite people down and drink champagne in the garden. It was fab.

The pace of life slows you down mentally. I'd walk down the high street and people would be so slow compared to London that I'd just want to push them! It takes you at least eight days to get into that pace and then you're in it and pottering around at junk shops, car boot sales and bookshops. I loved finding old recipe books in the bookshops down there. We'd go to Dymchurch from Hythe on a fantastic miniature steam train, then go to the funfair at the beach there. Lots of family stuff. Sometimes Simone would come because she also lived in Kent with her boyfriend who later became her husband. That was why I got that house – to have a hub for us all to congregate. Sissy was going to school down there so it was convenient. I'd go on a Friday, take the day off, get the train down and Rick would already be there.

Of course the next summer it just pissed with rain and I hate it when it's raining down there. You're just enveloped in greyness with the grey sea and the grey sky. I get depressed when I'm there and it's shitty weather. The consequence is I never go because we never have good weather. I remember one summer I went down there and I just said to Rick, 'I can't stay here.' I buggered off to Spain instead with the kids. Rick doesn't mind it so much; he likes the wind and the rain and mooching around. It's OK at Christmas because you're meant to be inside with a fire and so on, it feels normal, but not during the summer.

A few years ago – before the recession – we were offered £1 million for the house by a property developer and I was really tempted but Rick didn't want to sell. They were going to knock it down and build flats. I didn't care since my summers weren't hot but Rick wasn't having any of it. By the time I convinced him to sell the crash came and the investors disappeared. Eventually it will get knocked down, I'm sure of that. The children hate it there, probably again because it's become defined by all those terrible summers. Now for a lot of our family get-togethers we tend to gather at Simone's house, especially at Christmas and New Year. She knocked down her farmhouse and built another one. It's not quite the Old Rectory, but we've had some lovely times together there over recent years. I feel really fortunate to have the family I have and though we've had our share of ups and downs, I really wouldn't change a thing. You are your family – that's the truth.

20

NEW FRONTIERS

I brought in the new Millennium at the Tiger Inn in
Stowting with a big group of family and friends. We had
such a fun time – lots of dancing on the tables, merri-
ment and general horsing around. Rick and I sneaked
Sissy in – she was only eleven at the time. Then there
was Chris, Huggy and Olivia, Simone and her fella Steve,
plus a ton of faces from the village. It was definitely an
unforgettable night and a suitably raucous send-off for
an iconic decade.

The Noughties signalled another new beginning for
Premier, post Elite and the supermodel era. We had to
run a much tighter ship without that big network
support. There was a massive influx of new Russian and
Eastern European girls – the New Model Army! – and
we all had to get to grips with this fab new invention
called the internet, which none of us understood, or

cared to understand, at first. We resisted for a while but eventually we succumbed and it changed the industry totally.

After the split from Elite we went through a really difficult time financially. Basically we'd lost a big company that was behind us and it was hard to convince the bank that everything was fine. It was tough. I had to cash in my insurance policy, Chris had to find money and our houses were dangling precariously as backup, as always. Then we found this guy, Chris Guina, who was a parent at Sissy's school. He came in to help us and looked at our systems to see where we could make savings. When we were part of Elite, it was always like let's FedEx this, let's buy seventeen magazines we don't actually need. We'd be out for long lunches every day, drinking lots of expensive wine in the evenings, the whole nine yards. That was the Nineties, though – it was a time of excess. In the new regime we had to practically ask permission to have a wee! We certainly weren't sending FedExes every five minutes or getting cabs everywhere any more, that's for sure. It was actually a really good discipline for us – he helped us cut everything down to the bone. It was really just what we needed at the time. It was scorched earth for about a year and a half. I didn't let anybody go but I cut right back on frivolities. Before, we never thought about saving money. We were making a lot of money but we were spending a lot and much of it was on unnecessary things. After about eighteen months, things started to pick up. I'm not extravagant at all but I haven't got time to look at what's going out of the company and what's coming in, though I am better now than I was. It was a culture shock for us but also for Chris Guina – I'm sure he thought we were a bunch of crazies. I'll never forget one day him taking Paul Hunt, one of my bookers – and a really good friend – to one side and telling him not to call me a cunt, which Paul frequently did, jokingly. He said, 'You shouldn't call ladies cunts.' I just peeked my head around the corner and said, 'Oh, it's OK, I am a cunt sometimes!' That's kind of how we were, and still are, with each other. We swear and fight and cause a commotion sometimes but we all get on and get the job done. It's fun!

To put the industry in context for you at this time, the market had become very different thanks to the Russian invasion. It had started to happen in the Nineties but it was the 2000s when the new aesthetic, post the supers, really took hold. Suddenly the industry was awash with Eastern Bloc girls that could now get out of Russia and they were different and so beautiful. These models have a completely different work ethic, spurred on I'm sure by a feeling of 'get me the fuck out of Siberia, I'm never going back'. It totally changed the business and the internet compounded it. The market was swamped with these incredible-looking girls who were really young. The Russian and Ukrainian girls start modelling even now at thirteen or fourteen and they leave home to work in Paris, Milan or New York. We don't take them that young and it seems very exploitative but if you saw where they came from you could see why they wanted to leave. The girls just wanted to get out. And stay out. It was really poor there and there was no hope. Even now, Siberia is pretty grim. The culture is very different over there. I think many girls are brought up to try and get away from it and find a rich husband. I guess that becomes their raison d'être.

The influx of these girls came with a surge of Russian scouts approaching big agencies like IMG and Elite and so on. It was a vast empire where dedicated scouts find the girls. A lot of the American agencies would send scouts in there but it was quite dangerous still so we all relied on local people. Of course nobody could speak the language or knew the culture so we became very dependent on these scouts that popped up and I would think that some of them were pretty dodgy. Suddenly these Russians started filtering in and they were all very young but tall: even at the age of fourteen many Russian girls are like 5' 10".

The Russian look became very fashionable. It turned everything on its head. After the supermodels who were practically household names there were suddenly thousands of Russians – tall, skinny, young and beautiful – but faceless (or at least nameless) in a way. There was so much choice for the casting directors that we started losing our negotiating leverage, and the Eastern Bloc girls would accept much lower fees, because for them almost anything seemed like big bucks. These two factors started forcing rates down and they've never really recovered.

We'd all be saying 'no no no' but the client, instead

of saying, 'I've got to have that girl,' would go: 'Well, I want *that* girl but I'm not paying that price for her and if she doesn't want to do it then there are twenty others who will.' And so models eventually became less enduring. They might do a Prada campaign and everybody would be talking about them but then they'd disappear. Traditionally, if you did those big campaigns you became a big name, whereas now you can do them and still fade from view. Simply move on to another Russian girl. It did change the market and, if you'd like to call models a product, there was so much more product available. It wasn't as exclusive any more, except at the very top end. Models were becoming commodities.

I never went to Russia at this time – it scared the pants off me. I just remember a lot of horror stories. It was considered too dangerous to let women go. In the early Nineties, there were stories about an Elite scout who carried a gun! It was dangerous, like the Wild West. You had to pay people off. We were visited by Russian scouts who'd come in like carpetbaggers with DVDs of five zillion girls. It used to drive us nuts because you had to look at every bloody girl. It was very tedious. We tended to wait for the French or the Americans to get the girl and then say, 'Can we have her?' It was less costly for us because we didn't have the expense of bringing them in and setting them up. We'd bring a girl in from Paris when we knew she had a bit of experience.

Around this time, actresses also started to break into the industry more than ever before. You wouldn't have got that in the Nineties. Actresses like Jodie Foster or

Winona Ryder, they wouldn't do designer campaigns or model for a fragrance. It would be considered a bad reflection on their acting. In a way, models were sneered at. The heart of acting was about truth and you couldn't sell out. But once they cottoned on to the fact that models could earn £300,000 a day, suddenly they were like, ooh, we could do that. They wouldn't touch products for years but then it became gradually acceptable. And of course the clients wanted recognisable faces which is exactly why the supermodels were so huge. Modelling was all about the Russians but no one knew who they were. So what do you do after that? You go for actresses who people in Scunthorpe know. That's a much more powerful selling tool.

21

THE MODEL AGENCY

So here we are, almost back with 'Carole Shite', spawned from my, shall we say, 'colourful' role in *The Model Agency*.

I was approached in the spring of 2010 by this really lovely lady called Jilly Pearce from Maverick Television saying they wanted to do a documentary about the workings of a modelling agency. They envisaged it being a one-hour documentary filmed during Fashion Week and they wanted it to be a bit like *The September Issue*, the film about US *Vogue*. We discussed it and all decided that you couldn't do a show about a model agency during Fashion Week in just one hour so we said if they'd do two hours, we were up for it.

A week or so later, Jilly came back to see me with a new proposal – they were now thinking four or five hours would be more suitable, split into one-hour episodes. We had our reservations, thinking what can you do for four or five episodes? We thought it would be quite boring so we turned it down and off they went to look for another agency. But they kept coming back saying, 'No, we want you, we really love you and Annie [our head of New Faces] and your team.' We were really nervous at the thought of it because of course we had no idea what it would be like, and we had to speak to all the staff to see how they would feel about it. In the end, we decided: 'Well, let's do it because if we don't someone else will.' We agreed on six episodes and the main reason I agreed to it was because I was so impressed by Jilly Pearce (the producer) and Nick Hornby (the director), and I trusted that they would do a good job. It's all in the edit, after all.

So we'd agreed to do it but two members of staff said they didn't want to be involved. I said, 'OK, fine, we just won't have you in it.' It's the best way to deal with it because as soon as you say that, everyone else is thinking, 'wankers'. Eventually, the production team talked them through what was involved and persuaded them to take part.

One booker started winding everyone up, saying that Premier would be getting paid a lot of money to do it so suddenly everyone started asking me if they'd get paid. I said, 'No, it's not lawful in this country to do that, it wouldn't be a documentary show,' which was absolutely true. No one would be getting paid but it would be incredible PR for the agency and we'd all benefit from that.

Then suddenly the contract came in and they'd sneaked in a seventh episode. I thought that was a bit off but decided actually, what the heck, what's the difference between six and seven? The next bombshell was that it wouldn't be filmed by cameramen but by remote control cameras in every room – like *Big Brother*. Everyone freaked but I actually thought that would be great because I know, every time we've done a TV show before, the cameramen are in your way and you don't act like a real person because you're so aware of them and over-thinking what you're going to say. The way I saw it was, as long as they edit it in a fair and truthful way, you're fine. So we had to put a tremendous amount of trust in the TV company. We also insisted that 50 per cent of it was filmed out of the office so that there was a balance between the observational/reality stuff and other goings-on. Otherwise it would have been too much like a *Big Brother* thing.

In the second-to-last week of August the production team arrived and started drilling holes everywhere and putting in cameras. That's when we started to get a bit nervous. These mikes were coming down from the ceiling, from everywhere, lots of them. I think there were about six cameras in the meeting room, back office, accounts – but no sound in accounts. The only place they didn't have cameras was in the toilet. They even had cameras on the door outside because they'd caught on to how much we went outside to smoke and that's where everyone talked. And then we were all miked up as well. So that was a bit scary.

The first day of filming started and literally no one talked! Or if they did talk about something they considered highly alarming they'd go outside and talk on their Blackberries. Jilly Pearce started to get really pissed off. In the end she got everyone in a room and said, 'You guys have signed up for this. What do you want it to be? A complete disaster or do you actually want to be involved in it?' So then everyone sort of got used to it. Annie used to go in the toilet and talk sometimes but eventually the team twigged that they needed to make a commitment: a commitment to being normal. Do what you do. I didn't see the big deal about it, though in the back of my mind I was aware that potentially we could come across like complete plonkers. One thing they did have to do at the end was take out some extreme expletives, twenty-five 'cunts' to start with. There was a lot of swearing! They kept the fucks and arseholes, though. The intro sequence at the start of every episode had me calling somebody a 'fucking wanker' down the phone, Sissy saying 'that fucking girl' about somebody or other and Chris shouting at me, 'Stop being an asshole idiot!' All in a day's work at *The Model Agency*.

As a company, this wasn't our first time at the rodeo when it came to being on TV. We'd conceived a show in the Nineties called *Model Behaviour*, which was one of the first TV programmes about the scouting process. Our then New Faces booker, Angus Monroe, went around the country holding auditions and came back with various different girls. Most of them weren't right – some of them were too short and so on. From a modelling point of view it wasn't that successful but it did put us on the map. I found it quite annoying because it was mainly interview-based footage so no one acted naturally. I think that's why I was pretty relaxed about the remotes – I could see the sense of it. Also I could see that it would be a proper documentary if we had that and not people thinking what they're going to say next or having to repeat yourself if a lorry drives past.

They started filming two of our newbie models, Leomie and India, going to New York for the first time. The idea was to put into context the process of introducing new, young models into the industry. Both girls had been with us since before they left school so we were able to shed light on the coming-of-age process that Annie and Sissy deal with on the New Faces team. They stupidly didn't film them leaving the agency to go to New York – I don't know why, maybe they didn't have a cameraman on that day or something! So we sort of knew that we were going to concentrate on these girls and how the bookers get them ready. Then, as happens every show season, Annie and I go to New York ahead of the shows to find new models, so they wanted to film us in New York, and the two new girls.

On the day I was scheduled to go to New York, Corinne Day died. I will talk more about Corinne: we had been friends for years and been through a lot together, so of course I went to her funeral and agreed to join Annie and the crew in New York later. She went out from City Airport with a cameraman on some fancy plane and they lost her luggage so she was having a shit fit. I had to leave just after the ceremony and changed from my funeral gear into my comfy plane gear in the car.

On arrival into JFK, I got stuck in customs. It was the most bizarre thing because they put me in the detention room and kept asking me if I'd ever imported Prozac. I kept saying to them, 'No, I'm a perfectly happy person, I have no need for Prozac.' It was very odd indeed – I don't know why or how they had my name associated with importing Prozac! Anyway, I was let out of there after about an hour and the cameras were waiting for me to come through. Then I was taken and searched and my baggage was searched. Because I'm diabetic I had all my pills in there. Did I have a prescription to prove it? No. I also had my trusty Andrews Liver Salts in a Tupperware box, thinking what on earth are they going to make of this white powder? Luckily they missed it!

Then Annie and I just started to do what we do in New York, which is go around the different agencies looking for new models to bring back to the UK. Our first port of call was always Paul Rowland, who is somebody else I will talk about later, an extremely influential agent and creative director. He started an agency called Women and then another one called Supreme, which was famous for taking these really strange-looking girls and making them into stars. You trusted his judgement and nine times out of ten he was right.

He was approached by the new owner of Ford to come to make a high-end board because Ford is a very big agency that turns over a lot of money but it's not cool or trendy. So they made two Fords and had offices both downtown and uptown, which was all high end. His brief was to find new girls and inject some 'cool' into grand old Ford. So we went to see him at the uptown office and, of course, the film crew loved him because he's such a charismatic person and has this amazing look, too.

Then we went to a whole load of other agencies but I think the camera crew got quite bored of that because it's actually quite a repetitive process – basically Annie and I poring over a load of models' cards in an office. They also filmed India and Leomie. It was lovely and sunny and hot, and we were able to meet up with the girls, too, which was nice. Whereas in the office we weren't aware of the cameras, now we were being tailed by a crew 24/7, which I found the most difficult part. It was annoying, we kept telling them to bugger off! Anyway, they got some nice shots and they filmed in the hotel room that Annie and I shared. It was quite nice because we had this little entourage with us but when you're tired it can become irritating. Plus I'm not an actress, nor is Annie, so we were a little on edge.

The next episode was us coming back to the agency with our new model cards. Annie scattered all these cards on the floor in the meeting room over the weekend: why would you do that when the cleaner has to clean the carpet? I had a fit about that on the Monday, which made me look slightly hysterical. I'm not bothered. I do occasionally blow my top about little things like that but I soon get over it. Then we went through the whole process of what happens during London Fashion Week, bringing the girls in and how much you have to hustle to get them in to the shows. Then Sissy and Annette went to Milan, India vanished and Annie went back to New York to try and stop her vanishing!

The India story was pretty dramatic, as Annie will tell you, since she spent the majority of the first couple of episodes bawling! India had been tipped as one of the top five breakthrough girls and we just knew she was going to do really well, so she went to New York to do the shows. She seemed so up for it but then suddenly she turned into this marshmallow and lost her bottle. Leomie, on the other hand, who we knew was a fantastic-looking model and a great character but – we thought – a harder sell because she's black, did amazingly! The response she got was phenomenal. She did all these great shows including Marc Jacobs, which is a key New York show to get. Sadly, Annie was unable to persuade India to stay and give it a go. Her father ended up having to fly over and get her. It was a lot of hard work launching these two girls' careers, but sometimes a girl just isn't ready and we have to press the pause button and regroup, which is frustrating but necessary. We felt India was going to zoom but she was too young for New York. It is scary to go there for the first time, we know that, and we do try to give as much support as possible but sometimes it's just too soon.

Annie, of course, was really upset, I think she blamed herself, and meanwhile had got so used to the cameras that she probably didn't realise that all of her tears would make it on to the TV. She got quite a lot of stick for those first couple of episodes when it came out but I think it was good because it showed how hard we'd worked to get to that point, and the fact is we're dealing with human beings and humans have a habit of letting people down. It just shows the commitment from the booker and how much she was trying to help the girl. The most frustrating thing, I remember this, was Annie trying to talk to her to stop her leaving and in the end she said, 'OK, I've done my best, you need to go,' and then India gets in the car and calls her back and says, 'I think I've made a mistake,' but by then it's too late. The story has a happy ending, though – India subsequently went to Australia and was a big hit there and she still has a great career ahead of her.

As well as the observational stuff we also did some talking-head bits, where they interviewed each of us individually, trying to get the gossip. I wish I'd seen the lighting before because it was so harsh! Of course they reassured me it was brilliant. That was the confessional bit and I didn't like it so much, again because it's not that real. I prefer just being me – relaxed, swearing and smoking!

We filmed another episode in Paris, the fourth city in the show circuit. We stayed at the Westin, I think – a vile hotel. I ended up sharing a room with Leomie, I'm not sure why because it's not normal that I share a room with a model. They filmed her a lot in the bedroom – this disgusting, purple room. It was a good little narrative following her progression. She got some really nice shows in Paris too, plus Marc Jacobs had fallen in love with her, so she was all set to get Louis Vuitton as well, which is a huge deal.

We were told she was going to open the show too, though Leomie didn't quite understand the significance of that (opening a show is like opening a movie – it's what all runway models aspire to). They had her down to be wearing a bikini and she was working late every night till one or two in the morning on fittings and so on. Then, the night before the show, they dropped her – it was so cruel. But that's how it is. Maybe they culled the garment or the bikini didn't arrive or didn't go with the whole essence of the show. They often do that, pull a look at the last minute. So we always say, never celebrate until you're actually on the runway. Leomie was so upset but because she's very level-headed, she just dealt with it. Some girls have a meltdown – it really affects them. Leomie did some other shows after that but it would've been superb if she'd opened Louis Vuitton. For a designer to tell a model 'you're my number-one girl' and then drop her is upsetting, but the designer and the stylist and the casting director are looking at the whole picture. They're all about the flow of the show and the order of the looks, which you can understand. I just wish they were a bit kinder some-times. Occasionally, it also comes down to politics. A casting director might drop a girl because they can't get another girl who's at the same agency so they'll punish the agent.

It all ended well with Leomie, though, because she

got Ungaro, which we went to see. It was a lovely show. The Paris filming ended with us having a great lunch on the terrace of a restaurant called L'Avenue. It was a beautiful sunny day and all the Paris agents were swarming around Leomie, desperately wanting to get her on their books. Leomie is still soaring now.

After being so self-conscious at the start of filming, we really missed the crew once they'd cleared out. We'd sit there during show time and if we were hungry we'd look up at the camera and say, 'Can we have a pizza?' and it would just appear. There were twenty-five people holed up in a building over the road – almost as many as we had working in the office! They wouldn't let us see what it was like there until the show wrapped. It was weird to see it – banks of monitors everywhere. Very *Big Brother*.

The show had an amazing impact on our business – we suddenly started getting a lot more models. Then, I was asked to do interviews all the time. We won an award, too, at the National Reality TV Awards – that was hysterical. We went to the O2 and hung out with the guys from *The Only Way Is Essex* and people like that. Not in a million years did we think we'd win – we were up against quite a formidable bunch of reality documentaries – but we did! I kept saying to everyone, 'We're not going to win it so just get drunk,' which is quite hard to do actually because it's never that easy to get a drink at those events. Anyway, we weren't prepared at all when they called our name out. I wanted my men's division director, Christophe, to come up on stage with me but he wouldn't, he was too shy. In the end Paul Hunt and Sissy came with me!

As for the general reaction, most people loved us. We couldn't believe it. And thank God! My worst fear was coming off as naff. Plus, like I say right at the beginning of this book, it was our chance to tell a true story about the modelling industry. So often, our business is slighted and looked down upon whereas here we were giving it a human, humorous and warm face. I'm actually rather proud of us.

You may have seen me say (OK, shout!) to my team, in the opening credits of the TV show, 'WE ARE MODEL AGENTS!' What I meant with that somewhat obvious-sounding statement is that our job is to be there for the models. We are there to help establish and guide their careers, and to nurture them, too. Ultimately, why I get out of bed every day is for the girls that we look after and the next 'dream girl' we're searching for whose life could change in an instant and whose face has the power to define an era. I will never tire of that.

It's another reason I wanted to do *The Model Agency* – to show the commitment we have to our models. We try to encourage very young people who don't always get it to get it. If you put the time in as a model you definitely get rewarded, albeit for a relatively short period. Models come and go but if you're smart and work hard, you can save your money, buy a house (or two!) and set yourself up for the next part of your life. This is something I'm always trying to impress on our girls – they can be financially independent and build a great life for themselves. Sometimes it takes a long time for the penny to drop for a model to realise how committed she has to be to have a successful career in this industry. They think it's easy and it isn't, it's a tough business. But I never give up on a model. If I believe in a girl I'll just keep going. I'm stubborn like that. I hate to think of opportunities wasted or dreams left undreamed.

When I was that wide-eyed twenty-year-old, nervous and unsure what I wanted to do with my life, I would never have envisaged the life that I have now and the crazy adventures that I've had along the way. What better job could you have that you love every day? I know I'm incredibly lucky. I also know I have worked incredibly hard, and that I wouldn't change a thing. Life is a poker game and you have to play it.

EPILOGUE: HATCHLINGS

Bringing us right up to date, *The Model Agency* effect is still playing out at Premier HQ. Three of my current and brightest young stars all landed on my doorstep as a result of the TV show. I'd like to talk about them, partly because they're good stories to tell but also because they reveal a lot about this industry now, and the cycle of discovering, developing and nurturing a model from very young until she's strong enough to go out there in the world. I always think it's a bit like sitting on a nest waiting for your eggs to grow up. They're hatchlings.

During filming of *The Model Agency* our prominent 'hatchlings' were Leomie and India. I'm pleased to say both girls are doing brilliantly. Leomie has gone on to work with a host of prolific designers including Marc Jacobs, Tom Ford, Chloé, Giles Deacon and Vivienne Westwood. She has also shot for Italian *Vogue*, *AnOther*,

Dazed & Confused, *i-D* and *Teen Vogue*. Leomie's such a go-getter, too – and really on it with social media, which is so important now. An aspiring writer and presenter, her brilliant blog *Cracked China Cup* has loads of followers and explores her life as a model and her love of clothes, as well as interviews with industry insiders. India, after her little wobble that you see on the show, has gone on to work in Australia and is doing really well. I think she's going to do it this time!

When the first episode had aired I got a phone call from an excitable mum keen for me to meet her 'beautiful daughter'. I say excitable because she couldn't seem to get over the fact she was speaking to 'Carole from the show'. 'Oh my God, I'm speaking to Carole,' she said, which was so weird for me. I didn't realise then that apart from being an odd conversation from the get-go, her beautiful daughter was set to take our industry by storm. Her name? Malaika Firth. If you don't know it already, you will soon enough.

Malaika's lovely-sounding mother Jecinter sent over some pictures and immediately I said, 'Can I see her?' The next day the two of them came into the office. Malaika was only sixteen at the time. She wasn't so tall, probably about 5' 8", but so, so stunning and an unusual ethnic mixture of Kenyan and Swiss plus her father is half Seychellian. Her features were so delicate and she was very long-limbed. We just loved her.

I knew from that first moment that I'd found someone special. It's like love at first sight, the feeling you get in the pit of your stomach. And lovely as it is, it's only the beginning. The hard work is to come and with Malaika, it wasn't easy at first. We started doing tests with her and − I've said it before − it's much harder for black girls to get tests. You really have to sell the girl.

Eventually she started to do e:commerce work and was working for ASOS a lot. She loved it because she was suddenly making money. Then she was booked by Burberry, again to do e:commerce. It was lovely to see her thrive, start to earn a living and learn her trade. Much like when I went to Lucie Clayton's modelling school way back in the day, I feel like the world of online retailing is a great grounding for young models. They learn how to pose, and walk (for the videos), and generally be professional, work hard and turn up to work on time. All of that stuff is really important at the beginning of a fledgling career.

What this kind of work doesn't do is help to develop a model's book. To do that, she has to keep doing what we call 'test' shoots, which we did, with quite a lot of persuasion. Then, a break. Burberry had kept saying they were going to do something quite big with her and eventually they shot her for a make-up campaign and it came out on a huge billboard in Times Square but only for a week. We never saw it, and we were never able to see the pictures. Sometimes these things happen. So, after that little glimmer of excitement, she continued doing all her normal stuff.

Next we sent her out to New York with an agency called New York Models. She did bits and bobs but nothing major. Then the agency suddenly decided to put Malaika in its commercial division without telling us, so when we found out we just freaked and said, 'No way, get her off.' We knew that wasn't the right place for her. She was taken under the wing of Duncan Ord, head booker at New York Models, which is when it happened: she was cast for the Prada campaign and that was it. Her world opened up completely. I realise to those who don't work in fashion it may sound a little bit *Ab Fab* – 'Oh, she got Prada, darling' – but that really is a big deal in our industry. Especially for a black model. Before Malaika, it had been ten years – ten years! – since the Italian label had used a black girl in their campaign. And who was *that* girl? Naomi Campbell.

Suddenly it all got very exciting. She got to work with the photographer Steven Meisel – that was such a big deal – and during the course of that coming out, Burberry decided they wanted to use her for their campaign. She got a Valentino campaign, French *Vogue*, Italian *Vogue*, *W*, *Interview* magazine. She's worked with all the top people. She also did the Victoria's Secret show, which was so exciting for her because every girl wants to do that, God knows why. It's not my cup of tea but it seems to be a medal for models. I think she'll become very, very famous. She's extremely focused and determined. And she's still only nineteen.

For me, Malaika represents everything I love about this job and why I do it: discovering a girl and seeing her blossom and thrive. I love how on a day like any other she wandered into our offices – a schoolgirl living in Barking with her mum and brother – and within a matter of two years her life completely somersaulted into something new and exciting. She's probably going to live in New York next year; she's become an independent young woman. I just love all that, changing a girl's life. If we hadn't persevered with her it might not have happened but we knew she was special. That gives me so much pleasure. It's not about money; it's the Cinderella story. An entire family's life can change too, which is also lovely. Malaika has already bought her mum and dad a house in Kenya. How brilliant is that?

A discovery like Malaika isn't easily explicable. It's a sort of magic ingredient – a 'you just know' moment. She's not a quirky look; she's a true beauty. I think she works in this world because she's got the most beautiful honey-coloured skin and delicate features so she can cross all borders, if you like. No one's saying she's African, or she's English – she could be from anywhere.

I'm proud of what Malaika represents in terms of the race debate in our industry. I think it's fantastic that she's breaking barriers that have been invisibly set up. I think she's going to do incredibly well, like supermodel well. She's a special girl – the kind that comes along only every ten years. She's enduring, too. You can get a lot of girls that come up in the shows and they're very of the moment, whereas Malaika will go on for a long time.

Luna is another 'hatchling' who came to us thanks to the TV show. This time via Rotterdam in Holland. She's only just turned sixteen, and again her father watched the show with her and they just loved it. She was with a teeny agency in this town and he kept asking the agent to bring him and Luna to meet me but the agent never obliged. The father's a very strong man so in the end he said: 'If you don't ring her, I will.' He called and came into the office the next week. I remember chatting to him outside our office over a cigarette.

With Luna, it was that love-at-first-sight feeling again – she's a sexy Giselle/Lara Stone type girl – but because she was already placed with a Dutch agent we had to all sit down and work out what was best for her career. Discovery is one thing but the right development is vital. I asked the Rotterdam agent which agencies they had placed her with elsewhere and I wasn't sure they were the right choices. Long story short, we were able to get her out of the contracts she had in Holland and Paris and take her under our wing at Premier. I had a good relationship with Luna's father from the very beginning and that is always a good foundation for a young model's career.

Like Malaika, Luna has started out doing a little work for ASOS whilst she's still studying. She loves it. She's what we call a 'secret girl' – she's not being put out there because she's still young and learning. We'll probably start her properly at the end of 2015 when she's finished school. A secret girl is basically somebody who is hidden on your website – so she's not available to everyone yet. All agencies do that now – they have secret girls when they're really young. Then you launch them at the right time. If you do so too quickly they're dead and gone before they've even left school. Sometimes it can be frustrating for the girl because we hold her back at first and don't let her do a lot of things but for Luna, she has to be at school until she's eighteen anyway. That's the law in Holland. Luna is going to be a phenomenon.

Zarina is the third girl that knew about us from *The Model Agency*. She's Danish and one of our scouts found her at Madame Tussauds when she was holidaying with her family. She's an otherworldly beauty at 5' 10" with pale, pale skin and strawberry-blonde hair. She's like a fairy, very pre-Raphaelite. So far she's just been testing because she's still very young but I predict Italian *Vogue* for her very soon!

You find models in the most innocuous of places. From Madame Tussauds to Waitrose, which is where Sissy and I discovered Phillipa Hemphrey around three years ago when she was just thirteen. We kept in touch with her and brought her up from Kent in the summer to do the odd digital test. Then she started working this February and did amazingly well straight away. She opened the Christopher Kane show, which is a very big deal in this business. She also did J. W. Anderson (another hot London-based designer), and Alexander McQueen and Louis Vuitton in Paris. She's got the bug now, which is lovely to see. She just shot French *Vogue* and when that comes out everything will start happening for her and we will cherry-pick what we want for her. The French *Vogue* story is funny, actually. Phillipa has a phobia of snakes and it turned out a lot of the looks she had to wear were snakeskin. She had a minor freak-out on the shoot and had to go for a walk to compose herself! She's since gone to see a hypnotherapist about it which I hope has worked but she hasn't been on another snakeskin shoot yet. She'll be a high-end fashion girl because she's very tall. She's also such a lovely girl – a true English rose.

What about the boys, I hear you cry? We also have a thriving men's division. Callum Ward is our new hot superstar. He took London collections by storm doing Topman, Pringle, Richard Nicoll – he is definitely one to watch. Another boy, Aurelien, has shot with Mario Testino recently and is touted to be the next David Gandy, while Chuck just shot the new CK1 fragrance campaign with Mario Sorrenti. Men are scouted in the oddest of places. Another boy, Morris, was spotted by our scout Tom at Primark in Leeds. At the time he had pink and blue hair. Callum was discovered at Leeds Festival, knee deep in mud around the loo area!

It's such a roller coaster this industry, which is partly why I love it, of course. When you first discover somebody special it's like, 'ooooh': a guttural feeling. Then you go, oh God she's only fifteen, I have to wait. Or, worse, thirteen! Then you think, how old will I be when this one hatches? I don't think I'll ever retire for this reason!

It's all an unknown, of course, whether once a model has hatched she will be successful. And our industry can be very fickle. All you can do is draw on experience (in my case a lot!), trust your own instincts and stick with it. I wish more people were shepherds rather than sheep. Like with Malaika, we knew she was special but a lot of people were too frightened to take a risk on her.

Until Prada, that is. But to my mind that's what fashion's about – taking a risk. You have to move the story along.

If I could predict the future, which is part of this game too, I think girls will be launched slightly older in the future. In the UK, you can't do shows unless you're sixteen. It's eighteen in New York (or sixteen with an acting licence). Just from the hassle factor of getting a very young girl I think it will make agents look at girls from eighteen upwards to launch them, plus we've noticed a trend towards 'older' girls too. Agents are finally realising that the girls burn out, and the client burns out with the girl because they think they're 102 by the time they're twenty years old because they've seen them for such a long time.

The industry moves so fast and people are obsessed with what's new and what's next. It's a greedy world, isn't it? Because everyone's on a smart phone and constantly connected, everything is so instant for the consumer. There's a low boredom threshold, which can be tough for models and something I am really mindful of when developing our girls. I'm increasingly looking to video and the moving image, too. We're connected to a studio upstairs at Premier now so we're able to record high-quality video content, which is vital in an industry where print magazines are declining and social media is valuable currency.

It's 2014 – what's the look of the moment? What's the next look? Short answer: who knows! Every season you think it's going to be more conventional and then suddenly a quirky girl pops up. I don't think there's a particular movement at the moment, there are a number of tribes. You've got the Brazilian girls that are drop-dead beautiful with amazing bodies, the Dutch that are Amazonian and stunning blank canvasses, and the Belgians cutting a lean, high-fashion shape.

If I see a cool girl, with her own sense of style and a bit of swagger, I always assume she's British. Brit girls are different – cooler somehow. There are a lot of great British girls riding high at the moment: Cara Delevingne, Sam Rollinson, Edie Campbell, our own Lara Mullen (more on her in the A–Z). Cara's success has been phenomenal. She is going to become a big actress. And she is a huge personality. She's got balls.

That's what it's about, too – personality. Cara is so successful because she's got a personality. She's fun. She's like Kate Moss in that respect.

Britain has a habit of breeding cool and interesting girls. Ours is a culture born out of the best art and fashion schools, a thriving music scene and cutting-edge magazines like *Dazed and Confused* and *i-D*. If your girl gets in one of those magazines it's the coolest thing on the planet. There's just something very creative about Britain and what we produce. It's unique. And it makes me very proud.

Here's to the next generation.

THE WHITE ALBUM: CAROLE'S WORLD, WIT AND WISDOM, FROM A TO Z...

A IS FOR...

ASSISTANTS

Assistants see it all. They experience it all. They *smell* it all. Working in the fashion industry and looking after high-profile models is not for the faint-hearted. Some rise to the challenge (they are a godsend), some let it go to their head (they are a nightmare) and some get punched (they tend to get paid off).

Some models will go to great lengths to make friends with the people around them, whether it's their assistant, foreign agent, driver or bodyguard, but these alliances tend to be tempestuous – a bit like a love affair that burns brightly at first before it combusts, leaving bodies strewn everywhere and a right mess to clean up. It's all about who's the flavour *du jour*, and even I could go from best friend to skivvy in the space of half an hour, if there was a French fashion editor in the room that needed impressing.

I'd always say to the new flavour, 'Be careful, she's not your best friend – keep your distance.' And they'd inevitably go, 'Oh no, she's my friend,' and I'd say, 'No she's not, she'll bite you in the arse.' And then guess what would happen? She'd bite them in the arse (not always literally). Suddenly, the pursued becomes the jilted and they can't believe it because this so-called best friend who opened doors for them has suddenly publicly insulted them.

In the Nineties I always had an assistant because it was so much work with all the supermodels on our books, who took up so much of my time. What does assisting a supermodel entail, I hear you ask? Well, it's a many and varied job, often with anti-social hours and *always* with unforeseen circumstances. I've had assistants reduced to tears for not getting hold of the right shade of lipstick, being forced to stay overnight in hotel suites due to night frights (and then not allowed to use the bathroom), and even being called to a house party in the dead of night attended by Hollywood stars because a pet dog might have ingested harmful substances. Talk about running the gauntlet. I've had assistants accused of stealing jewellery and clothing, one poor woman who ended up carrying illicit powders through customs – not knowingly, she just happened to be carrying the bag – and another who was responsible for assembling a menagerie of sex toys ready for a play-date at a top London hotel.

Assistants – or any part of a model's entourage really

– stick it out because the wooing part is very seductive. At first the model can't do enough for them. She'll shower them with trinkets, take them shopping, call them up and say, 'Let's have lunch,' where of course they'll saunter in and be ushered to the best table and promptly stared at for the entire meal. How thrilling!

I'd sit there and laugh sometimes, knowing from bitter experience how quickly the tables would turn. I think some models behave like this mainly because there's really so much bullshit in the fashion industry, that they suddenly start realising that the people who tell them they're fabulous and this and that are actually disingenuous. They feel like they can't trust anyone so these new alliances are short-lived. There's a lot of suspicion and mistrust – I feel bad for them in that respect. It can be a lonely old life.

When a strong bond is formed and an assistant has worked with a model for a long time, even if that relationship is borderline abusive (which is rare, but it does happen), then that assistant will often still stick around. It's called Stockholm Syndrome and is usually applied to hostage victims that develop feelings for their captors but also to those who forge a strong emotional bond with their superior (for want of a better word). We've had a bit of experience of that with a couple of assistants who, even though they were bullied and treated badly by a model, and even resigned over it, were talked into staying. It's a very powerful and weird kind of alchemy.

Then there are 'assistants gone rogue', the ones who get so close that they get notions of grandeur. There are usually influencing factors: in one particularly thorny case, it was vodka, carried around religiously in an Evian bottle. This particular model and her assistant had become co-dependent drinking buddies. Chris was practically knocked out on vodka fumes on one occasion when he picked the model up from her hotel to do a job. He had to ply her with coffee and mints to get the show on the road. The PA, a deluded woman, wanted to become this model's manager, but honestly couldn't define the difference between assisting and managing. Sometimes these characters would really throw a spanner in the works with their snaky behaviour. It just makes everyone's job that bit harder when you've got some mad, drunken controller allegedly in charge of a supermodel.

Luckily, they're not all like that, so at this point I have to pay tribute to a couple of very special assistants who have supported me through the good, bad and the extremely ugly. First, there's Stephanie Pierre, who was with me for three years, but also for the overnights, the tantrums and the commitment to the 'Carole Special' sandwich, which you will find under 'C'. Carlton Gardner is another special mention. She and I have worked closely together on so many things over the years. We're still in regular contact now. She's such a lovely woman.

ASSOCIATION OF MODEL AGENTS (AMA)

Premier is part of the Association of Model Agents, or AMA. There are sixteen agencies that are members and we come together as an alliance to help create bench-marks for good practice in the industry and to get the best for our models. We meet eight times a year. I've been a member of the AMA council for a long time because I'm gobby. Then there's Simon Chambers (Sarah Doukas's brother) from Storm, John Horner from Models 1, Laurie Kuhrt from FM and Natalie Hand from Viva.

Effectively, Natalie and I are bookers and the others are strategic. At meetings we might discuss clients who don't treat us well; work paper issues, as we often have dealings with the UK border agency; ways to make model agreements fair and correct. If you're a model and you want to make sure you're with a bona fide agent you should choose an AMA member.

Simon and I are on the council representing the AMA with the British Fashion Council (BFC). Our input is particularly relevant when it comes to London Fashion Week, regarding working conditions for the models and show rates. The BFC will tell us what the rates are going to be and we'll reflect on the working conditions and tell them when and where they're poor. We've been very vociferous on how models are treated during Fashion Week.

BFC sets minimum rates for shows for LFW. We tell them that's their challenge because such-and-such a casting agent is trying to get a model to do a show for nothing. In New York, designers will often pay models in what they call 'trade', in other words last season's cast-offs. Often the model's so busy she won't even get the clothes so she's working for nothing and that's not right. A designer wouldn't let you walk into their shop and just take a dress, would they? So the AMA stopped that years ago in London. We've always had a minimum rate for shows in London and it goes up each year. Paris has minimum rates too, which are higher.

The next big thing is safety. The issue is that there is no travel day between the end of the New York shows and the beginning of LFW, and models may have as many as twenty-five castings all over London straight off the plane and they're often in dire places really late at night. It's not safe and it's not nice. A lot of these girls are foreign and don't know their way around London, so we have to provide a fleet of cars and drivers to get them to their castings and ensure their safety.

You wouldn't get that in Paris where the fashion houses are beautiful and usually centrally located – not like a council flat in Dalston. I don't think it's appropriate that these very young girls are going to these awful places. The BFC should be helping the designers have a centralised venue where they can cast properly and do their fittings and so on. If it's practical then that's what we're after next.

Thanks to the AMA, we also send staff once a year to BEAT, a fantastic organisation that teaches people about eating disorders. What else do we do? We talk about the rights on pictures. We used to collude on rates and we had a sort of dispensation from the government that we could actually set rates because it was easier for the client than to go to 75 million agencies – but we're not allowed to do that any more so they're just stagnant.

It's subject to market forces, which is probably great for some clients, but not for our models.

ANNIVERSARIES

I do love a party and Premier's twenty-fifth anniversary party was humongous. We held it at the Intercontinental on Park Lane. We invited about 1,500 people and it was totally rammed. Amy Winehouse, Kelly Brook and Robbie Williams turned up. Well, sort of. We had a Robbie Williams lookalike singer. That was my idea – I thought it would be hysterical. Of course everyone thought it was Robbie Williams!

Parties are important, for networking and for morale. Some of the best parties we've had have been at the office in Parker Street in the summer and they've spilled out into the street. They're quite famous – I've already mentioned the parties at the Wag and, before that, Café Pacifico, when we were starting out.

For the twenty-fifth party we took rooms at the hotel so people could stay the night. We really went all out. We had a Martini maker, a chocolate fountain, goodie bags that they actually forgot to give out – doh! – and a photo booth. What do I remember the most about it? My feet were absolutely killing me because my shoes were so high! And I spent the whole party trying to find people – it was one of those rooms where you can never find anybody so you wander around and around like a hamster on a wheel!

B IS FOR...

BLAGGING

When I started out especially, I felt like I was blagging everything a lot of the time. It's very much a learn-as-you-go job because so many random things can come up on any given day. This means you have to bend the truth a little sometimes to help things run smoother – everyone does it, from the model to the booker to the client . . . everyone! It's about smarts. I once took on a booker in the early Premier days and said to her, 'Right, now you've got to bullshit that client.' She said, horrified, 'I can't lie.' I said, 'What? You're a booker and you can't tell a little fib from time to time?' I mean it's a prerequisite! We have a list of excuses to tell clients. The more ridiculous the better.

Sometimes this can backfire, though, like when I gave

a client a genuine, albeit farfetched reason why one of my models couldn't make the shoot: 'She had to go and see the Pope.' It was true but still no one believed it! Then we've had things like 'she burnt her leg on a hot-water bottle'. My favourite had to be this model who hadn't gone to her casting. Her reason? 'I couldn't because there was this mouse and it ate through my handbag and into my purse and it ate all my money. So I had no money and I couldn't get to the casting!' You couldn't make it up.

BOOKERS

Bookers are at the heart of any agency and they tend to start off as juniors where they're basically runners – they get tearsheets out of magazines, they learn how to make a booking, or reserve flights and go out and buy flowers. Often they'll start out on reception and gradually a position comes up and we'll say, let's try them. I believe in giving people chances. I found Paul Hunt (the one who affectionately christened me 'the witch' in the TV show) at my hairdressers! He was on reception and I just liked his personality. He's worked for me twice now at different stages and is a really good booker. He also set up his own business for a few years and is now director at a casting agency. I love seeing people grow like that – it's all about personality. It's important to put faith in people. Paul and I are great friends too and I'm sure we always will be.

The prime things we look for in a booker are quickness,

efficiency, understanding of computers, that kind of thing. Then there's the really important bit, which is an understanding of what makes a good model and how to grow her career and make her better. It's about having the knowledge that her look should be shot by this photographer and not that photographer and the instinct as to when the time is right to strike with a girl. You don't want to overexpose somebody too early on, for example. It's also about being really personable and charismatic with the clients to build those key relationships. Then as the booker grows they get more confident.

Good bookers are really hard to find. It's such a small, bespoke business throughout the world, based mainly in the 'fashion cities' of London, Milan, New York and Paris. Countries outside of these four are often a bit looked down upon. Germany is sneered at in our business because there's not much high-end stuff, it's primarily a money market, though I think there's good stuff coming out of there. If somebody rings and says it's for so-and-so in Germany then nobody gets that excited but if it's a cool magazine in Paris everyone goes *woo*!

There are good bookers and there are baaaaad, lazy bookers. Sometimes you look at them and think, how on earth are you in your position? There can be massive egos within a booker's world and in some cases they live vicariously through a successful model, which is infuriating. The world doesn't have enough really good bookers. By good, I mean somebody with a great reputation, who clients like, who is considered cool or is just an excellent money booker with a talent for negotiating contracts internationally. Then, as soon as you get somebody like that, everybody's trying to poach them! It's a funny business, you can be fighting with somebody one year and best friends the next. It can be very snaky and it's still a very small business irrespective of what it turns over.

So what makes a good booker? To me it's a vocation. Bookers are very specialised people who are made by people like me. It's not a profession where you leave school and think, I'm gonna be a model booker, like you might a teacher or a doctor. It's probably not even a job you know about particularly. That might sound ridiculous because we're not saving lives or anything but you've got to love it. It's not about the money, it's not about travel – you have to live and breathe fashion. And the exciting thing about fashion is that it changes all the time. It's not static. There are two seasons in a year, plus you've got pre-collections, Cruise, you've got Brazilian Fashion Week, Australian Fashion Week – there's never *not* a fashion week going on. To be a good booker you've really got to be a good communicator, you've got to be über-efficient. It's sort of like being a PA with a character. You've got to know what you're talking about. And that's not picking up just one magazine and calling it research. It means reading French *Vogue* and *Twin* and *AnOther* and *Russh*. You've got to know everything, and you've got to know instantly, who's that photographer? I like him, I'm going to follow him. You've got to know about everyone that's up and coming, you've got to follow brand-new photographers who you think are talented and make them your next client. It's like being a mini detective. You can't just sit there reading emails and answering the phone. You've got to love it.

A good booker has to know when she's got a really good model and be able to develop her and put her on the right path. In our New Faces department we've got bookers with a really good eye for up-and-comers – both models and photographers. They know about style, and they nurture their girls – often from their early teens – into fully-fledged models: a bit like bringing up children! Then when they've done really good stuff we usually bring them onto the main board. Sometimes we never bring them onto the main board. Sometimes they've been a new face and then we know they won't have the capabilities when they're older. Sometimes they're just models when they're a really young thing and do quite well but it doesn't always translate into the mainstream of modelling, whether it's high-end or middle-of-the-road. Often we'll drop a girl after a couple of years on New Faces; she's done her school, we've done everything we can but we can't see her going onto the main board. It's all about development. I talk more about this under Y, for young girls.

Some bookers do a bit of scouting but some don't actually have an eye for spotting a model on the street. Either they're too lazy, embarrassed or they just don't see it. Not all good bookers are good scouts.

There are editorial bookers, who do the cool editorial stuff and the shows, and there are 'money bookers', who book jobs for catalogues and online stores. You're respected for being a great booker and making a lot of money but it's rare you become a name. It's the editorial bookers who become the names. They progress from picking a girl, making a girl, to really being hard-nosed about what editorial they do. It's about being strong and playing a giant game of poker every day – negotiating, holding your breath thinking, God, I could've blown that. It's the direction you put the star girl in that makes your name. It's all down to the proliferation of editorial. What you don't let her do, what you do let her do. As you deal internationally – because that girl will be working between New York and Paris – you've earned your stripes and people start talking about you because you've developed and made this girl.

Editorial jobs don't make much money (they are generally badly paid or not paid at all). The cooler you are the less you pay, or you don't pay anything. Like *i-D* and *Dazed*, forget it. But editorial is extremely valuable in other ways because it is (the right kind of) editorial exposure that builds a model's profile. Take Lara Mullen, a new-ish girl of ours who did a *Dazed* cover and an *i-D* cover, both out at the same time. She was unheard of at the time but she's incredible and soon after she got a *Dazed* cover again. So that has made her. She instantly turns that into money because her rate zooms up. That's when you can start negotiating.

BOYFRIENDS

We're always very aware of models' boyfriends, mainly because they can be a real pain in the arse. Traditionally, models always have yuk boyfriends: surprisingly, they can lack confidence and have low self-esteem and this is often reflected in their choice of partners, especially in the early days. They can be either controlling, or drifters who hook up with the girl for some kind of leg-up. Both types will often result in the boyfriend-turned-manager scenario, which rarely ends well. They're either meddlesome or they influence in the wrong way – maybe they'll get the girl into partying too much, or think they can advise her on business matters.

A boyfriend will often hold a model back, particularly when they're starting out, because he will object to them travelling a lot. 'I'll never see you,' he'll say. Then the girl worries she'll lose her boyfriend to Sally down the road when it should be the other way around – he should be worried! She could be on a boat in Capri doing a fantastic shoot but she'll be more worried about the boyfriend at home.

A really sad example of a controlling and jealous boyfriend happened around six years ago with one of our up-and-coming models who was destined for great things. We ran a competition where we scouted models from around the country and this girl won the regional heat in Manchester, where she lived, and went on to be the overall winner, too. She was stunning and only sixteen. Modelling was a fabulous opportunity for her because her background was such that two generations of her family had never worked; she'd been brought up in the benefits system, and her ambition was to get a council flat.

It started off really well. She started to do editorial in London and then went to Paris for some jobs. Gucci wanted to have her for their advertising campaign – she was very new but going to be big. The problem was her boyfriend – he was very possessive. She went back home to Manchester in November and went to a bonfire night party. Her boyfriend punched her in the face in a jealous rage. He knocked four of her front teeth out. So awful. That was the beginning of the end for her. Her career was only a year old but it seemed so promising. It was so sad – I was so fond of her. I loved her look and I also loved the fact that I could take her from one style of life to another. If she'd not had that boyfriend she would probably be living in New York now in a penthouse apartment. The boyfriend ended up in prison, which is what he deserved. He was a very violent man. The really sad thing is that she had ambition too – she knew she could get out of her situation. But he was intent on pulling her back. At first I think he thought he was going to make a fortune from her but then he got jealous. It was a classic case of the controlling, bullying boyfriend.

Money and status tend to be an issue because more often than not the girl has more money than her boyfriend so he feels inferior. Then what happens? The fella wants to become the manager because he needs to justify the fact he hasn't got any money. This is when they start advising the models on their career. God help us! So then you have to start advising the boyfriend as well – tell them something's a great idea, like you've never thought of it yourself. Bear in mind I've been seeing this cycle repeat and repeat and repeat now for many years. Model boyfriends should really be my specialist subject on *Mastermind*.

There are boyfriends, there are models' boyfriends and then there are supermodel boyfriends. Let's take this to the next level. Every genre of supermodel boyfriend has his flaws. I'd always hope and pray for a good one, but he never seemed to materialise, or the model would eventually frighten him off. She would travel all the time and when she did find someone she would inevitably over-compensate and smother them by calling all the time or showering them with gifts. It's strange, really: an extremely beautiful woman, desperate. But a lot of models are lonely because they don't have time to form proper relationships with anyone.

So to types. There are the rich guys: the sports moguls, the Russian business magnates, royalty, oddball magicians and even cricketers. These are more like business arrangements whereby the high-flying businessman who nobody has heard of suddenly has a profile and the big-spending model is kept in yachts, diamonds and lawyers' fees. There was one model who claimed to me she only ever had sex twice with one businessman squeeze, so she must've been getting it somewhere else. And one must assume the same about him.

Rock stars. It's the oldest courtship in the book, right? Well, a tradition that really gathered pace in the Sixties with some glittering examples – we're looking at you, the Rolling Stones. What self-respecting rock star *doesn't* have a model on his arm? And what does this mean for an agent? A lot of time spent backstage at places like Wembley and the Albert Hall for a start. Thanks to my models, over the years I've had dealings with a veritable who's who of rock 'n' roll: Adam Clayton, Bono, Eric Clapton, Bryan Adams, Mick Hucknall, Michael Bolton . . . And that's the pay-off here – the rock star doesn't really have to be attractive (or even be cool in some cases), just as long as he commands the biggest arenas and has a private jet fuelled up for every eventuality.

Actors. This is what I call the surreal category. What else can you call it when you're taking midnight phone calls, at home, from Robert de Niro, or orchestrating clandestine lunchtime trysts. I remember sending champagne to Paris. Like I say, surreal.

Let's not forget the 'completely out of his depth' boyfriend. One model went out with this guy who was wealthy, yes, but nowhere near wealthy enough – or experienced in the world of the jet-set – for this girl. She wielded so much power over him. She'd met him in Istanbul at a shoot and he was much older than her. He also had a wife and kids. When he came to London she made him hire the presidential suite at the Dorchester and buy her diamonds. He was so out of his depth. He didn't have a clue what it would cost him to have this woman. She'd make him buy all this food from specialist places, all that awkward stuff we were used to, and you could see him shitting his pants over what she'd demand next.

Which leads me to affairs. A lot of model relationships tend to resemble affairs precisely because they're so short-lived, but – shocker! – there are also quite a lot of extra-maritals going on behind closed doors. I've experienced jobs magicked out of thin air in order to cover up a *liaison dangereuse*. I've heard of models climbing out of windows in the dead of night to hook up with a bit on the side, and the rock star seeing two models at the same time, as well as his wife.

Is it all about making cynical alliances in order to further one's social climb? No, I don't think so. My tongue is firmly in my cheek. I think when models get to a certain level they're going to events and mixing with particular types – rock stars and actors and so on – so they just form an alliance. If they were meeting grocers they'd probably be going out with grocers. They're just in that environment.

Of course there have been mutually beneficial alliances, as I've mentioned above, and for the girl it might create a certain sense of mystery. As in, why the fuck would *she* be going out with *him*? Another interesting one that I remember more from the Eighties is when a model dates a pop star who's gay. We had a model who was 'dating' George Michael for a while. Obviously she wasn't really having a relationship with him but it was good for his press and good for hers too. I've never orchestrated anything like that but I've been asked to. And there are PRs out there who will do it. They'll set it up so a model is maybe going out with one of their clients.

There are also more romantic stories involving musicians and models, like Simon le Bon and Yasmin. He liked her so much that he approached her agency to get in touch with her. That pairing has a happy ending – they're still married. I think it happened a lot more in the Eighties and Nineties than it does now. Even before the supermodels, it happened a lot more. Bands and musicians would come to our parties and they'd meet models. They were a lot more accessible then. In the early days, Def Leppard were in and out of our offices in Goodge Street, as were half of Spandau Ballet.

Sometimes the boyfriend will do wonders for a model's reputation, or vice versa. Take Kate Moss. When she dated Johnny Depp, it made people look at her like she was a grown-up. It also made her global. Now she's the one who does the elevating. She's also fallen foul to the bad press generated by another boyfriend, Pete Doherty. But good for her – she goes out with who she damned well pleases.

C IS FOR...

'CAROLE SPECIAL'

I don't think I'm particularly diva-ish but I do like some things a certain way. The 'Carole Special', which is famous in the local sandwich shop, is toasted brown bread with mustard and mayonnaise and boiled egg and cress. Cut into four. I used to ring into the office on my way into work and say, 'Can you get my sandwich?' I'd get here and it would be on my desk, alongside a cup of Earl Grey with a 'cloud' of milk, in my special china cup and saucer. Does that make me a diva? I don't know. There are a few things that will really bother me, like I'll always notice and get really narked if somebody takes my chair. And blown light bulbs drive me mad. Pet hate. And the phone – if it isn't answered, I'll yell, 'Pick up that fucking phone!'

CASTING DIRECTORS

Casting directors are hugely influential, especially during show season. Jess Hallett, Katie Grand and Russell Marsh are currently three of the biggest names in the business and cast many of the big shows. They're all British and have a great eye for new talent.

Katie is highly respected and extremely powerful in this business – she works with Marc Jacobs in New York and Paris, and Giles in London. Russell Marsh was famous for trawling the Russian agencies, where he became very famous and everyone would send him these amazing girls. He used to do Prada so everybody wanted to know about Russell Marsh for a time. Now he does the casting for Christopher Kane and always has the best breakthrough girls of the season.

Russell is one of the most visionary names in this area. He took things in another direction and became very powerful when he was at Prada. Funnily enough, he used to work for me at one time, on reception! I'm sure he'll die to read that! Each show season we'll send him images of a girl we think he'd like and then he'll hopefully say, 'Yes, send her to me.'

Russell tends to want to be the first to see a girl and he doesn't really want you to send her to every other casting agent. It's that poker game again but this is why Christopher Kane's show always has the best cast show for new young girls. It's where editors look to see who's up and coming in our business. Russell also casts for Céline in Paris, and BCBG and Victoria Beckham in New York.

Then there's Katie Grand, who is first and foremost a stylist/consultant, as well as being a magazine editor at *Love* and general Industry Bigwig. She's highly respected and powerful and can make a girl into a name. She'll take the girl, put her in Marc Jacobs' show, then she'll come to London and appear in Giles's show, which can then lead onto the Louis Vuitton show, and if the girl's very lucky, a campaign.

Katie is not a casting director as such – KCD cast most of her shows – but she certainly knows what look she wants and she can resurrect people who are 100 years old and make them cool. She's exceedingly influential and has had a huge impact on British fashion and fashion in general.

So what is casting direction all about? From our point of view it's about where we want to place our girls – the casting director's personal status and the kudos of the designer they're casting for. There's a hierarchy.

A good casting director is like a conductor – he or she has to get the ensemble right. They're also a hustler. They have to hustle us and we in turn hustle them. If it's a girl everyone wants then we have the power and we're weighing up what her best options are – *could she do this? Has she got enough time to get to that show?* And then you're holding out for what you consider a slightly better show – the poker game. But then suddenly if the options drop off and you're in desperate need of your second option it's time to start hustling that casting director, who, of course, knows exactly what your game is! I LOVE it!

CORINNE DAY

I've mentioned Corinne already in this book but I really want to pay special mention to her here. I first knew her as a model, when she walked into the Bond Street office with her grandmother. Then she carved out an industry-changing niche as a photographer and, along with Kate Moss, turned the Nineties completely on its head. I worked with Corinne a lot, but more than that she was a dear friend. So it was devastating when she became ill with cancer.

It was 2009 when I took a call from Georgina Cooper, one of my models that Corinne worked with a lot, saying that Corinne's condition had worsened and that her friends were trying to raise some money for her treatment. I spoke with Corinne and her husband, and, along with her friends Kate Phelan, Neil Moodie and Karl Plewka, we came up with the idea of printing some of her pictures to sell. We decided to print an iconic Kate Moss image in a limited edition of 200. We called it 'Save the Day'.

All 200 prints sold in two hours and I think we raised about £40k at first. It was phenomenal – people from all over the world were coming in for these prints. We ended up doing five prints in total, with a couple more of Kate (with her permission), and also Georgina. It was the famous picture that was first published in *The Face*, with Kate wearing that feathered headdress, Corinne was too ill to sign it so we got her fingerprint instead and put it on the back of each print.

Corinne would come into the office but she wasn't

very mobile – her husband had to help her move around. She met her husband Mark when she was modelling for us in Japan. I think he was a model then but he was also a photographer so she learned how to take pictures from him. When she came back from Japan she started making a name for herself as a photographer and all of the iconic pictures started to happen. I really liked the way that Corinne wouldn't compromise on what she believed was right. She was like a little terrier – she just believed that you shouldn't do certain things. She would never compromise her work.

Corinne died in August 2010. The funeral was at a big house in the country. It was really lovely. They had the service in the garden. It was so sad but there were a lot of close friends there – Rosemary Ferguson, Sarah Murray, Kate Phelan, Kate Moss, lots of photographers. We weren't allowed to drink before the funeral because of Maori tradition – Corinne's husband is from New Zealand. Of course everyone wanted a drink; Kate was looking for beer and wine but we couldn't find a corkscrew!

Corinne was very influential because she changed how you saw beauty. She made you look at things in a different way. What is unconventional beauty? That's what Corinne Day taught me.

COURT

Let's just say I've spent *a lot* of time in court, or avoiding court. Or settling out of court. We do tend to win though, which is a bonus.

D IS FOR...

DREAM GIRLS

Bailey says there are only ever ten top girls and I'm inclined to agree with him. You discover models all the time but to find a really special one is very rare. And there are so many elements to her 'making it' – you can find a special girl that doesn't have any balls and just gives up when the going gets tough. They have to be so dedicated to make it work and the power that models once had has gone because actresses have taken over.

We've got loads and loads of beautiful young girls but we're always looking for the special one. When we found Lara Mullen we just knew she was going to be big. It doesn't happen every year or anything like that. It's hard to find the big gold nugget. I don't mean that in a financial way, I mean the extraordinary one. We recently found a fifteen-year-old girl called Zarina, who's Danish. She's quite unusual looking with strawberry-blonde hair and freckles. I think she'll be the next one to rise through the ranks. Tom, one of our sharp-eyed scouts, found her at Madame Tussauds on holiday with her aunt and uncle.

So who are my dream girls? Past and present, some I've represented and some I haven't, here goes . . .

Susie Bick

Susie Bick's look was so strong and of her time, yet twenty-five years on she hasn't dated one bit. You could plop her images into an ad now and it would still be perfect. There are some girls with a modern face like that. Certain faces of each decade depict the era to me and Susie does that for the Eighties. She was and still is my favourite model. To my mind she was the most beautiful individual, so naturally stylish, and she instinctively knew what to wear. She was radical – there is only one Susie Bick.

Christy Turlington

I love Christy and I think out of all the supermodels she's probably the most beautiful. Her face is incredible. She's also the most articulate and refined woman and very easy to work with – supremely professional, if a little cautious. Christy was 'raised' under the watchful eye of Eileen Ford and got her big break with Calvin Klein and those iconic campaigns. It's wonderful that now, over twenty-five years later, she is still representing the brand – looking utterly amazing in her underwear, no less! But then her beauty is very classical – she's elegant, flawless and timeless.

Kate Moss

I don't really believe in regrets but I'd say turning down Kate Moss was probably the closest I come to one. *I know*, shoot me now! Corinne Day brought her in when we were at Bond Street. Kate sat on the sofa and we all talked to her and looked at her. Corinne didn't think she was right for Storm or doing much work there and thought we'd be good for her. She realised she was special but I, stupidly, said, 'No, she's too short for me.' And that was the end of that – off she trotted. Now, twenty years down the line, she's probably the most successful model of all time with the most copied style of all time too. Why? She's beautiful but she's not unattainable; she's very cool, sexy and she doesn't give a shit (she also knows it's cooler to keep her mouth shut). She's the classic naughty girl that I love. Her character and oodles of energy make her a great performer – she knows exactly what to do on a shoot and has a chameleon-like quality. She also has a sense of humour and doesn't take herself too seriously, which is a great quality in a model. Who doesn't want to be Kate Moss or know her?

Naomi Campbell

What else is there to say? Naomi is probably the most powerful, globally recognised model ever. She's stunningly beautiful, a natural model, and knows exactly what to do once she arrives on set. She's an instinctive model, with a walk that has become iconic. How could it not with those limbs?

Linda Evangelista

I always thought Linda would end up as the editor of French *Vogue*. She's incredibly stylish and has a knack of knowing what's coming next – she's bright and determined. Linda was always a chameleon and that really contributed to her success. She reinvented her look all the time and kept people on their toes. She's not the tallest model in the world at 5' 9" but she knew how to make herself look good. She's clever because she's got a nose which you wouldn't say was conventionally beautiful and she must have struggled with it when she was brand new. But she was determined and she worked hard to keep people interested. Her hair became her story – she wasn't afraid to keep changing. With most models that would be a problem but with someone as strong as Linda? Not at all. It just added to her mystique, along with the did-she-or-didn't-she-say-it quote about not getting out of bed for less than $10,000. Chris says she did!

Stella Tennant

Stella is what I'd call a handsome woman. She's extremely beautiful: 5' 11", incredible skin, with an aristocratic and completely individual look, which she hasn't really veered away from over the years. Her career is very enduring. She's still doing very well despite having four kids in a Scottish castle. I like the campaigns she does, for the likes of Chanel, and she's cool – she's never debased herself with too much publicity. In a nutshell: thoroughbred class.

Lara Mullen
Right now, she's the one. Lara's one of my current girls – she's still a baby and hasn't found her style yet but she's so in demand. We discovered Lara in September 2011 from a little village in Northampton and she went straight to New York to do the shows. Having never even walked in high heels she did one of the hottest shows of New York Fashion Week – Alexander Wang. She appeared on the cover of *i-D* and *Dazed and Confused* in the same month before shooting the main fashion feature for British *Vogue*. She's been a phenomenon and I'm convinced she's going to do something amazing because she's got such a special face. It's almost girl next door but it isn't because it's quite androgynous and strong. She can go from cool, edgy stuff to quite strong commercial. And she's a lovely girl too!

Annie Morton
Annie's a Britpop girl, born out of the Cool Britannia era. I still represent her now and she's amazing. I had to fight like hell to get her. She was with Storm and DNA and I wanted her so I kept ringing David at DNA and saying, 'Have Storm booked her this year?' I never stopped and in the end I got her. I had a really good

time with her. She's a mum now but still very beautiful because she's such a unique girl and so much fun. She had the most incredible face with a little gap in her front teeth, and her body shape was not quite as androgynous as the waif that preceded her. She came in the next phase after Kate. Annie is a really approachable woman and I think that's why she was enduring as a model. She was wonderful to work with.

Helena Christensen

With Danish Helena, it's all about her eyes and lips – you could swim in those eyes. She's super-sexy too and not afraid to do daring things. Just recently she did a shoot for New York magazine *Future Claw* from her Manhattan apartment wearing little other than a delicately placed ornament in some shots! She's creative too, with a very successful career as a photographer. Helena was just so easy – an absolute joy to hang out with. I'd say that she was almost a supermodel. She's always been bigger in Europe and I'm sure her legacy will live on.

Catherine Bailey

Catherine is a friend first and foremost, and wife to a certain David (they are still besotted with each other and have three lovely kids), but to me she's always been an amazing model. She's quite stern in a way but stunningly beautiful. We looked after her quite recently, as an older model. She's still got it. There's nobody could just pull their hair back into a ponytail and manage to look as naturally stunning as Catherine. We're ladies who lunch now – when we get the time – and we've taken our kids on holiday together, without the men!

Claudia Schiffer
Claudia is one of the most famous blondes in the world – stunning, tall, a beautiful face and really lovely to boot. When she came on the scene in the Eighties she was an instant success. It was like Brigitte Bardot all over again. And as well as having a look that will always sell and that everyone adores, Claudia also has a dry sense of humour, is highly intelligent and very pragmatic so she was always a dream to work with. Chris dealt with Claudia mostly – he and Huggy had a friendly relationship with her because they all worked together on several big bookings. They had great times and, he says, some amazing adventures on safari, in Iceland, in Monte Carlo and in Montenegro on a particularly scary shoot, involving dodgy helicopters and shady gangster types! Claudia kept her cool though, as ever. Campaign-wise, who could forget those iconic shots for Guess jeans? Sexy or what?

DRIVING

Me and cars don't really go together. It took me five attempts to pass my test back in the Seventies. I drove a Mini that was an automatic and the gearstick was a bit dodgy. I remember putting it into drive but it went into reverse instead and I crashed it. So that was the end of the Mini. Then I got a Citroën – a big one – the fourth wheel never really worked so it just sort of limped around London. Anyway, I used to drive from Primrose Hill to Chelsea to work and one day popped into the underground petrol station at Park Lane. I drove up the ramp to get out and the guy was shouting at me because I'd left my petrol cap on the roof. I jumped out of the car in my four-inch stilettos but didn't put the handbrake on so I'm on the ramp and the car's now trying to run me over with all these people in Hyde Park looking on and shrieking at me. The attendant rushed out and managed to stop the car with his shoulder. But yes, I nearly got run over by my own car.

E IS FOR...

E:COMMERCE

E:commerce is such a huge part of our business now – companies like ASOS, My Wardrobe and Littlewoods Direct, who need models to wear the clothes they sell online. The demand for models is huge! You know the girls who sometimes have their heads chopped off in the pictures? We supply a lot of models to do that job. It means that across London ten girls a day, six days a week, are getting outfitted up precisely for this purpose. That's a lot of girls. And that's just one client! There are some models who have made a hell of a lot of money doing it. There are certain models, like Jamie Gunn who we used to represent, who have a certain look that works really well for online sales. It's all about having a good body and a pretty, non-edgy look. It also helps if you can't quite place where the girl is from – that way she appeals to a whole spectrum of customers. If a dress doesn't sell on one girl, they will shoot it on another, and that girl really has the power to boost sales.

EDITORIAL GIRLS

You can't survive without both money girls and editorial girls. There are agencies that just do money girls but they don't have that cool an image. The cool image is so important in this industry because then every agent in the world wants to work with you so they send you their best girls. And once you're sought after as an agency, the calibre of your girls grows. Cool girls earn nothing at first; we'll often fund them and give them spending money. Say it's a young girl from Siberia, we'll arrange work visas, fly her in to London and put her up in our model house. It's that poker game again – will she work, won't she? But you know I love a gamble.

F IS FOR...

FAMILY BUSINESS

Premier is a family business. Chris and I were brought up together in Africa, crossed the world aged just four and five to go to boarding school, set up the agency together in 1981 and we're still working side by side now. OK, so he may have called me an 'asshole idiot' on TV for seven weeks in a row (in the opening credits) but generally I'd say we're a good team. We each have our strengths and complement each other. Well, apart from when we're screaming and swearing at each other but that doesn't tend to last long.

Chris was a bit of a heartthrob in his day. He's so personable and very good-looking! Every PA we had fell in love with him but he's oblivious, he never notices. There were quite a few models with crushes, too. If ever I had a problem with a model I shoved them off onto Chris. He didn't get involved with the bookings but he was always interested in where he could take the model further. That is his forte. He was very entrepreneurial and ahead of his time. Eventually John Casablancas and Gérald Marie from Elite saw that, which is why they wanted him in America.

People often ask me whether it's a help or a hindrance partnering with family and I always say a help. It's by no means any easier than any other partnership. We have spectacular fights. He's a Leo, so he can never be wrong. I'm a Cancer and I'm never wrong either, so it's quite a clash. But it's actually good working with your family because you can say things that perhaps you wouldn't say to a business partner. And when times are tough you really come together. Even if one of you has made a mistake, it doesn't matter, you deal with it. You just close ranks and get out of whatever it is.

We started on very little capital and built it up. We had tough times at some points but we've always got through it. Together. We're a small business, about thirty-five people, but we punch above our weight. We're very well known worldwide and we're competing against big networks, which are the most difficult thing in this day and age for independent agencies. I don't really like networks. Elite was a network, then you've got Next and IMG and the Women Group, which is like a semi-network but they're not in London. I'm proud of who we are and where we're at – and the fact I've had my family with me all the way.

G IS FOR…

GÉRALD MARIE

Gérald Marie is from the old school of our industry – one of the original Paris playboys. He's always been what's affectionately known as a ladies' man and I for one love him, contrary to how he was portrayed (in my opinion, unfairly) in the BBC's MacIntyre documentary. He's also a fantastic model agent who has made numerous girls' careers, including Linda Evangelista who was his wife in the late Eighties.

I met Gérald in Paris when I'd first started Premier in the early Eighties and he had an agency called Paris Planning. We were swapping girls and I always thought he was one of the top bookers in Paris. We always had quite a jokey relationship – we had fun over the phone. Gérald mentored a lot of high-profile bookers in our business, such as Didier Fernandez, who's now at DNA, and Cyril Brulé who founded Viva.

Gérald was an excellent negotiator and he was also very good with the models – they always liked him. We'd tend to go out when either of us was visiting the other's city, but it was mainly a professional relationship. Back in the day he had really long curly hair and would wear leggings despite being quite a stocky guy. The best thing about him is his sense of humour – he's really witty. Eventually, John Casablancas, who had made a name for himself with the Elite brand in the US, approached Gérald to go into business with him and head up Elite in Europe. And so began one of the most powerful partnerships in our business.

Gérald is really good at reinventing himself. He left the business for a while and started up a yoga venture. He managed to get a flash mob of 10,000 people under the Eiffel Tower doing yoga one Saturday morning. But he's back doing what he loves again now, at a new agency in Paris called Oui. He was advising the owner, Steve, who is English, on what to do because he is so well connected in Paris. Eventually he went in as a partner and he's loving it. So he's back where he belongs and they're doing very well.

I have a fond memory of hanging out with Gérald and Peter Lindbergh at my place after some posh do or other, I think it was Pirelli. Gérald came with his girlfriend Linda who had been Miss France, a very beautiful girl, and Peter came with his wife. We were just getting a bit

Clockwise from top left: My 'secret Santa' present; on a scouting trip to Aarhus; Sissy on Shelley's scooter; Emily and Aidan decorating the agency; in our hotel during Paris Fashion Week; the bookers during London Fashion Week.

Clockwise from top: Chris and me; we never met after the trial but Mia left me this lovely note; another day in court.

Aunty Carole signs me...

premier

TURN THAT PEN
UPSIDE DOWN!

Clockwise from top: The Model
Agency, *Channel 4; behind the
scenes of* The Model Agency; *the
kippers went down well; inspired
by 'Turn That Frown Upside Down',
© Neil Kerber (Polly Bean).*

Telephone:
020 7938 6000

Daily Mail

Northcliffe House
2 Derry Street
London W8 5TT

Dear Carole —
Thank you for my lovely
kippers. I ate them for tea
with a few small boiled children.
Has Annie stopped crying yet?
You are all MONSTERS but I love you
Best wishes. Jan Moir x

Clockwise from top: I am usually in the office from 8 a.m. every day; Emily and Sissy scouting at Benicàssim Festival; Annie and me in New York, by Paul Rowland; at the Irish Pub in Paris; backstage with Giles.

Clockwise from top: At Marylebone Registry Office on our big day; Rick and me; a selfie of Sissy and Simone; Simone and Steve.

Clockwise from top: Sissy and me smoking outside the Park Hyatt in Paris; outside Corso Como; Sissy with Jonathan Saunders and Nick Dorey at the *Garage Magazine* party in Paris; at Sissy's wedding dress fitting.

Clockwise from top: At Sissy and Aidan's wedding in Tuscany; Sissy and Rick – father of the bride; my grandchildren – Ella and Henry.

Top: We won a TV award.

Above: My lovely bookers, 2015, photo by Tom Mitchell.

pissed at my place and Gérald and Rick ended up playing pool into the wee hours because our dining table converts into a snooker table.

H IS FOR...

HEDONISM

'The pursuit of pleasure above all else.' Now I don't think that's a bad mantra to live by but it does have its downfalls, especially when you're staring down the barrel of a massive show, with royalty in attendance (and all the restrictions that entails), and at least ten big-name models due to appear in said show are still up at 9 a.m., wandering wide-eyed between suites on the top floor of Claridge's, and facing a call time that's an hour away. Not fun. For them or the agent.

There's a lot of cat herding to do in this business – and some cats are fiercer than others. I've been in this business for forty years so I've seen a lot of pleasure pursuing and I'm no stranger to it myself so I'm not judgemental. *I get it*. But I've also come to realise when is a good time to pursue pleasure and when is not. See above.

Another funny-on-reflection-but-not-fun-at-the-time experience involved two big models and a Chanel show in Paris. They'd been up all night doing God knows what. I had to rouse them at their hotel and they were still drunk or whatever and they decided they weren't going to do the show. I took one of them aside and said, 'Look, you've got to do it. And if you say you'll do it then she will do it too.' Eventually I convinced Model Number 1 to do it, which meant Model Number 2 would also do it. Then I got them almost to the venue and they decided to go to sleep on some bench. A bench! In the middle of a garden in Paris. Two really quite famous women, about to do Chanel. *Jesus.* 'Please get up, please get up!' I was literally pleading with them. Karl Lagerfeld was seething because they were so late, but he got over it. They always did get over it because who could argue when faced with such beauty? Meanwhile, I risked a heart attack on an almost daily basis.

I remember Chris telling me a story about when he went to Cape Town to oversee the organisation of a major charity fashion event that was happening back in the late Nineties. Twenty-six supermodels, basically behaving like they're on holiday. He took a call from one particularly mischievous but very likeable model at 6 a.m., saying, 'Chris, I'm off my face, I'm not going to make the rehearsal. Pleeeease can you tell her.' Chris took the flak attack but fair enough, it was the rehearsal. She made it for the real event. She thanked him later by jumping on him after the show, legs around his waist, and inviting him to the toilet with her. Chris tried to explain he had a major Japanese client with him (who watched this greeting in bewilderment), to which she said, with a twinkle in her eye, 'I don't fucking care.'

The Nineties were particularly hedonistic. Let's just say it's a very good job camera phones weren't around. I shudder to think what kind of shit storms we would have faced. A designer held a party once where there was just a massive plate piled with white powder – very *Scarface*, I must say – that all the guests kept nipping over to. It was pretty extreme but there was so much money flying around.

The industry was full of nutters, or at least it seemed that way. It's so much more businesslike now. I must admit I love naughty girls, or people with an artistic temperament. It keeps things interesting. It was fun back then. Everyone was going out all night and turning up for work looking like shit and the make-up artist would sort it out. You can't do that now because there are too many models!

One final gem of a story involves a newish model who'd ended up pulling an all-nighter with a much more famous (and experienced in the ways of hedonism) model and a music mogul. This music mogul, I should point out, is an agent's worst nightmare because you just know, as soon as one of your girls ends up spending an evening in his company, she ain't emerging any time soon so you may as well kiss goodbye to the job. I used to beg this guy sometimes, 'Don't let her stay up all night.' To no avail of course. When has that ever worked? It's always the night before a big important thing when you do your very best to jeopardise the big important thing.

Anyway, it's the morning and my new little model comes into the office with an idea. She's clearly not been to bed and is all over the place but proceeds to tell me that having spoken to music guy and big model last night they all agreed it would be a brilliant idea if she changed her name.

'Okaayeee . . .' I reply, wondering what the fuck she is going to say. 'What name did you have in mind?'

'1981.'

Speechless.

I IS FOR...

INAPPROPRIATE BEHAVIOUR

Very rarely but occasionally you do get a girl who will say that a guy has been a bit too 'handy'. At that point, I would probably talk to other girls who've worked with the same guy to find out if they've had similar experiences and then call up and make a complaint. Sometimes it could be a bit delicate because the offending person would more than likely be your client – your boss, in other words! You wouldn't want to piss him off but then you would warn girls, don't flirt with him. I'm going back a few years, decades probably, when lines were more blurred or women put up with the odd grope. I'm not trivialising here, but things were a bit different in the Seventies and Eighties.

It tended to happen with promotional girls when I

worked at Alfred Marks and then Bobtons but the same would happen with models too. A lot of models flirt to get the job. And then these bald fat men think they're in with a chance. I mean, how unintelligent are they? They need to look in the mirror! I've had to talk to some men and say, 'Look, you can't do that, they're very young girls and it could be misunderstood. I'm sure you didn't mean it and you were just being friendly . . .' Etc.

Nowadays it would be 'shock horror, call the police' – and we do sometimes. Girls are quite funny, they don't mention it when it happens and you only hear about it a month later when one girl will gossip to another girl and then you ask her about it and she'll say, 'He asked me to get my tits out and was touching me inappropriately,' and you're like, 'Hold on.' Not that long ago we had this photographer who was a client but also doing test shoots with the girls so he was doing us a favour. We help him build his book. He also started to work for one of our clients and they thought he was fantastic but then I started hearing these stories from the girls and I realised he was making them take their clothes off and touching them, asking them to look sexy, and it wasn't what the test was about.

It takes a long time to get to the heart of the problem because a lot of girls just think it's normal and they're scared or too embarrassed to say anything. One girl had left her shoes at his studio and daren't go back and collect them. I'm like, 'Why not?' And she said, 'He was a letch with his hands.'

'That's not right. Why didn't you say something?' I said.

335

I started to ring up the other girls that had tested with him over a year and they all had a story. He was quite a young guy. I could destroy him in five seconds. This guy was starting to work and become a client so I brought him in. I said to him, 'I can call the police, you know. We're putting you in a position of trust. The only thing I can think is that you don't really get what you're doing and you think it's all like *Blow-up*. But it's a different era now. If I ever hear about any of it again there will be serious consequences.' He was mortified.

I'd spoken to his photographic agent first and we'd decided that was the best approach. A lot of the models will do pictures where they'll take their tops off and don't have a problem with it but they're always asked beforehand if they're OK with it and invariably they are. Their mums are asked, too. We tend to establish how models feel about nudity in the questionnaire all new models complete when they join the agency. The question is: 'Will you do semi nude?' Around 99 per cent will say they'll do it. Other questions we ask are: 'Will you wear fur?'; 'Do you have piercings?'; 'Do you have a tattoo?'; and 'Do you have scars?'

Over the years I've had words with a few photographers and told them to watch it. Occasionally you get a client who is a bit 'fresh' (for want of a better word) and you have to deal with it. If they have a boss it's easy but if they're the boss then you have to be more careful. In that case you warn the girls and you warn the other agencies. Some girls say, 'I can handle it, don't worry.' Others, you wouldn't send them there. In Bailey's

Models Close Up documentary, Kate Moss and Susie Bick both tell stories from early on in their careers when dodgy photographers asked them to take their tops off when it wasn't appropriate. Susie ended up climbing out of the window, after saying she was going to make coffee, because the guy seemed dodgy, and Kate, who knew it wasn't right because his 'studio' was basically a grotty north London flat, point-blank refused.

How was it in the Sixties? In the brief time that I was modelling, occasionally you were aware that if you gave off the wrong signal you may be pursued. Some girls were good at managing that – I wasn't. I was too timid and found the whole thing uncomfortable. I've made up for it since! In general, it's a really safe business now, though cultures can vary from country to country. Whenever my girls travelled to Italy I used to tell them to wear mirrored sunglasses because some Italian men have a habit of following you if you catch their eye. Mirrored shades prevent this!

Occasionally, there are some very high-profile photographers who agents and clients know have a reputation for being inappropriate. In these rare cases, it's common for the agent to send the model with a chaperone and warn the model in advance. A model is unlikely to turn down the opportunity to work with French *Vogue*, for example, so she'll take her chances – armed with support, of course.

It's quite a difficult one because we aren't the girl's nanny but we do put things in place to protect and advise them. We always make sure we know who we're sending them to. It's not really in a photographer's interest to step out of line because they'll lose their job. You'd just ring the police and then they're on the sex offenders list – just like that. So everyone's careful. And we try to keep communication channels as open as possible.

J IS FOR...

JOHN CASABLANCAS

John was the agent provocateur of modelling; he was a charismatic, competitive visionary who took the model business by the scruff of its neck and into the real world. At the time when John was rising through the ranks in New York, Ford treated models like they were school-girls whereas he treated them like powerful, sexy women. He gave them a voice and hyped them so much they became big commodities with sky-high rates. It was his unrelenting entrepreneurial drive that kicked off the supermodel phenomenon. He even said it himself – he created a monster.

In 1991, we set up Elite Premier and John, Alain, Gérald, Chris and I worked as partners for seven years. Our partnership was undoubtedly the best and worst thing to happen to Premier. We gained so much invaluable experience at a critical time for the whole industry right at the dawn of the supermodel era.

We had a brilliant relationship at the beginning – full of fun, good times, laughs, fights, stress, exhaustion and frustration – but we always worked well together and had respect for each other. In the end it became more difficult due to the 'empire's' internal politics, and extracting us from the Elite network 'spaghetti' was a real nightmare. But despite all that, once it was over John and I always had time for each other.

John was the most charismatic character in the model business – handsome, charming, funny, extremely clever and utterly engaging. Everyone wanted to know him and be around him. He was always very clear and direct and he put his money where his mouth was. He achieved an incredible success with the Elite Worldwide network (twenty-nine agencies and an-all powerful Elite Look of the Year in every country) and the amazing models he created and represented. Along with Alain Kittler, the genius 'Money Guy', and Gérald Marie, the wiliest agent in Paris, these guys were unquestionably the leaders of the model agent pack at that time. They transformed the model business into a real profession and unquestionably put models and modelling firmly on the map. Despite this incredible achievement and success, they also made disastrous mistakes and just wouldn't or couldn't listen or learn from some of them, which inevitably brought them down.

K IS FOR...

KIT

A model's kit is very important. We give all our girls a list of must-have items they need to look professional for castings and to be prepared for jobs. It's not bad as a capsule wardrobe for any working woman though, really. The list goes as follows:

- Black or grey skinny jeans
- Warm coat for winter in a dark colour (preferably black)
- Simple black high heels
- Simple black handbag big enough for carrying a book
- Plain T-shirts in white, grey and black – no logos
- Plain skirts

- Trainers or black pumps for walking
- Tank tops in black, grey or white – no logos
- Black tights
- Nude underwear for castings and jobs
- Black blazer
- Simple black dress

L IS FOR...

LAWYERS

Our lawyers, Dan Bright and Jamie Singer, have been absolutely brilliant. Well everything really. But in general, I really question some lawyers' morals. This snippet from an exchange I had with one such character just about sums it up. I can't share the actual details (for obvious reasons) but the conversation led to me questioning the lawyer's moral stance. It unfolded thus:

Me: 'Well, you need to get your facts straight instead of listening to rubbish from your client and your client's entourage. That's so morally wrong. Do you have conflict with morals? As a lawyer surely you must have some morals?'

Lawyer: 'No no, I just take instructions, it's very difficult.'

Me: 'Your client has no morals so therefore you have none?'

Conclusion? Lawyers don't have morals.

M IS FOR...

MODELS CLOSE UP

In 1997, when Chris was in New York, he created the concept of *Models Close Up*, a documentary on the history and the nitty-gritty of modelling, and persuaded David Bailey to direct it. They brought Chris Evans on board with Channel 4 and it was produced by the brilliant Liz Warner for his Ginger Group. The production was actually based out of my brother's office at Elite for much of the time. It exposed the good and bad side of the model industry – the struggle to make it, the ones who got there and the interesting variety of characters involved. Bailey was at his cheeky-and-prosecutorial best. Only he could get away with some of the questions he asked, such as asking Gérald Marie how many models he'd bedded (to be fair, Gérald was quick to quip 'probably about the same as you' back to him).

Anyone passionate about fashion and our industry should definitely check it out. Some of the vignettes were brilliantly set up and directed, from the scouting guy posing ominously in the hot tub, Linda's 'panic attack' (she stood Bailey up when she was supposed to be interviewed), Gérald brazening it out, and John Casablancas' bitter denouncement of some of the talent he had helped to make international celebrities and millions of dollars. Most of the supers are featured. There's Claudia's interview in what looks like a wheelchair, and Kate Moss's explosive charm.

There's also an interesting discussion about the culture of the supermodels around this time – the infighting and some might say resentment being felt in the industry thanks to their stranglehold. On the one hand you have Cindy Crawford slagging off model agents and clients for what she calls 'double dipping' – taking double the commission – and then there's the designer Isaac Mizrahi who, with his tongue firmly placed in his cheek, describes the girls as 'the biggest pain in the ass. Society calls them supermodels but in reality they're the biggest bunch of messes . . .' He goes on to say he would give them whatever he could afford because 'water seeks it level', and that really sums it up.

MODEL FLATS

We started to bring in more foreign girls in the mid Nineties and you need somewhere to put them. Usually they were German or Swedish, they weren't from the Eastern Bloc as much then. We had a network of friends who would rent rooms, so often we'd put them up there.

Then the Eastern Bloc girls started to arrive and there was more demand for them so we needed to find *more* friends with rooms. Eventually, we reached critical mass so I decided it made sense to rent an apartment, which I did, right next to me on Elgin Avenue in Maida Vale. That could sleep about five girls at a push and it was often full, especially during Fashion Week. It's a two bedroom but it's got bunks. Now, because the demand is so huge because of e:commerce, we have to bring in so many girls. Eventually I started to rent another flat but realised it wasn't cost-effective so I bought a house. Now we have two houses and still use the odd friend's place, too! If they go and stay with one of our friends it will cost them £150 or £200 a week, which is very cheap for central London – much cheaper than a hotel.

Model flats are really important now but they're notoriously horrible. You've got young girls who aren't really taught how to cook or clean or look after themselves so they're always quite messy. Usually what happens is girls will come and stay for a couple of months and there's always one girl who is quite houseproud and kicks them into shape. If you're unlucky and nobody is particularly tidy then they all whinge and moan and say that the cleaner isn't doing her job properly. I'll say, 'She's not your skivvy – you've got to wash up.' The cleaner's there to change the bed sheets once a week and make sure it's hygienic to some degree. If the flats are not full they're quite nice but if they are there tends to be a lot of squabbles about people taking things from each other's rooms, etc. I always tell them to have a lock on their case.

In the house that I have in Maida Vale, my junior booker Annie Lou lives there so she acts as chaperone and makes sure things run smoothly. It's really good to have somebody there as the models often don't tell you things for ages. You'll go in one day and it's in complete darkness. I'll say, 'Why don't you change the light bulb?' They'll say they don't know where the light bulbs are so they've been using their laptops to see in the room. So dim! Literally! I remember going in once and there was no showerhead. Somebody had stolen it. And the loo seat! Towels are always swiped, and often there'll be a random suitcase left behind and nobody knows who it belongs to. The mind boggles. On the whole, they're quite good fun and my two places have gardens, which is lovely for them in the summer months.

The flats are part of our duty of care to the models. It might feel daunting when they're young and perhaps new to the city, so we make sure they have clean sheets, sterling to get around and buy their travel tickets, and tell them where the nearest shops are so they can buy some food. Then you have to make sure they have a map to get from the flat to the tube station. It takes up a fair amount of time before you've even booked a job.

I'm sure you're dying to know what the house rules are in the model houses? Well, the two main ones are that there is no smoking allowed indoors and the girls are not allowed to have boys back, but of course they do. One summer's morning I was looking out of the window at the model house next door and I saw this boy coming out of the garden shed! He'd obviously been living there. All the other girls know there are not supposed to be any boys but there'll always be one who goes, 'You don't mind my boyfriend being here?' Or you'll sit outside and hear a boy's voice. I remember one night there was a boy singing to them with a guitar! You're thinking, do I go and tell him to piss off or just leave it? He seemed quite harmless. And then you bring it up at a later date and they all close ranks and say he just popped round because they're too scared to tell you. To be fair, I'm not sure I would've played by the rules back in the day.

On the whole, the girls usually get on, and it tends to be the ones who have boyfriends who cause the most annoyance. Occasionally there's one bad one they all loathe. It's almost like a social experiment – all these mini groups of nationalities under one roof. Like *Big Brother* meets the Eurovision Song Contest, every day. Take the Russians – they never go to sleep and they tend to smoke inside the house when they're not allowed to. And they go on Skype all night and drink vodka. I'm generalising of course but it does tend to be the girls from Russia who keep everyone awake and are quite bolshie. All the girls go out, of course – somehow they find time to have a social life in London. Then they're not turning up for their jobs, or they're late for a casting. That's when you start asking what's going on in that model flat and tell them off, like a mum.

I don't advertise the fact that I'm next door but one year a girl came ringing on my doorbell and said, 'You've got to come, you've got to come! We've got a ghost!' They even convinced me, too. A house full of panicked girls at 10 p.m., in hysterics, crying! I bought the house in the area I live in so that if there's a terrible emergency I can be there.

In New York it works slightly differently. All the agencies have model flats but they rent them off other people. They're notoriously bad in New York, with rumours of cockroaches and all sorts. Some of them don't have cooking facilities. So the care element isn't as good over there. I try to keep my models away from apartments in New York and I'm looking into finding my own places. The standards are really quite poor and why should they put up with that? It's depressing for the girls, who are often young and vulnerable in a new, big city. New York's a scary place the first time you go.

A MODEL FOR LIVING

A Model for Living was a book written by the psychiatrist Julian Short that addressed common problems people face every day that are particularly pertinent in our industry. I wrote the foreword to the book and we use it as a reference point when advising new models and their families when they enter the business. It looked at issues like how to cope with rejection – a biggy! – and improving self-esteem, as well as dealing with family relationships or workplace dynamics. These are issues that can be really tough for models and it's important to highlight them and offer advice and support. The book helps to address this and I'm proud to have been associated with it.

MONEY GIRLS

'Money girls', as we colloquially call them, are the models who do the more commercial work in our business. That's the catalogues, online (ASOS, Littlewoods Direct) and swimwear. Or big brands like Lynx and L'Oréal. Without money girls agencies wouldn't survive because it's this revenue – the bread and butter, if you like – that keeps things ticking over and provides a monetary cushion that enables us to invest in young models and take chances on edgier girls. The whole thing about being a good commercial model is that you have to be hard working, in super-fit shape and reliable.

In some ways I think money girls are the heroes of modelling because they know their trade so well and they really take care of themselves. A lot of the work depends on their being in good shape, especially for lingerie or swimwear, so they'll be at the gym a lot to keep fit and toned. They tend to be more 'sexy' and their bodies aren't as skinny. Money girls can get away with being 5' 9" – most of them are 5' 9" or 5' 10" – but they're fit and lean. They also have boobs, which editorial girls don't tend to have. We have some money models that are a D-cup. That would never have happened years ago – no one would touch them. B-cups were the highest they'd go. I'm quite fascinated by boobs because I remember when I first started, if a model came in with a C-cup she couldn't get a job. It was 'ooh no, too big, clients won't like it', then gradually, into the 2000s, we started being asked for Ds. Not on the catwalk, though – flat as a pancake is what works there.

Money girls know what's needed to get the job done, and I really respect that. We had one model who was a very successful e:commerce and catalogue girl and she knew she needed to have a bit more of a bust so she went out and bought chicken fillets for her boobs and also a fake bum! And it worked. The clients all loved it and thought how clever she was. She didn't just think, 'Oh, I'm a bit flat-chested and I haven't got a bum,' she worked out how to deal with it. I like that work ethic. I think at first she didn't tell the client but then they knew and admired her for it and she's kept those clients for years and years.

A problem that money girls have is that their books don't look good because they don't do editorial, which keeps a model fresh and up to date. To make up for this they have to do test shoots a lot but they don't want to because they don't have time, they're always travelling. A lot of commercial girls would like to be doing more high-fashion work but they struggle to make that transition and occasionally don't accept what they are, which is a brilliant model within the category they're in. Commercial work is not as creative and everyone hankers for editorial because it has more prestige. You can have a girl earning £500,000 a year but it's still not enough if she wants the prestige.

Big money girls we've had include Jacqui Ainsley, whose partner is Guy Ritchie. She's a brilliant model – so pretty, an amazing body, always looks immaculate. Jacqui was in the Virgin ad where all the models walked through the airport as air hostesses. Lisa Snowdon was also a very successful commercial model. She came to us from an agency that did glamour modelling and we saw the potential in her. She did a lot of lads' magazines like *FHM* and made a fortune with catalogue work and underwear modelling. We got her the Triumph bra campaign. Lisa, of course, has gone on to do TV and radio presenting. She's got a good personality and a strong character. We got Lisa her first presenting gig at Channel 4 and eventually she flew the nest.

There was a batch of girls around this time, like Sophie Anderton and Kelly Brook, who were sexy models with fun and ballsy personalities who broke through onto TV. Not drippy. We had Kelly Brook as part of our 'special'/celebrity division. Sophie Anderton joined us from Models 1 and we turned her career around. She was a beautiful girl, really well turned out. She did do a bit of editorial and then she'd do big money jobs, not necessarily catalogue but high-profile brand stuff like Lynx. She has a personality as well – she's a strong-minded girl and a good model.

N IS FOR...

WHAT'S IN A NAME?

Remember the story about the model who came to me with the bright idea of re-naming herself 1981? Well, she had a point. Names matter in this industry. OK, so 1981 is taking the unusual angle a bit far but it pays to have a name that stands out. Models tend to be referred to by their first names so if you're one of a zillion Irenas, for example, then it starts to get tricky. I don't think any first names will ever resonate quite as powerfully as Naomi, Linda, Claudia and Kate, but there's a Cara and Lara whose stars are shining brightly just now, along with Leomie and Malaika.

A memorable (and cool) name makes life easier for a frazzled casting director during show time. I mean, who could forget Bambi? Or Drake? I for one will *never* forget

Drake, mainly because she was a model who got away. Annie and I met her in New York. She was older, at twenty-seven, and an actress. She was amazing-looking but we hesitated and were pipped to the post securing her. She opened Christopher Kane that very same season. *Drake*. We also have a new girl called Doug (a.k.a. Sarah Douglas) who's riding high at the moment – she has the most incredible walk and very 1960s look. She's very specific and quirky, with the name to match! Hedi Slimane at Saint Laurent absolutely adores her and I'm sure he won't forget that name, either.

Mak is another name I won't forget in a hurry. Mak is a model who left us recently after twenty-five years. Of course she's memorable because she was with us for such a long time – an amazing high-end girl who was super-professional, loyal and a shining example of a career model. But she had the name, too – how many Maks do you know?

Sometimes names are memorable for slightly different reasons. Back in the Eighties we took a model on from Belgium called Fanny Rasch. Yes, you read that right. She came to London and we must have been a bit slow as it only dawned on us when we were ringing clients for appointments how funny her name was. Let's just say she got lots of appointments and everyone was very amused. She also secured plenty of jobs. There is a lot in a name for a model – if you have a clicky name it sticks in people's mind so those models can go far!

O IS FOR...

OPERATION WHEATSTONE

In 2012, I got a call from a detective inspector and immediately started worrying about what I might have done.

'Don't panic,' he said. 'I'm ringing you because I'm involved with Operation Wheatstone. We found your name and your movements in one of the reporter's notebooks, so we think you've been hacked.'

I said, 'Well, that wouldn't surprise me, I've looked after some pretty big names. I'm sure everyone was hacking us.' Suddenly, everything fell into place – all those times stories came out and I was baffled as to who was the leak.

The inspector advised me to get my lawyers to contact News International's legal team and make a compensation claim. So I rang Jamie, my lawyer, and said if I could get two grand for my holiday in Turkey then that would be good. He said, 'We can try.' The next step was assembling an evidence file – any emails/correspondence that could point to hacking. Natalia, my assistant, spent a week trawling through years of emails and we passed it all on to the lawyers. Soon after, Jamie called and told me they would offer a settlement. On Monday he called me again. He said, 'Within half an hour of me sending this email they made me an offer so they've obviously allocated the money.' Then, like any good lawyer, he said, 'I think we should go back for a bit more.' I didn't want to go to court but I was happy to leave it in his hands to see what he could get. In the end, we were happy with the settlement we received but more than that I'm just pleased that there is some kind of justice. When certain stories came out I was genuinely bewildered as to how they had come to light. It caused many rows – people became convinced that somebody in the office was being indiscreet. Who could blame us for thinking that?

On some level I think we suspected that hacking could be taking place but then we always came to the conclusion that surely they *wouldn't* do that? They *couldn't* do that? Well, now we know. Lawyers always used to say to us, don't talk on your mobile phones, don't leave messages, and now we know why. They knew it was going on, too. The invasion of a person's privacy is bad enough but it's also the knock-on effect that hacking has on those close to the person being hacked. It causes mistrust to set in and relationships can irrevocably break down. In some cases, never to be fixed.

P IS FOR...

PHOTOGRAPHERS – MY TOP 10

Photographers are so important in the building of a model as the prestige, name and calibre of the photographer rubs off on the model. Some girls would crawl through the Sahara desert to work with certain photographers. And vice versa. I've worked with a lot of photographers over the years. So who are my top ten? It's hard to narrow it down, of course, but these names have really shaped my eye and enriched my life over the decades . . .

David Bailey
What's the key thing about Bailey? Well, he changed everything, didn't he? For me personally, he represents the Sixties and my youth. His images kicked off the spirit of the decade with his candid portrayals of his

then girlfriend Jean Shrimpton, who was all long legs, short skirt and fringe.

Bailey's style of photography was different. It's how you wanted to look if you were a teenager – it felt like you could recreate that life. It was real. And radical. Bailey kind of stormed into the industry and immediately set his own rules. He would do it his way, with his choice of model and if you didn't like it, well, you could forget it! He was at once rebellious, cheeky, sexy, disrespectful, risky . . . He was also working-class, along with Donovan and Duffy – the three East End boys made good. That was a big thing as well in the Sixties; suddenly you didn't have to be part of the establishment to become successful. Everything was attainable to anyone if they had a talent. That was the whole drive – youth, opportunity and bucking the system. The establishment hated it but it changed Britain and put London on the map. Prior to Bailey, photographers' only outlet was *Vogue*, *Tatler* and *Harpers & Queen* and they'd be asked to photograph debutantes and aristocracy. Then suddenly, along with these photographers, came a new wave of girls who didn't have to be posh. It was about what they looked like, not who their parents were or what school they went to. It became about personal style and attitude.

I think I first got to know Bailey properly in 1981 or 1982 when I'd just started Premier and I was asked to do a shoot along with some other agents. We had to choose our best model and Bailey would photograph us alongside the model. I turned up in Dr Martens and a long skirt and he really liked that. Everyone else was poshed up but I was like, 'I really want to keep my boots on.' He agreed – I guess we bonded over our single-mindedness! After that we worked together quite a bit, and we always got on and had a laugh. He's wickedly funny.

I admire Bailey because he's endured, too – he's remained relevant, which is so crucial in this business. He once asked me what I thought he should do next. This was probably towards the end of the Eighties. I told him I thought he should go back to how he used to shoot with Jean Shrimpton, those very strong, iconic black and whites. Now, at seventy-five, he still works all the time, and for hip magazines like *i-D*, too. The problem is if you stop, you die, and I'm sure he knows that. So he's brought in to 'do a Bailey'.

Steven Meisel

Meisel is like God in this industry. If a model works with Meisel he can make their career and they will learn a lot from him because he's so inventive. It's impossible to pin his style of photography down because he's always changing. He's a bit like a painter, always creating. He does radical things too, which I love. I adored the shoot he did with Linda Evangelista for Italian *Vogue* in 2005. The fictionalised narrative showed Linda bandaged up, as if she was post-plastic surgery, in various upscale places. It was brilliant – a witty commentary. Then he did another one recently with a plus-size model with no clothes on. It was amazing. So all of a sudden plus-sized girls were in vogue. He's a thinker – he dreams it all, he creates it all. He wants to know all about the hair and make-up; everything. What does this mean for the model? He teaches her things about herself that she didn't even know. He'll often take a brand-new girl and somehow get her to become a model. Nobody actually teaches you how to be a model in this business: you've either got it or you haven't. Or that's the received wisdom anyway. I don't fully agree with that. With a bit of guidance from a photographer, a Svengali-type figure, you can be taught or at least shaped. That's Meisel – he's the model whisperer.

Herb Ritts

If I may, I'd like to borrow from Anna Wintour's words, written for Ritts's eulogy in US *Vogue* in 2003. 'In a fashion world inevitably given to fluctuations of taste, he stood out for his absolute commitment to making models and actors and friends look gorgeous and happy and like themselves, only better.' Actors and friends included Richard Gere (it was candid shots of Gere taken in front of their broken down Buick during a desert road trip in the Seventies that launched Ritts's career), Elizabeth Taylor, Jack Nicholson and Michael Jackson.

He's responsible for so many iconic images that contribute to America's mythology, it's difficult to single one out. How about Madonna's *True Blue* album cover? Or the shot of five supermodels – Naomi, Christy, Cindy, Stephanie Seymour and Tatjana Patitz – woven naked around each other? Ritts had a way with bodies – creating these fluid shapes and silhouettes, and using shadow in a really graphic way.

His style was also firmly rooted in his home and birthplace, California (specifically LA), where he made use of the abundant natural elements from the beach and the sea to the desert and the mountains. This use of light, texture and shape really gave him his distinct aesthetic. I'll remember his beach shoots the most, where the model is having fun, and looks healthy, relaxed and beautiful. That's the Herb Ritts signature.

Peter Lindbergh

If you think about a Peter Lindbergh picture you remember the face. It's always about the woman that he's shooting – she is so much more important than the clothes. He's a bit of a rebel really because he kind of went on strike in the Eighties, refusing to do those over-styled, over-made-up shots, with models and their slicked-back hair and all that artifice. He wants the woman's natural beauty to shine through and this 'new realism' kind of changed our ideas of femininity in fashion. His style is very modern but also timeless; it doesn't date. It's all about the movement of the clothes and the hair isn't too 'done' or anything. He doesn't do poshed up. It's all very free.

I love the fact that Peter didn't start out in his profession until his thirties. There's something really inspiring about that. It also means he's lived outside of the industry which makes him more interesting company. We've hung out socially a lot. Like the time he was at my house with Gérald Marie and his wife after a Pirelli event and my toilet broke. We all had a big laugh about that as we attempted to flush using a coat hanger.

Mario Testino
Mario Testino is the opposite of grunge. As he told the *Guardian's* Jess Cartner-Morley in 2001, 'Grunge came from a group of English photographers, and they were documenting their own reality . . . I'm South American – we celebrate life.' Mario moved to London from Peru in the mid Seventies (rather hysterically if I think about him now, living in a wing of the abandoned Charing Cross Hospital) and had a bit of a slog trying to establish himself as a photographer, but in the Nineties, after a move to New York, he became a superstar. He developed a candid but beautiful way of shooting his subjects – maybe they'd be tucking hair behind their ear or biting a nail. I see his style as beauty in vulnerability.

His work with French *Vogue's* Carine Roitfeld was a turning point for him: he shot a Gucci campaign in 1995 which caught Madonna's eye so she requested him for her Versace campaign, an album cover and *Vanity Fair*. Then, in '97, he took those now-iconic shots of Princess Diana, shortly before she was killed, and the rest is history. In terms of my personal relationship with Mario, he used to come into the agency quite a lot when he first started until he became too posh! I like him a lot, though – he's very friendly and charming – a genuinely really nice man. I like the fact he still wants to see new girls too, such as India, our errant young thing in *The*

Model Agency, who manages to stand him up three times – one of the biggest photographers there is and she blanks him! He was charm personified about it, though. Of course, how could he not be? It's Mario!

David Sims
Born in Sheffield and displaying a rebellious streak from a young age, David dropped out of school as a teenager to begin assisting photographers (Robert Erdmann and Norman Watson, no less) and continued his rebellion as a key player in the punkish Nineties realism move-ment, along with Corinne Day and Juergen Teller. He worked with one of my favourite models Annie Morton a lot – he loved her. A 1995 campaign with Yohji Yamamoto was his big-league turning point and he hasn't looked back. Now, I'd say he's one of the biggest – and coolest – names we want to associate with our models.

Juergen Teller
Juergen and Corinne Day changed the world. I'm not sure if Corinne got there first but their brains are the same. I like Juergen because he sees things with humour. Everything was stripped back into nakedness – he even used to take a lot of pictures of himself naked, which I just love him for. He doesn't take himself too seriously like people often can in this business. His collaboration with Marc Jacobs has been very prolific, placing celebri-ties as models but again in that grungy Juergen way. Counter-culture poster girls like Sofia Coppola and Chloë

Sevigny want to be taken into his world and the results are fantastic.

Juergen is not frivolous. His style doesn't deviate much from his original street-style aesthetic. We wouldn't have *The Sartorialist* if we didn't have him. He's the god of the straight-up – simple, irreverent, understated, cool.

Mert and Marcus

Mert and Marcus (the duo Mert Alas and Marcus Piggott) are like fashion's mad scientists – their work is over-styled, over-retouched and crazy-sexy-beautiful. As Grace Coddington puts it: 'It's very fakey, fakey, fakey, but that's what it's supposed to be.' They are huge campaign photographers because the world they're selling, sells. It's a hyper-real wonderland featuring magnificent, sexy women in hyper-colour poses. It's very attractive to the eye. Their point of difference is prob-ably the work put in post-production. 'It's like a painting,' Alas said in 2004. 'You can paint a scene. The next day, you think, I wish I had a dog. So you draw a dog on it. You can achieve what you want eventually, even if you didn't do it that way.'

Paolo Roversi

When we were at Bond Street, Paolo came into the office once and we thought he was making a delivery! One of the bookers said, 'Delivering or collecting?', then I real-ised who he was. The poor man. We went through the big book of all our models so that he could take his pick. He worked a lot with Susie Bick – they both had the same artistic approach to fashion. He's very painterly in his style and has an interesting way with colour. He always shot quite blue pictures (as in the colour!). He used to shoot for French and Italian *Vogue* and he's just one of those photographers I have always loved. A lovely memory from the Susie days, too.

Jamie Hawksworth
Jamie is one of the new breed of young photographers who I absolutely love because he's not afraid to take a risk on new girls. He's not a sheep. You can sit on a girl for a long time and it's frustrating knowing you've got something but no one is biting and then suddenly one photographer will come around who'll get it and that will change everything. Jamie's that person. We work with him by showing him new faces and he'll push for a model and stick by a girl he really believes in. Like Lara Mullen. He took shots of her for me and he just knew she was brilliant. He loved her. He's now doing everything, from French *Vogue*, *W* magazine and *i-D* to J. W. Anderson's campaign. He sticks to his guns and is not compromised by this business.

PICK UP THE GODDAMN PHONE!

My biggest bugbear is the fact that nobody uses the phone any more – it's all email. I'm genuinely concerned that it will get to the point where we will become mute as a race, able to communicate only by passing fingers along a keyboard. In the past, before email and the internet really took hold, an agency's success was judged by how often the phones rang. Sometimes you'd have clients come in, or foreign agents, and we'd all ring each other within the office and talk baloney just in order to look busy!

Now every agency is dead, literally. The bulk of the workforce is typing away furiously. To me it's quite an alien thing. It's dangerous to not talk to your clients and agents because primarily you're selling a product. However hard you try to sell a girl on an email you can't. We have these endless arguments with me saying, 'You need to ring these guys and say, "I loved your last shoot, blah blah blah," and then you've made a friend.' This way, you get a rapport that's personal and you're far more likely to get something out of that client in the future, but the bookers are very reluctant. They're actually scared to speak to clients. How ridiculous in a job like this!

There's a lot of cold calling in this job because you could open a magazine and think, *I haven't heard of this photographer or this stylist*, and so then you've got to find them. In that situation I would always call that person up but now my staff will email them. Can you imagine, every agent from around the world sending pictures of girls to the same line-up of photographers, stylists and editors?

Sadly, the art of conversation is being lost. My skill when I was a booker was that I could charm anyone. I did it all verbally, a bit of flirting on the phone goes a long way. Heck, it's how I snagged my husband! But it's a skill that's being lost, and it's terrible because nobody will know anyone any more. I think it's sad. So we have big fights in our staff meeting and my team will always say, to placate me, 'Yeah, we'll do that,' but they never do.

PAUL ROWLAND

Remember early in my story I talked about Gillian from Bobtons who helped me 'develop my eye'? Paul Rowland, a prolific model agent and scout, is another person who has been very influential in how I perceive beauty and its ever-evolving cycle. I first knew Paul through an agency he started called Women in New York, then another called Supreme, which was hipper than hip. Supreme was famous for taking these really strange-looking girls and making them into stars. I'd go and visit the agency and Paul would say, 'Have you seen this girl? She's beautiful' to which I'd inevitably say, 'Are you sure?' But nine times out of ten he was right. You trusted him, and then, after a while, you got it. As they became successful they became more and more beautiful because success breeds confidence, which in turn breeds beauty. And with this, an agent's eye changes and grows. I'm grateful to Paul for his insights because there really is no one else quite like him. He always works very closely with his partner Mohammed Fujar, who is an amazing booker, and together they are quite the team.

Unfortunately Paul is not around at the moment because he was let go from Ford in New York where he had been approached to create a high-end board. Traditionally, Ford has always been a very big agency that turns over a lot of money but is not necessarily cool or trendy. Paul's brief was to find new girls and establish a new, high-end division. Unfortunately it just fell apart so he's on a year's gardening leave at the moment. For me it's quite sad because I found him so inspiring and I loved his talent for finding exciting girls. He never played it safe and without him I suspect the industry will probably go through a period of being quite conventional. Also, during times of recession the models tend to be more predictable – or recession-proof – blonde hair, blue eyes, etc. Then, struggling out of that people reject it because they think it's boring and you get a new look. Paul also has a gift for taking amazingly arty Polaroids of his models. He is inspirational and he changed how the whole world took those candid snaps our industry so relies on.

I'll give you a good example of the Paul Rowland magic. In September 2011, Annie and I went on our usual scouting mission to New York ahead of Fashion Week. September is the breakthrough season when all the new girls come through. We weren't having any luck finding new girls and then we went to Ford to see Paul and Mohammed and saw ten amazing girls, just like that. We were sitting in the Ford lounge meeting a lot of the girls because when you meet them it's easier because you sort of get it. Paul was saying, 'There's this beautiful girl called Athena.' Then one of his bookers came in and showed us her book and we were like, 'Are you sure?' Now Annie has a great eye and she wasn't sure either. He said: 'Take this girl, she's amazing.' We hadn't met her at this point but we said, 'OK, we trust you,' and we took her for the London shows. Of course when she came over we immediately loved her. We just knew she was going to do well. Lo and behold, come December she was shooting main fashion for British *Vogue*.

If you can find somebody like Paul who has that talent and you can tap into it then you see different things. Each season your eye changes and if it doesn't you die as an agent. We do find these 'strange' girls ourselves at certain points but Paul was very prolific and a lot of them were American, which was unusual.

Within the industry Paul's seen as quite cuckoo, which of course I love and mean only kindly. He's a maverick, too, because he knows what he wants and won't deviate from that. Within this business he is held in high regard in that respect. People think he's iconic; a genius for how he picks up beauty. Everyone knows what a classical beauty is but to find strange beauty when it's embryonic is quite a difficult thing.

Paul is like a brand you can trust. Sometimes a brand will bring out a pair of shoes that are quite radical and you think you really don't like them but because it's that brand, and it's powerful and you trust it, you buy the shoes. It's the same with him.

He's fond of transforming a girl, too, often with a dramatic new haircut. Suddenly, it becomes obvious what he'd seen in her – his vision. He would even cut Annie's hair if he thought she needed it. He'd pick up the water spray they used for the plants and chop chop chop! Amazing. Paul is a spiritual soul who has seen and done it all – he's full of charisma, wit and charm. Secretly I think he's many people's hero and I'm pretty sure we all fancy him too!

POLITICAL CORRECTNESS

The PC movement drives me mad because it gets out of control. It makes people scared to speak the truth and stifles thought because we've become so worried about offending somebody. In our bid to not leave people out we're destroying individualism. There's a culture, especially in Britain, that has us shying away from celebrating achievement or beauty or not being fat (i.e. being slim and fit) and so on. I think this is why models – and our industry – get a lot of stick because the business is beauty, which isn't necessarily shared by all. And it means that models have been a little sidelined from mainstream advertising as a result. Think about the Dove adverts that use 'normal' women (are models not 'normal'?) or the prevalence of actors. Personally, I think this is actually condescending to the public and, frankly, bollocks. Who can be an original with PC?

Q IS FOR...

QUITTING – IS NOT AN OPTION!

I'm not one for quitting and I'm not fond of those that do. It takes a lot for me to give up on a girl who has promise. Often my bookers will be getting fed up – maybe the girl is a bit moody or difficult or she isn't getting as many jobs as they'd like, so they'll want to give up on her. I see that as a challenge and often end up saying, 'Give her to me, I'll sort her out.' I think some people see it as me being stubborn (probable) or potentially that I have too much faith or trust in people (possible). It's probably a bit of all of that but I think it's important not to quit at the first hurdle. Or even the second. You don't get anywhere in life by giving up on things too easily.

I think how I was brought up really drummed this into me. I had to learn to be independent from such an early age and that kind of experience makes you pretty resilient. Also, when you have your own business, you can't be somebody who quits too readily. You'd never stay afloat!

I will add a disclaimer to this; there is something to be said for knowing when to quit, too. I think this is probably one of my weaknesses. I have been known to back the odd lame horse and it's usually people who I've hired and had high hopes for who ultimately let me down. It's the challenge, though; it's addictive!

QUIVER

I said this at the beginning of the book but it's worth repeating here. When a model is really exceptional, she quivers, like a thoroughbred racehorse. Very occasionally you'll meet a new young girl and just know they're special for this reason. They vibrate on a special frequency. You don't see it very often but when you do it's very exciting. You get goosebumps and you just know she'll be a star. Susie Bick was the first girl I saw quiver. And Naomi, too.

R IS FOR...

RAGE

It's not just models who throw a shit fit, sometimes it's the client. We had booked a major supermodel for an appearance at Seoul Fashion Week. It involved a short TV commercial and the fee was huge. Too good to turn down, in other words.

Chris had flown in via Frankfurt with our supermodel and found himself faced with the client's producer, an extremely intense, nervous and stressed man, prone to talking to himself and seemingly in a permanent state of 'lost in translation'. It transpired that the client was insisting on a personal visit by our supermodel to every stand at the event, to meet and greet all his sponsors with a photo op and interview. Now apart from the fact that this would take hours, it had not been pre-agreed or even discussed and certainly wasn't going to happen, however many times the stressed-out guy pushed Chris on it. The answer was always the same – no chance!

He was obviously under orders and extreme pressure from his collective of sponsors so the stress levels only continued to climb and he just wouldn't give up. This ongoing argument came to a head as the event was near to closing. It finally became heated to such an extent that the organiser snapped and went into full-on 'event rage': shouting, crying, screaming, falling down, crying some more, screaming and finally squaring up to Chris in full karate stance outside our supermodel's green room.

Then, like a saintly apparition, our cool girl – Claudia Schiffer – appears. She's calm, she's immaculate, she's Claudia. With a reassuring hand placed on karate man's arm, she soothes him and the situation by graciously agreeing to meet *some* of the sponsors. His face, and possibly his job, are saved, just like that. The power of the supermodel strikes again. And all credit to Claudia here – she had a great presence of mind and an understanding of how to keep clients happy under extreme circumstances.

ROLLER COASTERS

Roller coasters are my kryptonite. I *hate* them! They scare me. I remember when I first started going out with Rick, we were at Disney World in Orlando and he wanted to go on the new Space Mountain ride, which was a big deal back then in 1980. Now I knew I hated rides but I also wanted to impress my new boyfriend so I was telling myself, *I can do this, I can do this*. We get in and the rocket thing you're in basically shoots up like a bullet as if you're boosting off into space. Well, I'm totally hysterical and actually try to get out of our carriage, to the point where Rick has to get hold of me by my neck and frantically hang on to me for the duration of the ride. If he hadn't, I could well have died but I just panicked. Years later, Chris's wife Huggy took me to Iceland with Sissy and we went to a funfair. I got on one of those teacup rides for kids and ended up hysterical, screaming and crying. A grown woman! Meanwhile Sissy and cousin Olivia were loving it. When the ride finally came to an end I thought, thank God, I can get off. And then they went, 'Wasn't that great? Let's do it again!' Nooooooo!

S IS FOR...

SKINCARE

We devised our own, really rather brilliant, Premier Model Skin range – the Model Kit – to tie in with the release of *The Model Agency*. I wanted a great promo to go out when the show was first broadcast. Chris and Michael were working on various licensing projects and took the opportunity to pilot the Premier Model Kit idea. We found a cosmetic manufacturer and distributor who really liked the idea. We licensed and put the models' travel kit together in nine weeks – just in time. We did all the research and development in-house with the models. We loved the product and even managed to get a hint of my favourite witch hazel into it. This is a great concept and still very popular with all our girls. If you want to give it a try yourself, find out more at premiermodelskin.com.

SCOUTING

Scouting new models is a big part of what we do. You always need new talent coming into the agency and often this means bringing girls in when they're pretty young – like thirteen and fourteen – and then nurturing them until they've left school and are old enough to start modelling. Scouts need to have an incredibly good eye and they have to be able to recognise a special quality in a girl at a young age. We usually have a full-time scout on staff who will spend some time in the office and the rest out and about scouting for girls. We also have freelancers who we may pay on a retainer to be our 'eyes' when they're out and about. For example, we have a session hairdresser who we use who's very in tune.

Scouts go all over the country to find girls – from gigs and festivals to shopping centres and Topshop on Oxford Street. Girls can be found anywhere. Leomie Anderson was found at a bus stop in Wimbledon on her way home from school, and Lara Mullen was at a gig in her home town of Northampton. It's actually a very difficult job because it's so hard to find a genuinely good model. Sometimes we'll do specific scouting events to try and drum up some interest, like last summer we set up stall at Benicàssim music festival in Spain because lots of cool young girls hang out there. There are competitions too, like Elite Model Look that we did in the Nineties when we were part of Elite. There are regional heats, a bit like *X Factor*, where girls from different towns around the UK (they also did them worldwide) would turn up for an audition and the best from each region take part in a glitzy final in London, with the winner getting a modelling contract. Elite Model Look was very prestigious back then and we always secured top-quality judges for the final and put on a big glitzy event.

The first year, Linda Evangelista was one of the judges and Naomi and Kate came along – it was a big deal. That famous picture of Kate wearing a long, bias-cut silver see-through dress? That was our first Elite Model Look in '92 at the Connaught Rooms. The two we did there were huge actually, upwards of 2,000 people came. Judges over the years have included Vivienne Westwood, David Bailey and more celeb-type people like Lily Savage (somewhat hysterically), Piers Morgan, Robbie Williams and even the footballer Ian Wright.

With scouting, the girl's age is always the first challenge because often it's really difficult to ascertain how old they are. Sometimes they could be as young as thirteen so our scout will always approach the parents first and present them with a business card so it at least looks official and not like some strange man is asking weird questions about their kid! So our first question is always, 'How old are you?'

And what are we looking for? It's that gangly girl from school who's really good at netball and who doesn't want to be that tall. When models are interviewed they'll often recount experiences from school where they felt too tall, skinny or awkward, or they'll use the phrase 'ugly duckling', which the general public finds a bit nauseating, but it tends to be true. These are the girls who turn into models.

Sometimes you can spot a face, chase them, and you don't know how old or how tall they are, and then suddenly you'll be talking to them and realise their teeth are all wrong, or something else is not quite right, so you have to back off a bit. It's a bit like trying to find a romantic partner – the right ingredients are just very difficult to find. Like sometimes you might find the most beautiful girl but she's 5' 5", then it's 'bye bye!'.

It goes in spurts as to how successful we are. On average we might scout ten girls per year. It's so important to have new girls. When Annie and I go to New York to find new faces over there, that's all anyone wants to see – 'What new girls have you got?' An agency is judged by the calibre of the new girls so it's a big pressure.

SIZE ZERO

The Size Zero debate has hung over our industry for too long now. I think it should be pointed out that obesity kills three times more people than malnutrition, worldwide, and that women in the UK are now Europe's fattest. These were the findings of the Global Burden of Disease study, published in a special edition of *The Lancet*. One of the lead authors of the report, Professor Majid Ezzati, chair of global environmental health at Imperial College London, said to the *Telegraph* in December 2012: 'We have gone from a world twenty years ago where people weren't getting enough to eat to a world now where too much food and unhealthy food – even in developing countries – is making us sick.'

'Sick.' I want to pick up this word because it's one that's used to describe models on a regular basis and has become a synonym for thin, or skinny. This is not right or accurate, as there are now more 'sick' people who are overweight. Another year-long study carried out by the Academy of Medical Royal Colleges and reported in the *Guardian* in February 2013 identified an 'obesity epidemic', stating that doctors are 'united in seeing the epidemic of obesity as the greatest public health crisis facing the UK. The consequences of obesity include diabetes, heart disease and cancer, and people are dying needlessly from avoidable diseases.' To spell it out, one in four adults in England is obese, and the figures are predicted to rise to 60 per cent of men, 50 per cent of women and 25 per cent of children by 2050.

I say all this upfront because I've spent such a lot of time defending our industry, and defending our models, when the facts are, in my forty years in the business, I have never sent more than five girls home for being too thin (or 'sick') and surely, in light of the above, we're having the wrong debate? To be very clear, I'm not saying anorexia, bulimia or any kind of eating disorder is trivial, far from it. I'm not even saying that it isn't something that model agents deny but I am saying that under the catch-all banner of 'Size Zero', it has been blown out of all proportion when it is, at best, a sideshow to the real threat to the health of young people in the UK today:

obesity. At worst, it is a deliberate attempt to distract our attention from the dramatic rise in obesity in this country. With the latter in mind, I'm guessing that certain media outlets don't want to bite the hand that feeds them – attacking the causes of obesity wouldn't go down well with certain fast food and drink advertisers.

I just think there needs to be some perspective. It's too easy – and dangerous – to take a pop at a model who is thin because she's born that way and it is her job to be slim and fit, just like a ballerina or a runner. It incenses me when certain factions of the British press stir things up. Instead of being proud of an industry that brings money to this country, it's like a spiteful, nagging jealousy. That's how it comes across to me anyway.

I'm often asked to be a talking head when these issues come up – from general anorexia debates where blame is laid at our (or the fashion industry's) door, or the recent time I went on *Daybreak* because a young girl had committed suicide. She was bulimic and it was such a tragedy – she had been bullied at school. But the reason why I was on TV talking about it? The coroner for some reason blamed it all on fashion models so then that became a huge news story. This girl wasn't a model. I was arguing with a doctor, also on the panel, that there will always be tragic losses like these but it doesn't mean that every model in the world is responsible. I was defending the industry, saying that we're very health-conscious nowadays – because we are. We want fit models; we don't want 'sick' models. No one wants a sick girl but I think they vilify models so much that now the public associates a skinny tall girl with being 'sick' and that's so far from the truth. I think the press also insinuates it's got worse these days. But I don't think models are any thinner than they were fifteen years ago.

It's like looking at a beautiful portrait in the National Portrait Gallery. You might look at that painting and think, that's the most beautiful woman. But the artist has probably flattered that woman – they're not going to make her look horrible. You might think, *that's beautiful*. You might even think, *I'd love to look like that*. But you know you're not going to actually look like that because at the end of the day it's a piece of art, it's bound up in artifice. And anyway, why should you expect to look like that? I think the same about fashion and modelling. Modelling's about ethereal beauty, it's about a dream. It's saying this is how you can put your clothes together but it's also like a painting as well. There's an art to it. I'm talking about high-end pictures here, by the way, but I don't believe that anyone goes: 'I've got to go on a starvation diet to look like that.' I really don't.

I think the reason that there's so much press about it is we're more aware these days because of the increased communication. They say we never had anorexia until the Seventies or Eighties. I'm sure we did but we just didn't know about it. I have some models here who are very slim, like a girl from up north who is actually an athlete; she's a runner, and immensely fit. People stop her and vilify her in her hometown at the bus stop, saying, 'You're sick.' And she's not sick. It makes me so mad. The sweeping pompous statements from MPs and doctors who have never met a model, and certain members of the media giving it all a good stir.

When I volunteer to be a spokesperson like this, my staff always say to me, why are you doing this again? But I really do think it's important. The last time I was on *Women's Hour* there was an MP who made a statement saying all models up to the age of eighteen should be chaperoned. I said to her, who's going to pay for that? You can work legally at sixteen, you can get married at sixteen, you can fight for your country at sixteen . . . but no, she wanted them chaperoned around. Why? So I ended up asking her if she'd ever been to a model agency. She said she hadn't, so I invited her here. She came and I told her how we deal with our models and in actual fact we lined all our models up to show her how fit and healthy they are.

We actually fib about our models' measurements. So the cool girls, who are the girls that do all the e:commerce catalogue advertising, I bet you if you measured their hips they'd be about 37" or 37.5". We're saying they're 36" or 35.5" because that's what our clients want to see but we know damn well that they fit the clothes and the clients aren't going around with a measuring tape. So the bog-standard statistics are that a model is 34, 24, 35.5 and a show girl is 32, 23, 34.5–35. In New York and Paris it's more strict. But these are not the measurements of 'sick' people. They're the measurements of professional models whose job it is to be in shape. To me it's a no-brainer, of course a model has to be thin. It doesn't mean she's sick, though!

When *The Model Agency* came out the Size Zero debate was reignited because it's a quick story with a catchy title that immediately resonates with people. It's like 'credit crunch' or 'Britpop' – one of those natty media slogans that's stuck. We don't even have Size Zero in this country so it's bollocks.

I think with the TV show people got offended by how frank we were when it came to discussing the girls' looks. But it's the same as many other jobs: if you were a football coach you'd be analysing your player's game and assessing their fitness. It's the same with us. We expect our girls to feed themselves like athletes and exercise like athletes because we want healthy girls. So I've got a bee in my bottom about the press and how they attack us. Yes, there are difficult things in our job but there are difficult things if you're Wayne Rooney or a gymnast. You're not going to be a fat gymnast, are you? You do things to make sure you're fit and healthy and not overweight.

I'm not saying our industry is without fault but I am saying that we're the best we've ever been. Models in the UK are looked after in a phenomenal way. The London agents in particular are better than anyone at developing a model from a young age, pulling her through and getting her into the international circuit. In the past, we agents didn't really know very much about diet and nutrition but now we've all educated ourselves. Maybe fifteen years ago we'd have just said to a girl, 'Don't eat, cut everything out.' As a nation though, if you think about it, the foodie revolution is only relatively recent, as is the health and fitness knowledge that a lot of people have now. Model agents are no different.

Now our approach is very formulated. We have personal trainers who will look after the girls and gyms that offer us discounts. It's all about healthy eating and exercise. We're very careful that we don't push a girl too much. Body shape is very important, there's no getting away from it; they have to be skinny, particularly the high-end show girls, which is why you look for younger girls. But they're not sick, they're tall, gangly adolescents. It's an innate body type.

When I was a teenager I weighed six stone. My parents always worried about me. I was called 'the Stick'. Even prior to that they used to put stuff on my food because I was always skinny as a kid. The most I weighed at sixteen was seven stone. I ate like a pig but my metabolism was buzzing. That is what happens with these girls and as they develop into women, they get a bit bigger. I didn't start to put on weight until I was about twenty-seven then it just all changed. If you're looking for a rugby player you're looking for big guys, if you're looking for a flyweight boxer it's small and lean, a jockey . . . I could go on. In every aspect of sport you're looking for a body shape. Call it discrimination if you want but it's actually selection.

So why does modelling have such a bad rep? I think this brings us back to my original point – it's probably because there are so many overweight people in this country. It's like we want to mollycoddle anyone who isn't thin and criticise those who are as being unhealthy 'role models'. There's something wrong here. To use the sport comparison again, if you've got some guy who's not as good at rugby as the England captain you don't cuddle him and say 'there, there'. But if you're not as attractive as the girl who's in the Burberry ad then the argument is that you're damaged by unrealistic representations of beauty.

If you go back to the Thirties or Forties and consider how people admired film actresses, did people think, 'Oh my God, I really resent her'? I doubt it. They may have aspired to be her. Fashion is about aspiration – the look of the model is about how the photographer and the creative director and the designer see the clothes. Why not aspire to it? You didn't understand Marilyn Monroe but you didn't hate her for it. We've got this culture where everyone's supposed to be the same: you can't win a race so everyone's got to lose. That's bad. We're a unique society in the UK, and we do amazing things out of nothing. We should celebrate this instead of pulling people down.

SOCIAL MEDIA

Social media is now so important for our industry. We have a Premier blog, we're always tweeting, we have a Facebook presence. We even scout some girls via Facebook. I've already mentioned how key social media and particularly Twitter was for the TV show and then there was the whole 'Carole Shite' phenomenon. Well, it's also becoming important for our models. We really encourage them to build up their followers on Facebook, Twitter and so on, so that they have a fan base. If you've got a brain and you're a model you need to build up a following. In the not-too-distant future, I think clients will start looking at selecting models based on how many followers they have. One of our new girls, Leomie, is excellent for this. She started a blog and has tons of followers. That's currency for her.

STRANGE ACQUAINTANCES

I have a tendency to find myself in WTF? situations *a lot* and it usually involves the people I meet along the way. Take for example Howard Marks, or 'Mr Nice' as he was known in his bestselling memoir (and subsequent movie starring Rhys Ifans) about his life as the biggest hash dealer in the world. Rick and I actually hung out with him and his family while we were on holiday in Mallorca, where he lived. Rick knew his wife from before but I didn't and I certainly didn't know he was such a wanted man! I remember he had one of those giant early mobile phones with the huge batteries that you have to carry around with you like a suitcase. We had no clue what he was up to. We just thought he was a big pothead and also very intelligent.

We got really friendly with the whole family. We had our nanny with us so we'd go off and have a fun time in places in Palma and he was ringing on his funny phone, and it was hysterical. We knew he was dabbling in a bit of hash but we didn't think it was that big a deal until we got back to the UK and it all kicked off. He was arrested and splashed all over the tabloids. We got in touch with his wife Judy eventually and he used to write to us from prison in America where he'd been extradited. He asked Rick to write him a character reference, to appeal for a more lenient sentence (he was looking at forty years at one point), which Rick did. We're not in touch any more but I do have fond memories of 'Mr Nice' and his family.

I forged another unlikely friendship with the comedian Alan Carr. Annie and I had gone to Miami to visit the agencies there and scout some new money girls. We were eating in Balans restaurant and Annie was saying to me, 'There's Alan Carr, I'm sure it is.' She's like, 'don't look', but of course I looked and then she's telling me off for making it too obvious. Anyway, we carry on eating and he comes over to our table with his boyfriend Paul. I look up and he says, 'Hi, Carole from *The Model Agency.*' Paul told us they'd watched every episode and loved it. And then he looked at Annie and said, 'And you are Pru.' She said, 'Pru?' and he said, 'I know that name's not right.'

So, somewhat hysterically, Annie was worried about us staring at them and it was the other way round! We were staying at the Mondrian and they were at the W and they were going to see some friends so they invited us to have drinks with them. We didn't necessarily think it would happen but said, 'OK, cool, we'll be by the pool.' We got back to the hotel, went to the pool and suddenly Alan's shouting, 'Come here, come here!' in that famous voice of his and we all got totally legless together. The year before in Miami we ended up being invited to Craig David's party and were hanging out with JLS. I didn't even know who they were. Almost as surreal as having lunch with Kevin Spacey that time or when Robert De Niro used to call up my house: 'Hi, it's Robert.' Funny.

SWEARING

I swear a lot. So sue me.

SMOKING

I have been known to have the odd fag. I know it's not good for me but I do love it so. It's become my signature now since the TV show, a bit like Charlie Chaplin's hat or something – 'Oh yeah, Carole from *The Model Agency*? The one with the big gob who's always smoking?'

As Jan Moir kindly put it in *The Daily Mail*: 'Carole smokes like a chimney, has skin like a kipper and doesn't know how to work a camera.' What did I do? I sent her a box of kippers.

I was once responsible for the fire brigade being called to a West London hotel where I was at a shoot for a Philip Treacy campaign that included Grace Jones. Paul Hunt (one of my bookers) and I disappeared off for a fag and the next thing we know the alarms were going off and fire engines were on the way. 'Oh no, not again,' said the hotel staff. Apparently it was a regular occurrence. The whole hotel had to be evacuated and the none-too-impressed fire fighters, knowing what had happened *again*, had to go and do their investigations. 'It was me, it was my fag!' I said to them. 'We still have to go upstairs,' the chief replied through gritted teeth.

T IS FOR...

TOP TIPS

There has to be something to show for being sixty-three years in this world. So here it is – some of my top life tips for you. The little tricks I've picked up along the way to make life run that bit smoother . . .

Travel
Anyone travelling to New York should seriously consider checking out Kuwait Airlines. You can fly to New York *first class* for £1,000. Business class is even less and economy around £300. If I don't have enough air miles I'll fly Air Kuwait and it's brilliant. It feels a little like going back to the Sixties. They don't have completely flat beds, they're probably about 75 per cent, like huge armchairs, and they won't serve you alcohol but you can take alcohol

on board with you. It's hysterical – a bring-your-own booze flight! And there's never anyone in first class, except maybe one businessman and Annie and I, swigging our wine.

Medicinal must-haves
Four things I always carry with me, and which don't always go down that well at US customs . . .

Andrews liver salts: this is made up mostly of bicarbonate of soda – the Victorians swore by it and it's really good if you're feeling nauseous. You know how some people drink Coca Cola when they're feeling sick? Well, this is much better. If you have one spoonful it's an effervescent drink; two spoonfuls is a toilet aid! If you're travelling a lot and your diet changes and you find you can't go to the loo, two spoons makes it all work. I always travel with it. Chris also tells me it's a powerful cancer deterrent too but I didn't know that.

Beechams Powders: this is my failsafe cold remedy. As soon as I feel even the slightest sniff of a cold I'll reach for the powders, never the capsules. I make all my bookers take it, too. If they've got flu or a cold I'll be wafting a sachet under their noses.

Witch hazel: this is my skin saver. It's an astringent but made from a flower so very natural and brilliant for getting rid of spots. If you get a blemish, put witch hazel on it with a piece of cotton wool and the spot will vanish. It's also a very good toner for your skin and super cheap from the chemist.

TCP: my cure for a sore throat. Gargle with it and you'll be cured!

Beauty heroes

Moroccan oil: it makes your hair grow, stops split ends, makes your hair thicker and isn't oily. It's fantastic.

Premier hand cream: I'm not just saying it but Premier's hand cream (from our skincare range) is *the best*. My daughter Simone and all her mates in Kent absolutely love it. As soon as they see it anywhere online for sale they snap it up. It smells so good and it's non-greasy. The worst thing about hand creams is when you put it on and then can't open the door because your hands are so slimy!

U IS FOR...

UNDISCIPLINED MODELS

What's wrong with a bit of drive and discipline? Without wanting to go all Victorian school ma'am on you, I really think it's a problem – or certainly one of the biggest issues I currently have with my younger models – in that they don't have any.

Some of these girls are so beautiful but they're lazy and give up too easily. They don't want to go to the gym to keep in shape, they don't understand that you have to commit and have some willpower. I wonder if it is because kids today tend to get too spoilt and things come a little too easily for them? A lot of girls don't seem to have any guts any more. They don't recognise the opportunity they have at their fingertips and it really frustrates me.

This is in stark contrast to girls from Russia and the Eastern Bloc who can and do take it seriously. They have massive drive to seek out opportunities and improve their lives so they work hard and are dedicated. I'd like to see more of this grit from our girls, I really would.

V IS FOR...

VERSACE

Versace is so woven into the DNA of the supermodel phenomenon that the label, and the family, have been a big and regular fixture in my life. I'll never forget the lavish shows and the fact the girls were paid with wads of cash, showered in gifts and put up in the most expensive hotels. I also won't forget the case of one model who got so smashed after the show, she walked into a glass door and had to be rushed to an emergency dentist, order of Gianni, to have her front teeth replaced. Like I say, lavish.

It was an extremely sad day when news came of Gianni Versace's death. We were about to go to South Africa to shoot with David Bailey and visit Nelson Mandela's charity and I thought, *we're never going to do this*, but we had to get this job done because it was all arranged with Nelson Mandela and the Soweto kids. We then had to leave early to fly straight to the funeral in Milan.

When we arrived in Milan, we were directed to the hotel where everyone was staying. Linda was there, and all the big models who worked with Versace. In every girl's bedroom, Donatella had laid out their outfits for the funeral. I think they all had a lace veil, black suits and high heels, tights . . . Everything had been thought of, down to the lingerie. The service was at the magnificent Duomo in the city. Princess Diana was there, and Elton John and Sting sang 'The Lord Is My Shepherd'. It was very moving and meticulously organised down to every detail.

At the end of the service I went to shake hands with the family. Then we had to go back to the Versace House and sign the condolence book. It's such a beautiful place – we went through this huge doorway that revealed a beautifully carved stone room, filled with scented candles. Then that led into an incredible courtyard – it was stunning, like a movie. The supermodels and Gianni Versace kind of made each other. It was a very clever thing. He adored them and they loved him back. And now Donatella carries on his legacy, and she feels the same way about them. Only recently Naomi walked the Versace catwalk again to a rapturous reception. Some things never die.

W IS FOR...

'THE WITCH'

Paul Hunt can take credit for my charming nickname, 'the Witch'. It's something he said in jest when they were filming *The Model Agency* and lucky for me it's one of the bits, along with Chris calling me an 'arsehole idiot', that was played in the opening credits every week. I suppose I can be a witch sometimes so I don't really care.

WOMEN RUNNING THE SHOW

The modelling business in this country is pretty much run by women. I think it's a really good thing especially because history tells us that ours is an industry open to abuse when it falls into the wrong, usually heterosexual male, hands. Because a lot of women are mothers, they see things in a 'what if?' way. We'll automatically think, what danger can this girl get into? I don't think men naturally think like that whereas it's a natural instinct for women.

Women tend to be sensitive to the fact young girls don't speak English well, or that it's their first time in a foreign country or they're not familiar with London. We do chaperone them a lot – we'll tend to send junior members of staff with them until they find their feet. In this country it's a very safe business. We know all our clients, we know the photographers. As it evolves you might meet a brand-new photographer and you make sure they come and visit you and build that relationship and if you feel there's something wrong you don't entertain anything with them. It's sort of like a sixth sense.

Eileen Ford was of course the original matriarch in this business, at the helm at Ford in New York and famous for her strict, school-like protection of her girls. From a business perspective, and for her sheer balls and bohemian spirit, Gillian Bobroff from Bobtons was a huge inspiration to me. She made me believe and was the push I needed to set up on my own. And now it's mainly women in power here in the UK. There's Sarah Doukas at Storm, Clare Castagnetti at Select who has two other women partners. Union is run by Rachel Du Preez. The London branches of IMG and Next networks are both headed up by women. In France it's slightly different and in Milan it's mainly still men.

It's a business that seems to attract women. It's a

fascinating job but also a tough one, too, so you have to be tough to do it. With the toughness though there also needs to be sensitivity. I instinctively know when a model's unhappy. Sometimes I don't have a big role with the models initially but I can always tell when there's something wrong. You just pick it up. It's something a guy wouldn't do.

X IS FOR...

X-RATED

Now I honestly don't remember this but Suzanne, my partner in crime at Bobtons, insists that in the late Seventies I would wear long, floaty hippie skirts and . . . no knickers! I mean, what if there was a strong wind blowing? And I thought I was such a lady, too.

Y IS FOR...

YOUNG GIRLS

In the mid to late Nineties nobody really thought about age. If a young model had been started in America or Italy at thirteen or fourteen, especially if they were Russians, for some reason it was acceptable at that time. In the UK nowadays, and this is testament to the duty of care and rules put in place thanks to organisations such as the AMA, the British Fashion Council has clamped down on girls working before they're sixteen. New York has also recently tightened up its rules regarding age.

I think it's bad for the girl to start out too young because they become 'old' too quickly, as well as burned out. They lose their childhoods because they've been mixing with adults the whole time and it means they're often finished at nineteen. Casting directors often think if a model hasn't made a name for herself in the first couple of years then she's had it. Or she's old. But she's not old – she's only sixteen or seventeen! This business moves on so quickly though, it's greedy. People always want 'the next big thing', which is why I'm very careful and strategic about when I launch a new girl. You can't do it too soon, for the sake of her sanity and career prospects.

To this end, we're very mindful of when we make a new girl public on our website. Sometimes we've been working on a girl for two years but we keep them secret because if we release them too soon the internet is so powerful that when you actually start pushing the girl and want her to start working, people already think she's old! This has definitely been more of a problem for models from poorer countries, who are really keen to get working as quickly as possible because their situation at home is difficult and perhaps the family doesn't have much money. Russian girls, who potentially haven't been protected either by the state or their parents, will flood the market for a short period and then burn out quickly. Nobody is advising or caring for them. It's not how we do things in the UK. Model agencies have a genuine duty of care to the young girls starting out.

At Premier, we will make sure we chaperone our young ones. Some parents insist on this, but not all. Girls are scouted aged anywhere between thirteen and sixteen but they don't start working properly until they're sixteen and have left school. Or often, they'll be doing A-Levels too and will work around those commitments. They're like little apprentices. We're teaching them how to be a model in between their studies. They might come into London in their holidays and somebody from the office will take them around some castings or they'll go with their mum and we'll put them up in the model house.

The use of young models is getting up there in the controversy stakes with Size Zero. In the past, there has been huge outrage at London Fashion Week thanks to pre-pubescent girls being used to model 'women's clothes'. The BFC has really clamped down on this. We have to prove their age with their passports. *Vogue* won't use a girl under sixteen either.

Age is a very tricky thing in this business because girls are often scouted young. The way to deal with it is to go really slowly. Much like with the casualties of young Hollywood, 'too much too soon' is disastrous in this business.

I take my duty of care very seriously. Our whole ethos is to make sure these girls can gain confidence, can get around the city safely and understand the job. Initially they don't make any money so I support them. They're doing test shoots to build up their books and then suddenly someone says 'I love this girl' and they get a job.

If a foreign girl comes in we provide them with a phone and somewhere to live. If a girl has absolutely no money we give her pocket money. If it's an English girl from a poor background we always make sure they've got enough to feed themselves and get on the trains and stuff like that. Most of them haven't got a clue about cooking, or how to work a washing machine. We teach them that, too.

At any one time we'll usually have about eight to ten young models in training. Once they're old enough they'll start out on the 'New Faces' board and then maybe be moved up to the main board. This doesn't always happen, of course, it depends how they develop. But that's certainly our aim, and we put a lot of time, effort and money into each girl with a view to making her a decent career. But it's that poker game again. You're trialling her. You don't know who's going to work. You're waiting for them to grow. That's why you have to be patient and caring – you have to give them time to do that, instead of chewing them up and spitting them out before they've even had a chance. That is *not* how we do things.

Z IS FOR...

ZOOLANDER

I'd like to say that 'Blue Steel' is my invention but I'm afraid all credit there must go to Derek Zoolander (a.k.a. Ben Stiller). If you want a laugh at the expense of our industry, it's a must-watch!

INDEX